"Elaine has done a masterful job of presenting the most important part of consulting: How to stay in business. Drawing on her wealth of experience, she shows how to find your first client, what to charge, and how to build relationships with clients who will rave about you to others. If you want to start a business—and stay in business—*The New Business of Consulting* is an essential read."

—Daniel H. Pink, author of *WHEN, DRIVE,* and *FREE AGENT NATION*

"In today's world, everyone will have fifteen minutes of fame and spend six months as a consultant. This book does a great job of bringing a business sense to professionals in the difficult position of creating a business where they, themselves, are the product. It is practical, compassionate, and a good alternative to an M.B.A."

—Peter Block, author, *Flawless Consulting*

"Is it time to start your own consulting business? Don't start without first reading Elaine Biech's *The New Business of Consulting*. The book, paired with her 35 years as a successful consultant, form a perfect guide for your success."

—Marshall Goldsmith, #1 *New York Times* bestselling author of *Triggers, MOJO,* and *What Got You Here Won't Get You There.*

"With 35 years in the consulting industry, Elaine Biech is the best person I can think of to write a book like *The New Business of Consulting: The Basics and Beyond.* Not only is she a successful consultant, but her engaging writing style will inform, entertain, and challenge readers—and then leave them with the knowledge and confidence to move forward in the world of professional consulting. Elaine doesn't sugarcoat; she lists pros and also cons, gives encouragement and also reality checks—the straight scoop. Whether you are an aspiring consultant, a novice building your clientele, or a pro looking for advice, read this book! I guarantee you will learn a lot from Elaine—and you'll enjoy the ride."

—Ken Blanchard, coauthor of *The New One Minute Manage®*
and *Leading at a Higher Level*

"Elaine Biech combines her twin passions for consulting and learning and development to produce an extraordinarily insightful and actionable playbook. If you want to launch a consulting career or take your performance to another level, make this book your personal coach."

—John R. Ryan, president and CEO, Center for Creative Leadership

"Why would anyone consider consulting without devouring this book? A great blend of solid information on consulting A to Z: the operational issues, the business and emotional risks, the personal discipline required, along with the tremendous payoffs of the profession! Applying the start-up thinking alone should increase first-year revenues four-fold."

—Dianna Booher, speaker, Hall of Fame, author, *Communicate Like a Leader* and *Creating Personal Presence*

"Don't start a business without it! *The Business of Consulting* is full of insightful tips and exercises to take you from intellectual comprehension to practical application. More sage advice + actionable ideas – inflated guru ego = a must-have tool for any consultant."

—Halelly Azulay, president, TalentGrow and host of The TalentGrow Show podcast

"When Elaine Biech speaks, I listen and learn. You will, too! She is the consummate professional, and she truly knows all aspects of consulting. Her advice is a must read for established as well as new professional consultants."

—Cutler Dawson, former CEO, Navy Federal Credit Union, Vice Admiral, US Navy (Ret.)

"If only I had been offered a course like this when I was building my business! I learned how to start and grow a company through the proverbial school of 'hard knocks!' You don't have to! Elaine has worked hard to share her wisdom and put it together in one place. The world of consulting takes a lot of hard work and guts, but you'll learn from her journey as she guides you in building or enhancing your own company. Still, after all these years, I continue to learn from Elaine."

—Beverly Kaye, CEO, Bev Kaye & Co.; author, *Help Them Grow or Watch Them Go and Up Is Not the Only Way*

"Elaine Biech just made a great book even better. *The New Business of Consulting* will become a classic in its field, with many useful, productive tools and advice. This is a must resource in today's consulting environment. We recommend that you read the first chapter and then scan the rest of the book and read the last chapter. Then, if you still want to be a consultant, use it as a how-to guide to manage, grow, and sustain a consulting practice."

—Jack J. Phillips, chairman, and Patti P. Phillips, president and CEO of ROI Institute, Inc., and coauthors, *Maximizing the Value of Consulting*

"This book is informative, will add value to the work you do and, most importantly, help you position your approach so that it is relevant in today's ever-changing business environment."

—Janice C. Kreamer, chairman of the board, Ewing Marion Kauffman Foundation

"*The New Business of Consulting* is from one of the best minds in this business. Elaine Biech is the most astute businesswoman in the consulting world today. She speaks the language, has seen it done in all environments both in and out of the U.S., and has helped shape organizations everywhere. Elaine has been that one person inside my personal inner circle in everything I've done for the last ten years. When you want the hard work done, call her."

—RADM (ret.) J.B. Godwin III, vice president, Athena Technologies, Inc.

"Hesitating about whether this is the *right* book for you? This is the only book you will ever need in order to start, maintain, or grow your consulting business. Elaine uses her years of experience—plus updated info and practical advice—to guide anyone contemplating or already in this profession. Buy the book now and save yourself time and money—you won't regret it."

—Ann Herrmann-Nehdi, CEO, Herrmann International: The Whole Brain Company

"Despite the fact that I have greater access to information than I have ever had before, my most trusted resource when it comes to my professional life has been *The Business of Consulting*. Elaine Biech has captured, organized, and articulated the heart of the matter when it comes to consulting. This new edition provides an expanded blend of practical insights, along with a realistic optimism about how to succeed. *The New Business of Consulting* is my go-to resource."

—Pamela J. Schmidt, executive director, ISA, The Association of Learning Providers

"Elaine and her team did an outstanding job coaching our region through our quality management journey. Her approach to consulting is refreshing and right-on for today's and tomorrow's business needs. Read her book. She shares all her secrets!"

—Gail Hammack, former regional vice president, McDonald's Corporation

"There is a substantial gap between possessing subject matter expertise and possessing the skills to apply that expertise in a way that adds value for clients. Then, once across the gap, there is need for a well-charted course to negotiate the challenges of simply doing business successfully. Elaine Biech has bridged that gap again with an even more reliable crossing to the realm of integrated expertise and consultant skills, and then provided the essential roadmap for reaching our business goals. This is my go-to book."

—Joseph G. Wojtecki, Jr., senior fellow and business manager, Center for Risk Communication

The New Business of Consulting

THE BASICS AND BEYOND

Elaine Biech

WILEY

For general information on our other products and services or for technical support, please contact our Customer Care Department within the United States at (800) 762-2974, outside the United States at (317) 572-3993 or fax (317) 572-4002.

Wiley publishes in a variety of print and electronic formats and by print-on-demand. Some material included with standard print versions of this book may not be included in e-books or in print-on-demand. If this book refers to media such as a CD or DVD that is not included in the version you purchased, you may download this material at http://booksupport.wiley.com. For more information about Wiley products, visit www.wiley.com.

Library of Congress Cataloging-in-Publication Data:

ISBN 9781119556909 (Hardcover)
ISBN 9781119556923 (ePDF)
ISBN 9781119556947 (ePub)

Cover image: © Aukid Phumsirichat/EyeEm/Getty Images
Cover design: Wiley

Printed in the United States of America

V10008930_032119

For Shane and Thad
My first two consulting projects

CONTENTS

EXHIBITS AND THE COMPANION WEBSITE

You must know right up front that consultants are an odd bunch. Most of us love downloadable templates that will make us more successful. That's why I've included all of the exhibits in the book, plus some additional ones, at www.wiley.com/go/newconsultingbiech. I want to do everything I can to get you started on the right foot, and making these worksheets easily accessible is a small way I can contribute to your success. Here's a list of the exhibits included in this book; the ones marked "(online only)" can be found at the above URL.

FOREWORD

I will always remember Johnny Smith. Johnny was my very first supervisor in my very first full-time, salary-paying job.

I had returned from two years in the Peace Corps and was fortunate to find work in a consulting firm that had landed a contract from the U.S. Office of Economic Opportunity. I was part of a team that traveled from city to city in the southwestern United States to conduct training programs, facilitate team-building sessions, and consult on organizational issues to newly formed Community Action Agencies. Our group was made up of mostly young, inexperienced, but highly motivated behavioral scientists who wanted to change the world. It was a perfect kind of job for us, but without Johnny we most likely would have gone broke.

Johnny was a Texas Instruments manager who had decided to take on the temporary assignment of leading this small band of do-gooders. He, too, wanted to do good, but from his years at Texas Instruments, he also knew that to be of service we had to stay in business. Johnny brought a discipline that was absolutely essential to our survival.

I vividly remember one consulting gig in Dallas, Texas. We had a meeting with the director of an agency to talk about the goals and roles for the assignment, and the director was called out for a few minutes. Johnny said to us, "This guy is very organized." I asked, "How do you know that?" He said, "See all those file folders lined up neatly on the credenza behind his desk? That's how." And, he was right about that. The guy and the agency were very organized. Johnny paid attention to detail. He was all about the little things that, when you added them up, either made something work or caused it to fail. I also remember what a stickler he was for filling out expense reports and submitting invoices. He used to say things like, "You'll get my thanks when you fill in the blanks." Corny, but it worked.

Johnny Smith would have adored Elaine Biech. He'd have wanted her on our team. And, had it been available back in 1969, I am confident that Johnny would have handed every one of my colleagues and me a copy of *The New Business of Consulting*. It's the kind of straightforward, no-nonsense book that he would have wholeheartedly embraced.

But since Johnny isn't around to give you that advice, permit me to offer it instead. If you are just starting out in consulting, or if you are at a place where you're growing but not making enough money, you must study this book. *The New Business of Consulting* is vital to your success. You can be extraordinary at what you do, but if you do not know how to run your business, you will be out of business quickly.

Just take a look at what you'll find in *The New Business of Consulting*. In Chapter One Elaine asks, and helps you answer, the question, "What are you getting yourself into?" The chapter enables you to come to grips with the myths and realities of the business and asks you to seriously consider whether or not consulting is right for you. Chapter Two is about the talents and tolerances you'll need to succeed in the profession. Chapter Three discusses money—what you think you'll need to earn, how much you should charge, and how to make ethical pricing decisions.

Chapters Four, Five, and Six focus on starting—and staying—in business and the cost of doing business. These are the meat and potatoes chapters about running the operational, marketing, and financial sides of your practice. Need to write a business plan? It's here. Need a marketing plan? This book has guidelines for developing one. Need to calculate your cash flow or deal with bad debts? Elaine offers wise counsel on these and more.

Chapter Seven addresses clients. From the first meeting to maintaining the relationship after the project has been completed, Elaine coaches you on how to create value for your customer. Chapter Eight describes the pains—sometimes welcome, sometimes not—of growth. One of the most vexing issues you will have to deal with during the life of your firm is how to manage it as it matures, adds people (and costs), and becomes more than just a hobby for one person. Elaine talks to you about the advantages and disadvantages of key aspects of growth.

Elaine and I share a passion for ethics. Elaine is adamant about how we conduct ourselves in business, and Chapters Nine and Ten are calls to action. As Elaine puts it, "Your reputation as a consultant will be created by thousands of actions, but may be lost by only one." She reminds us that it is imperative that we act as role models for how business should be conducted. We always have to practice what we preach. All this takes continuous professional learning and personal growth.

In the closing Chapter Eleven, Elaine poses the question, "Do you still want to be a consultant?" She helps you answer it by giving you a peek into her own daily life as a consultant, a dose of reality for anyone daring to answer "yes" to the question. Of course, we all know what Elaine's answer is, because it's the profession she chose for herself. She's not a journalist who just writes about it; she lives it every day. She's a role model for the advice she gives others, and she's personally helped hundreds of people start consulting practices with the information in this book.

And you can understand why so many people benefit from her wise counsel. *The New Business of Consulting* is complete and easy to use. The advice can be put into practice immediately. No theory here. Just real-world examples and proven tactics to build and grow a successful consulting practice. Elaine does not hold back; you don't need to read between the lines. She is straightforward and candid, and she shares openly all that she knows. This is a compilation of all the lessons she's learned about running a consulting practice during her 35 years of being in the trade. There are over 50 checklists, tables, forms, and other useful tools. It's all between these pages, but as an added bonus there are forms available in a downloadable format that can be easily personalized.

Elaine also offers tips that are meant to help you tap into all the resources beyond the book. Many of these tips are based on the technology that is currently available. They are designed to help you save time and money, tap into ever-changing information, identify resources to build the business, and find tools to keep you on the cutting edge of what you do. Given the extraordinary developments in technology in the past decade, these ideas make this book exceptionally valuable in the virtual ways in which you now work.

But there's something else that you need to know about Elaine, something that comes alive when you read the book and is even more evident when you talk with her in person. Elaine loves consulting, loves a challenge, and loves her clients. As you will understand when you read this book, these are perhaps the only three reasons why you should get into consulting in the first place.

The spirit of this book is best captured in a comment that Elaine sent to me when we first corresponded about *The New Business of Consulting*. I asked her to tell me what she most wanted others to know about her book, and one of the things she said to me was, "I feel I owe so much to the industry and to people who have helped me along the way. This book is one way for me to give back to the world that has given me so much." That is quintessential Elaine and is at the heart of who she is. It's why those of us who are privileged to know her and work with her so highly respect her and the work she does. This book is Elaine's gift of experience to our field, and I invite you to open it with great glee, read it with delight, and use it to help grow and sustain your business.

Jim Kouzes
Coauthor of *The Leadership Challenge*

April 2019

ACKNOWLEDGMENTS

The New Business of Consulting was authored by many wise and wonderful people. It is a delight to thank everyone who helped me write this book.

- Consultants who led the way and taught me all that I know: Geoff Bellman, Ken and Margie Blanchard, Peter Block, Elliott Masie, Ann Herrmann-Nehdi, Bev Kaye, Jim Kouzes, Peter Senge, and Jack Zenger.
- Matt Holt, editor and friend, for sending subliminal messages and then making a phone call to confirm the deal.
- Vicki Adang, Zach Schisgal, and Shannon Vargo, the team that answered all my crazy questions and made time for me. You make me look great.
- Dawn Kilgore, the best production editor in the business, for caring about her work and her authors.
- Rebecca Taff, for unraveling my entangled sentences, cutting contrary commas, and reducing redundancy.
- Dottie Dehart, publicist extraordinaire, and her team, who create beautiful book music.
- Dan Greene, for keeping the world at bay while I wrote.
- Mentors and friends who believe in what I do: Kristin Arnold, Halelly Azulay, Dianna Booher, Justin Brusino, Steve Cohen, Kris Downing, Admiral Godwin, Linda Growney, Jonathan Halls, Shirley Krsinich, Jenn Labin, Robin Lucas, Toni Lucia, Jennifer Martineau, Cat Russo, Pam Schmidt, Judye Talbot, and Kathy Talton.

- Clients for allowing me to practice the business of consulting with you.
- And especially to Peter Block, for responding to a plea for help in 1987 with "flawless consulting."

Elaine Biech
ebb associate inc
Virginia Beach, VA

April 2019

INTRODUCTION

Are you thinking about starting your own business of consulting? Your timing couldn't be better. The world of work is changing rapidly. Gone are the days of lifetime employment with traditional, stable organizations. In its place is the gig economy. You have most likely heard predictions that more than 50 percent of the U.S. workforce will not have traditional jobs in this decade. Whether you've heard these new roles called freelancers, crowd workers, contractors, solopreneurs, free agents, agile employees, on-demand labor, giggers, side hustlers, portfolio careers, or some other endearing name, consulting fits the definition.

The term *gig* originally comes from the jazz players of the 1930s, who called each separate performance a *gig*. Today, all types of freelancers and consultants use it to describe work that they've been hired to do that has either a time or scope parameter.

Consulting is a profitable $250 billion industry and growing. Millions have taken the initiative to create their own livelihood and do what they want. As the gig economy infographic designed by Robert McGuire of Nation1099 (Exhibit I.1, at www.wiley.com/go/newconsultingbiech) displays, 86 percent of professional freelancers choose freelancing. That means that they are not in traditional jobs by choice; they didn't lose their jobs involuntarily.

THE TIMING IS RIGHT

Consulting is more respected now than ever. Freelance consulting is viewed as a win for companies and consultants alike. Companies can hire expertise for the time or project duration that is needed. Consultants can provide the expertise on demand and can be reimbursed for the amount of effort they contribute. Several changes have influenced how business is conducted. This has led to the increased approval rating of those in a 1099 tax arrangement.

- Organizations need an agile workforce to keep up with the ever-changing demands of their missions and the intense competition.
- Technology has empowered consultants to work from anywhere, to connect with clients, close a million-dollar deal, or build a brand from their mobile phones.
- An increasing number of consultants are not just surviving, but thriving, earning a six-figure (or more) income. A 2016 McKinsey report found that 75 percent of consultants were making more or the same amount of money than they did in their traditional roles.
- Professional apps, online marketplaces, marketing opportunities, and other business operating options are readily available and easily connect consultants to clients.
- Large consulting firms are getting in on the gig economy, recognizing that they cannot support the large cadre of consultants they've had on staff in the past. In fact, in 2016 PricewaterhouseCoopers (PwC) launched its Talent Exchange, an online platform that matches independent consultants with relevant skill sets to work on PwC projects.

Is the timing right for you, too? The dream of being self-employed, being your own boss, and striking out on your own is not new. For many employees, an entrepreneurial spirit strikes no matter the societal or economic trends. Unfulfilling work, temperamental bosses, and unhealthy organizational cultures have spurred entrepreneurial dreamers to quit their jobs to pursue their passion, to do the work they love. Your reasons for becoming a consultant might include some of these.

- You desire an increased sense of meaning and fulfillment from your work, to make a difference where you think it counts.
- You want to trade the hassles of a corporate career, a desk job, and a commute for more control over your time, doing what you love on your terms.

- You want to work with the organizations and people you choose.
- You know this is the direction the workplace is heading and you want to prepare for the ongoing gig economy.
- You see that stability is being redefined and you want to be in charge of your own future.
- You want to learn and develop your skills and expertise more broadly than you are now.
- If you have expertise that is in demand, consulting is a relatively inexpensive and easy business to break into.

Or perhaps you are like me and you just want to prove that you can be successful on your own. Of course, there are drawbacks and we will point them out throughout the book. But the bottom line is that consulting in the gig economy is healthy and growing. It is a satisfying arrangement for both consultants and the clients who need them. This book will help you prepare for your half of the equation.

LOGICAL CONTENT FLOW

The chapters are presented in the same order that you will likely require the information as you move into a consulting role. Each chapter begins with a short story. Whether you are a millennial who is looking for purpose and meaning in the work you do or a baby boomer on the verge of retirement, you will relate to these stories. Don't think that they are just made-up fiction. Every story happened in real life to me or my consulting colleagues.

Tips are sprinkled throughout the chapters to give you ideas that meet your specific needs or resources where you can search for the ideas you still need.

Each chapter ends with a section I've called "For the Consummate Consultant." It presents three actions you can take that go beyond the content in the chapter—beyond the basics. Think of these ideas like "extra credit" that you may have had in school: optional additional activities that will boost your rate of success.

We are all consultants—all experts in something. Oh, I am not trying to come up with an impressive ad campaign or a slogan to sell this book. I mean it. But being an expert at what you do isn't enough. You need to be an entrepreneur to stay in business. I grew up on a Wisconsin dairy farm and believe that farmers may be some of the original entrepreneurs. Farmers need to be good at animal husbandry and raising crops, but if they do not focus on their businesses with wise capital investments and maintain healthy cash flow, they will not be farming for long.

You are no doubt a very fine consultant, but like farmers, being good at consulting is not enough to keep you profitable. You also must manage your business. This book focuses on the business side of consulting: how to develop a business plan, how to market your business, how to charge for your services, how to build a client relationship, how to grow the business, how to ensure your continued professional growth, and, of course, how to make money in the profession.

The New Business of Consulting is written in the first person—singular and plural. Although I've authored the book, the employees of ebb associates and all my colleagues have played a big part in shaping the content, so I'll use "we" on occasion.

HELPFUL AND PRACTICAL CONTENT

My goal in writing this book is to provide as many practical tools and sound ideas as possible. Most were learned through trial and error, and I hope this book will prevent you from making some of the same mistakes.

- The book has been written for several kinds of readers: the individual who is considering a consulting profession and wonders whether it's a good decision and how to start, the new consultant who may have mastered the client-consulting role and now realizes that there is also a business to run, and the experienced consultant continuing a lifelong learning journey who is looking for a few practical tips.
- Being a successful consultant means that you not only provide excellent advice for your clients' businesses, but you also implement excellent advice for your own business.
- To be most helpful, dozens of checklists, assessments, templates, financial forms, and other tools are included. To make it even easier, all of the tools are available at www.wiley.com/go/newconsultingbiech. You can personalize them with your company name and print them out to project cash flow, plan marketing campaigns, track your time, identify your aptitude for starting a business, or a dozen other things.

BEYOND THE CONTENT

This book delivers everything you need to manage a successful consulting business. However, just reading it will not make you a successful consultant. Three things are required for your success.

You Need to Do the Work

In some cases I present suggestions. In other situations I offer pros and cons of each decision. And at times you will need to do your own self-discovery to determine what's best for you. You'll need an entrepreneurial approach to take risks, focus on your client, and make a profit to be most successful. The book is your guide to do what's needed.

Start with Your Own Expertise

The book is not about the content of your consulting. That is entirely up to you. Whether your expertise is in accounting or zoology, you will still need to run your consulting efforts as a business, using entrepreneurial skills. The business philosophy I present is one of a relationship consulting business—not of a grab-the-money-and-run relationship! So you do not need to be concerned that your reputation and expertise will be tarnished by the business processes I suggest.

Your Attitude Is Everything

It begins with your mindset. I am a huge believer in positive thinking. To paraphrase Henry Ford, "Whether you believe you'll be a successful consultant or not—you'll be right!" Combine your consulting expertise with the business tools in this book and believe that you will be a smashing success.

So You Want to Be a Consultant

A person who never made a mistake never tried anything new.

Albert Einstein

Kayla was livid. She really wanted to do stellar work, but how could she when she never knew what was happening? This was the third time in a month that she had to hear bad news about her department from Amy, who was in the contracts department, instead of from her own manager. Didn't he understand that anything less than total transparency was not acceptable to her?

She started this job four years ago, right out of college with her MBA and the expectation that she would use what she learned and continue to learn and grow. But that hadn't happened.

She had been turned down four times for the additional training she wanted. Granted, the first time it may have seemed like a selfish request because the only rationale she provided was that "she wanted it" and she hadn't tied the content to her job. But every request after that was directly related to problems and issues that occurred on the job. The last time, she even put together a cost-benefit analysis that clearly showed that what she would learn would save the company money. Instead, her manager told her to wait because next year she would be in line for the leadership development program. He seemed to be shocked when she told him she wasn't that interested in being a leader, and that she was more interested in being a top performer and expert in her field.

Leadership wasn't for her. The previous month, the CEO had signed off on the new innovation policy with, "I'm interested in hearing all your ideas. Come see me." But when she went up to the fourteenth floor, she was turned away by the chief of staff, who said that her actions were improper. Leadership was hypocrisy! She didn't want any part of that.

Kayla wanted to keep learning. Heck, she'd settle for some coaching, but her manager didn't seem to have time—or the inclination. After all the articles that had appeared about millennials, didn't he get it yet? Without figuring out what she valued, he didn't stand a chance!

Why was she here? She disliked the slowness and bureaucracy; she didn't want to be "managed." She wanted a job that had purpose and meaning and that connected directly to the company's mission. She'd been thinking a lot lately—perhaps the corporate environment didn't suit her. Then again, she'd heard from some of her friends who had struck out on their own and found out that "doing what you love" doesn't always put food on the table.

But she'd been studying the whole freelance, gig thing for over a year and found that consulting might be different. She pulled out her "How to Rule the World" journal and perused some of the pages: write a business plan, buy liability insurance, charge what you are worth, choose a good name, clarify your niche, select an accountant, develop a marketing plan, plan your transition, get a federal EIN, check on a city license. Well, there certainly was enough there to keep her busy.

She knew she would love the freedom of being her own boss, but she had an enormous student loan to pay off. If she could only figure out how much she might be able to make and a few more details about how consultants charged. She read a Randstad report when she was researching the company's agility article that more than half of the workers surveyed believed they could make more money as consultants than in their current jobs. Well, money wasn't everything. She wanted to do something more enjoyable, too. And she certainly wasn't getting any younger; she'd be 30 next year! Besides, she deserved to be happy! Maybe her friend Mason would know. He knew everything. She'd text him now. Maybe he could meet her after work.

■ ■ ■

Do you admire consultants who zip into a company, capture everyone's attention, accomplish in days what you've been struggling with for months, and waltz out with a big check?

Ever thought you might like to be a part of that glamorous profession? This book will help you determine whether you have what it takes to be a consultant, as well as whether the consulting profession offers what you desire as an individual.

WHAT IS CONSULTING?

Consulting is the process by which an individual or a firm assists a client to achieve a stated outcome. The assistance can come in the form of information, recommendations, or actual hands-on work. A consultant is a specialist within a professional area who completes the work necessary to achieve the client's desired outcome.

Whether companies need help developing an agile workforce, increasing competitiveness, reducing turnover, increasing engagement, installing a new computer system, building an executive team, breaking into the Chinese market, or solving almost any other business problem, they can call a consultant to assist with the effort. The organization requesting the assistance is usually called the *client*. The term can refer to the entire organization or to the person who actually made the call.

Consulting is not a descriptor that identifies a profession in itself. Unlike doctors or accountants, highly skilled consultants come from a variety of backgrounds. A qualifying adjective may be required to identify the form of service or the area of expertise, for example, management consultant, engineering consultant, or performance consultant. Although consulting is not a profession by definition, it is often referred to as "the consulting profession." For the sake of convention, I will refer to the *profession* in this book.

The actual work of a consultant can vary quite a bit, depending on the area of expertise offered. Every consultant must be a subject-matter expert in some area. The expertise might be in the form of general content such as management development, organization development, leadership, or family business. Expertise might be in a specific profession, such as engineering, cybersecurity, writing, marketing, or a thousand others. Expertise might also be in the form of how the consultant delivers services, such as facilitation, training, strategic planning, or team building.

Even after you determine an area of expertise, you may need to select the actual work method you wish to conduct. For example, if you decide to focus on the talent development field, you could develop and deliver your own material or subcontract material development to another person while you deliver it. You could design material for others, or you could deliver others' materials. You could even be certified to deliver others' courses, especially for the large training supplier firms.

If you are a generalist, such as a management consultant, you will need to determine whether you will focus on a specific industry, such as manufacturing, banking, aerospace, military, or hundreds of other industries.

WHY CONSULTING NOW?

Like all businesses, consulting has its peaks and valleys. Consulting grew most rapidly, at double-digit rates, from the mid-1970s until 2000. When the economy weakens, consulting generally declines as well—especially in large firms. An independent consultant can take advantage of declines in a way that large firms cannot. As a small entity, a consultant has the opportunity to design the future. As an independent consultant, you can make changes faster than a large 10,000-employee firm. If organizations no longer need your expertise to nurture innovation, but need someone to help them plan for their high retirement rate, you can make that switch. Wayne Gretzky, the hockey player, is famous for claiming that his success is due to skating to where the puck "is going to be." Consultants too can skate to where the work is going to be. During a downturn, many consultants stick with doing only what they know, as opposed to what clients need.

Over the past 15 years, growth has been healthy, though few believe the rate will mirror the growth rate in the last century. As a consultant, you can economy-proof your business by providing services to at least a couple of industries that are rarely affected by the economy, such as healthcare, pharmaceuticals, and pet products. As compared to other industries, consulting continues to be one of the fastest-growing professional areas.

Why Get into Consulting? Why Now?

Turbulent times have increased how often consultants are used to help organizations make their way through the processes of implementing technology, going global, improving processes, applying lean principles, and negotiating mergers. The consulting projects have increased in dollar amount and duration. Since the early 1990s, large-scale projects that cost more than $50 million and last over a five-year period are common. As Charles Stein (1994) of the *Boston Globe* states, "Once upon a time, consultants were like dinner guests: They came for a brief visit, gave advice, and went home. Now they are like guests who come for dinner, move into the spare bedroom, and stay for a year or two."

Business Trends

Two trends in the business world continue to bring tremendous implications for consulting. First is the trend toward a need for organizations to be more agile. Corporations will continue to hire more temporary professionals to assist when needed, as opposed to adding highly paid, permanent staff. Consultants temporarily provide the "people power" to complete the work at the time it needs to be completed.

Even though many baby boomers will work past age 65, many retire every day. According to the AARP, 10,000 baby boomers are turning 65 every day, and this will continue into the 2030s. Gig workers fill the need for positions as diverse as sales representatives, engineers, healthcare specialists, information technologists, and accountants. But due to their expertise, consultant roles are in high demand.

Dan Pink, author of *Free Agent Nation*, was one of the first to alert us to the growing number of employees who would have alternative work arrangements. According to the Workplace 2025 study released in 2017 by Randstad US, one of the largest human resources (HR) services and staffing companies in North America, by 2025, a majority of the workforce will be employed in an agile capacity, as consultant, contractor, temporary, or freelance employee (Heisler, Southhall, and Cardec 2016).

The Workplace 2025 report surveyed more than 3,100 workers and 1,500 HR and C-suite executives across the United States and found that as early as 2019, as much as 50 percent of the workforce will be comprised of agile workers. The misconceptions about agile employment are disappearing, with about half (46 percent) of workers saying that they personally chose to become an agile worker. When asked why, employees responded as follows.

- Sixty-eight percent believe it is a better fit to their lifestyle.
- Sixty-three percent believe working as an agile employee will make them more qualified in the future workplace.

- Fifty-six percent agree agile work makes them more money.
- Forty-eight percent agree agile work offers them better career growth than working as a permanent employee.
- Thirty-eight percent agree they feel more job security working as an agile worker than they do as a permanent employee.

Although some of these comments may surprise you, it is a definite confirmation that employees' beliefs about the flexible needs of organizations will benefit them, too.

The second trend is that rapid changes occurring in the world make it almost impossible for the executive team to remain knowledgeable about their industry, remain focused on their customers, stay ahead of their competition, and know instantly what to do when these factors collide in a negative way. Consultants offer the knowledge, information, data, other experiences, processes, and systems to solve the puzzle. They fill in the blanks. When the task is complete, they are on their way.

Several other trends continue, so they are perhaps less "trend" and more a way of life. For example, consulting engagements continue to be larger and last longer. It is not uncommon for a contract to cost over $20 million in consulting fees and last for multiple years. Other continuing trends that affect consulting include: a continuing increase in the rate of change; a heightened concern for the security of intellectual property, and the safety of a corporate workforce; limited preparation to adequately address an increasingly diverse workforce; a higher ethical bar; the global economy; technology efficiencies creating heavier workloads that are expected to be completed immediately; and employees' belief that they are on call 24/7.

Talent management is a continuing trend that offers lots of opportunity for consulting. It focuses on the recruiting, retention, and rewarding of members of the workforce. Although it is focused mostly on the work that the HR department is supposed to do, it often encompasses training, diversity, and other aspects of people needs, focusing on the total employee experience. The field hasn't been around long enough to completely define itself, so don't be surprised if you actually start by helping your clients with a definition (Biech 2018a).

Healthcare is one of the faster-growing industries. This is a trend you should watch, as I expect the need for consulting to grow. Healthcare payment and delivery systems have been changing, which has generated a high demand for consultants to help healthcare organizations change through alliances, innovation, access strategies, and quality improvement. IT requirements continue to increase the demand for consultants. Other fast-growing industries for consulting include telecommunications, the Internet, environmental areas, and finance. Service industries and government agencies continue to implement lean principles. So if you practiced your skills in manufacturing, there is still more to be done in other areas. Not-for-profit and government organizations also continue to use more consultants.

Consulting Trends

Trends also exist in the kind of work that consultants are doing. Coaching continues to be on the rise. Although at one time having a coach was a sign that something was wrong with an executive, now the opposite is true. Employees think it is a sign that something is wrong if an executive does *not* have a coach!

Some consultants have become contingency workers. These consultants work full-time for months for a single employer, collecting hourly wages, but minimal benefits from an outside staffing agency. They are paid well while they are working, but the work is mostly short-term. Companies benefit with lower costs and the flexibility of easy termination.

That's the demand side. What about the supply side? The same organizations that are cutting permanent staff to keep payroll down are providing a steady supply of people who need jobs and find that they can do consulting. In fact, many people cut from their jobs today may be placed in the same company as temporary employees.

Why this shuffling of the same bodies? Consultants are often more cost-effective for the organization, which can hire the skill it needs on an as-needed basis rather than train and educate staff for skills that may not be used again. Consultants can usually complete projects faster as well.

Client Perspective

Clients need consultants for a variety of reasons. Several are listed here:

- *Lack of expertise.* The skills necessary for the growing and changing needs of an organization are not available inside the organization. Therefore, organizations turn to consultants to complete projects or solve problems.
- *Lack of time.* Even when the skills are available in the organization, staff members may not have the time to complete special projects or research.

A consultant can be a part of the organization just long enough to complete what needs to be done.

- *Lack of experience.* Certain professions are experiencing a shortage of trained employees. Consultants can fill in until demand is met by training or hiring new employees.
- *Staffing flexibility.* Consultants can be brought in for the short term to complete a project. When the work is completed, the organization can terminate the relationship easily and quickly without severance pay or other obligations.
- *Objective outside opinions.* Consultants usually provide fresh perspectives. Outsiders can look at a problem in a new, unbiased way.
- *New ideas.* Consultants bring with them ideas from other firms and industries. This cross-pollination is a surefire way to tap into many resources. Staff members may be too close to the problem to see a new solution.
- *Speed and efficiency.* Hiring a consultant who has experienced the same type of project in the past at other locations may be faster and more cost-effective than bringing staff members up to speed.
- *Assessment.* A consultant can provide an objective assessment, define the problem, and make recommendations.
- *Resolution.* In the case of a merger or other change of organizational structure, an outside consultant can act as an independent mediator to resolve differences.
- *Compliance.* An organization may not have enough time and may lack the expertise to comply with legal expectations. Hiring a consultant shows that an effort is being made to correct the problem.

Consultant Perspective

I frequently speak at conferences on the topic of becoming a consultant. The title I use is "So You Want to Be a Consultant." I always ask, "Why do you want to be a consultant?" The responses I receive are many and varied. Perhaps you'll relate to several of the following:

- *Be my own boss.* I want to be my own boss. It has always been a dream of mine. I will no longer need to take orders from anyone else.
- *Eliminate a set schedule.* I want to be free from daily routine. I am bored with corporate life. I've worked all my life. I've been a good employee. Perhaps it's

just this midlife thing, but I feel financially secure and I want more than just a paycheck. I want something outside of the routine.

- *Availability of greater opportunities.* I see more opportunities now than ever. There seems to be a growing need in every company. I see consultants in our company every week.
- *Do my own thing.* I have skills that I believe others will pay me for. I have a lot of experience and expertise and I'd like to set my own agenda, rather than follow someone else's.
- *Take advantage of technology.* Technology has made it easier to create a fully operating office quickly.
- *Easy start-up.* I think it's a business that I can afford to start. I already have a computer, and I can work out of my home office. The relatively low-cost start-up makes it possible for me to own a business. Most other businesses I checked into required over $100,000 to open.
- *Freedom.* I want to work in my pajamas if I choose. This is as good a reason as any. Besides, there is a new prestige in working out of your home. At one time the consultant working from home was seen as less than professional. This is no longer true.
- *More money.* Consultants appear to make big bucks, and I want to get in on it. I'm working for a company that does not have a retirement plan. I sat down with the numbers and I believe I can spend my last 10 years in the workforce doing something I like and putting money away for my retirement.
- *Out of work.* I don't have a choice; I was downsized out of a job. Actually, I'm beginning to think I'm lucky. I don't think I would have made the move on my own. I think I can make just as good a living as a consultant.
- *Greater good.* I want to make a difference. I'm not even concerned that I might not make the salary I am presently making. There is something greater calling me. I want to make a difference in the world and work with nonprofit organizations that will appreciate what I bring.
- *Security.* Corporate America isn't safe anymore. I want financial security, and I can think of no better way to ensure that than to take matters into my own hands.
- *Creativity.* I want to have the opportunity to be creative. I've always wanted to try something new, but in my job I am frequently told that it can't be done. I want to find out for myself.

- *Travel.* This may be a frivolous reason, but I want to travel. I know it may get old after a while, but I'll deal with that when the time comes.
- *Challenge.* I need a greater challenge, but it isn't going to occur where I am now. There is virtually no room for promotions, and I could be doing the same thing for the next six years with very little professional or personal growth.
- *Self-preservation.* I need to look out for myself. I'm in an industry that is fraught with mergers and acquisitions. I need to take care of myself and what I want out of life.
- *Location.* I want to live where I choose. The way I look at it, as long as I'm near an airport, I will be able to reach my clients.

What do people look for in a job so that they rate the job as being highly satisfactory? The four attributes cited most often include intellectual stimulation, high job security, a high level of control and freedom, and extensive direct contact with customers or clients. As you can see, consulting rates high on all four of these aspects.

Why did I join the ranks of the independent consultants over 35 years ago? The four aspects that others identify are all important to me in my career. In addition, I have always said that it was because I am not a compliant employee. I do not like to be told what to do; I like to march to the toot of my own saxophone; I like a challenge and I like to take risks; I like to work directly with clients; I am a self-starter and hard worker, but I want to work during the hours I choose, not on someone else's time clock; I want to express my creativity; and I prefer to control my own destiny.

> **Tip: WSJ resource.**
>
> Check www.careerjournal.com for other information about the consulting profession and business in general. It's sponsored by the *Wall Street Journal*.

What about you? Have you explored why you are considering a move into the consulting profession?

FOUR WAYS TO GET STARTED

Taking risks. Embracing ambiguity. Practicing flexibility. Balancing both process and people issues. Managing multiple responsibilities. Tolerating extensive travel. Communicating effectively. Learning continually. Proving your worth again and again. Does this describe you? If you responded with a resounding "Yes!" consulting may be an ideal career move for you.

If you decide consulting is right for you, what opportunities exist? Think about your ultimate goal. Do you want to be a partner in one of the "Big Four"? Will you eventually own your own firm? Do you think you will always want to consult as a sole practitioner? Do you want to teach part-time at a small university and consult on the side? There are at least four ways you could enter the field: as an employee, as a subcontractor, as a part-time consultant, or as a self-employed independent consultant.

As an Employee

Numerous employment opportunities exist for you. You could join a large national consulting firm. You could also join a small firm or even partner with someone in an even smaller firm.

Large Firm. If you just graduated from college, this is your best bet to experience the consulting profession. You will need experience. As an employee in a large firm, you will be an extra pair of hands on large projects—a great way to get experience. Consulting is typically listed as one of the top-paying jobs. With a bachelor's degree, you can land a gig in one of the major firms and expect to earn between $60,000 and $90,000. For a select number of firms, the salary can approach $100,000. These figures include base salary, a signing bonus, and relocation expenses. If that sounds like a high salary, keep in mind that first-year consultants work as much as to 14-hour days and travel most weeks.

Tip: Search salaries.

Glass Door lists the average consultant salary at $88,395, which is excellent as an average. The site also lists average salaries by company. You can get up-to-the-minute data at www.glassdoor.com for details.

And if you stay in school longer, the rewards are greater. MBAs from top schools can expect to be offered a base salary hovering around $145,000 to $150,000 as new consultants with firms such as Deloitte, Accenture, McKinsey, and others (Consulting.com 2018). About 75 percent of all consultants are eligible for bonuses and signing bonuses in addition to their salaries. The demand for consultants and a high starting salary have led to a strong competition for talent.

As a consultant for a large national firm, you would be able to focus solely on consulting and generating business. Someone else would complete tax forms, hire secretarial support, and pay the rent. You would have instant name recognition and a clear career path. Although this may sound advantageous at first blush, the greatest drawback is that you might become so comfortable with your job that you would never experience the world of the independent consultant.

These jobs generally come with a great deal of pressure. Usually you are expected to generate (sell) a certain amount of consulting services. Travel is another drawback. If you choose this route, learn more about these large firms, who they are, and what they do. I've identified several arbitrary segments. The same firm may be represented in more than one of these segments.

- The "Big Four" international accounting firms also offer professional service. They handle the vast majority of audits for publicly traded and private companies. Members of the Big Four are PricewaterhouseCoopers (PwC), Deloitte, Ernst & Young, and KPMG.
- Large national and international strategy firms, such as Accenture, Booz Allen Hamilton, The Boston Consulting Group, or McKinsey & Co., provide strategic or operational advice to top executive officers in Fortune 500 companies.
- Boutique strategy firms that specialize in a specific industry or along a functional line, such as Cornerstone Research (litigation support) or Gartner (high-tech research), are smaller, but many have excellent reputations.
- Firms that focus on human resources issues, such as designing compensation systems, change management, mergers, or conducting employee satisfaction surveys, include firms such as Korn Ferry, Aon Hewitt, and Towers Watson.
- Technology firms that design, implement, and manage information and computer systems are involved in work that is time-intensive, requires large teams, and usually takes place behind the scenes. These firms are less prestigious, but offer more opportunities for undergraduates. A sample of firms includes CGI, HP Enterprise Services, Oracle, SAIC, and SAP. Note that it is not always necessary to have a technology degree, as many of the jobs require other skills.

Prepare for the Interview

Are you thinking about applying to one of the larger companies for a job? If yes, examine these sample questions they are likely to ask you. I've added a couple of notes about what they'll be looking for.

- *Why are you interested in consulting?* The interviewer is testing how committed you are to bringing value to the firm. They are also interested in learning how much you know about the profession. Research the profession. This book is a good start.
- *Why do you want to work for this firm?* This is to test your knowledge about the industry, the firm, and consulting in general. Be sure to check the company's website before the interview.
- *Can you provide an example of when you displayed leadership and teamwork?* Leadership is a key skill in consulting. Give an example that includes a team and a result.
- You will be given several case examples in topic areas such as segmentation, data analysis, value propositions, or others. These are to test your ability to assess a situation and provide a structured, solution-based answer. There is no right or wrong answer. You are expected to ask questions to gather data. Then respond with your answer, explaining your thought process and even what you still might need to do to obtain more information.

Small Firm. As a consultant in a small, local firm, you would experience similar advantages to those of a large, national firm. One added benefit might be that you would probably experience a wider variety of tasks and be given more responsibility sooner. If you want to travel, a drawback may be that you are often limited to working with businesses in your locality. Although your salary would be only half what it could be with one of the Big Four, you would have less pressure, more opportunity for a variety of projects, and more involvement in the entire consulting process. Find these companies by location. Check your local industry-specific association chapters in the city where you live. Many small firms do not find value in advertising, so your local librarian or Chamber of Commerce can help you. Ask for a listing of local businesses broken down by industry.

Partnership As a partner with one or more other consultants who are already in the business, you would be able to share the burden of expenses, marketing, and the workload. The biggest drawback is the potential for conflict over numerous business and personal preferences. These conflicts can vary from an unbalanced workload to communication to decision making. How do you find a partnership? Well, more often than not, they find you. You may be able to join an already formed partnership (expect to buy in with cash or reduced pay for a specified time period) or identify others who, like you, want to get into the consulting profession. When I was just starting, I joined a small firm with the promise of a partnership. After two years, when the "partnership" never materialized, I left and chalked it up to a learning experience. Read more about partnerships in Chapters Four and Eight.

As a Subcontractor

Rather than becoming an employee, you could subcontract with a firm. Many businesses and consulting firms are looking for subcontractors who will fill in the gaps left as a result of downsizing or launching new initiatives. As a subcontractor, you may have a less secure position, but you will have flexibility while gaining rich experience and developing a sense of the market. The work will most likely not be full-time, but this allows you time to develop your own business. Who might hire you? You could consider the larger companies listed previously. They will most likely want you to dedicate time to one specific project. The scope will be larger and more full-time. If you like the idea of being a training consultant, consider some of the leading training suppliers such as AchieveGlobal, AMA, DDI, Franklin Covey, Herrmann International, and The Ken Blanchard Companies.

Side Hustle

If you're not ready to take the plunge, you could consult part-time while keeping your present job. Some people use their vacation time and weekends to conduct small projects—with their employers' approval, of course. For example, if your specialty is team building or facilitating decision-making meetings, you might be able to do weekend retreats for boards of nonprofit organizations. Consulting is natural part-time work for college and university professors. If you are in the teaching profession, you have summers and vacation days that you can dedicate to part-time experiences. Part-time work will not give you the full flavor of what it will be like to be solely dependent upon consulting as a career, but it will give you an idea of whether you like the work.

Self-Employed Independent Consultant

You could also start your own consulting practice. When you develop expertise in an area, you might choose to build and run your own business around that expertise. The expertise being sold can be virtually anything. Specialties might include management, IT, marketing, financial, healthcare, environmental, social media, software, or hundreds of other specialties. The emerging gig economy is encouraging many people to start their own businesses.

Independent consultants might be called different things in different industries: freelancers, contractors, management consultants, or 1099s. In the United States, a 1099 worker is the IRS designation for someone hired on a contingent basis, not an employee whom the IRS classifies as a W-2. A consultant is generally thought of as the highest-skill end of the gig economy spectrum.

As an independent consultant, you have an opportunity to make all the decisions, do what you want when you want, and receive all the recognition. The drawback, of course, is that you would assume all the risk, be responsible for all expenses, and have no one at your level readily available with whom to discuss business plans and concerns. At least 20 percent of full-time independent consultants earn six-figure incomes. According to Consulting.com, the average annual revenue of an independent consultant is $97,000. MBO Partners found that 20 percent of professional consultants make more than $100,000 per year. Your revenue potential is wide open and completely uncapped. With a good plan, you can break through to a seven-figure income.

Who Wants to Be a Millionaire?

In her book *The Million-Dollar One-Person Business*, Elaine Pofeldt (2018) shares multiple examples of small-business owners who have been successful building a seven-figure, lean firm. Although not all of her examples are consultants, Pofeldt deftly presents the possibilities and the advantages. Pofeldt also sells the likelihood that the number of firms with no paid employees other than the owner that generate $1 to $2.49 million in revenue continues to rise each year; the number was 36,161 in 2016. Can you become a millionaire with a consulting practice? Sure. You don't have to make a million dollars every year to become a millionaire. You do have to be consistent and thoughtful. Build these concepts into your plans.

Who Wants to Be a Millionaire?, cont'd.

- Believe you can do it. Set your mindset to success.
- Determine what you could do better than anyone else.
- Verify your intuition.
- Own a narrow niche.
- Create very clear, specific goals.
- Practice discipline and focus.
- Consistently and constantly produce value for your clients.
- Consider passive income to supplement your hours.
- Pay attention to both income and expenses.
- Keep your business and marketing plans fresh.
- Stay connected.

Finally, realize that if you are just doing it for the money, you will likely fail. As John D. Rockefeller, America's first billionaire, said, "If your only goal is to become rich, you'll never achieve it."

The focus of this book is on the final way of breaking into the field—independent consultants who open their own businesses. If you have decided this is the route you will take, you can still begin slowly.

One way would be to obtain experience as an employee in one of the national or local consulting firms mentioned earlier, or to work part-time as described in the third option, or to take work with you when you leave your present employer. Chapter Four provides more detail about how you can do this effectively while starting your own business.

Tip: Job hunt the Internet.

Looking for a consulting job? Check the web for job listings. Try a consulting match up. Check out PwC's Talent Exchange, where they connect independent consultants with PwC opportunities. Go to TalentExchange.Pwc.com and MBOpartners. com. Other sites for consultants include www.Top-Consultant.com, EXPERT360. com,TalMix.com, and www.consultingmag.com. At least two sites, www. TheLadders.com and www.ExecuNet.com, post only jobs with annual base salaries of $100,000 or more. You may have to pay a monthly membership fee to access some of the data. Although the last two do not focus exclusively on consulting, a fair number of consulting jobs are posted there because of the salary.

MYTHS ABOUT CONSULTING

Some of the common myths you may believe about the field and the realities connected with them are listed next.

Myth 1: "Consultants charge over $1,000 per day; therefore, I will become rich consulting."

Let's take a realistic look at this myth. It may seem like a huge sum of money for a day's work, but let's examine what that $1,000 covers. Let's imagine that you are the consultant. If you work an eight-hour day, you would make $125 per hour. However, as a consultant you are now an entrepreneur, and it is more than likely that you are putting in a 12-hour day. That brings your hourly rate down to $83.

Of course it's not possible to bill for 365 days per year. Take out weekends. Remove holidays and a two-week vacation (remember, there's no *paid* vacation). We can conservatively reduce your hourly rate by 8 percent. That brings it down to $76 per hour. Still not bad.

As a consultant you will not be able to consult five days every week. You will need to use one day for preparation, one day for marketing, and one day to take care of administrative jobs such as taxes, billing, research, and professional development. So now one day's billing covers four days of your time. That's 25 percent of $76 an hour, or $19 per hour.

Murphy's Law states that all your clients will select the same two days in September for their off-site meetings and the rest of the month you will catch up on reading your *Harvard Business Review.* This won't happen just once each year. It may happen several times. In addition, you can bet on December as a notorious down time because of the holidays. No one wants you then. I've often wondered what really happens that month. Does no one work? Do employees turn into elves? When you add December to another bad month, you can expect to turn down 25 percent of all work because your clients' desired dates do not match your available dates. So deduct another 25 percent from the hourly fee. You are now down to $14 per hour.

You must cover all your own taxes. There is no employer to share the burden. As a consultant, quarters will take on a whole new meaning. You will not think in terms of the football score, but of the check you must write to pay your quarterly taxes. In rough numbers, let's say that you will pay 33 percent in various taxes. That leaves you with just a bit over $9 per hour.

You are on your own, so you must pay for your own benefits, such as health and life insurance and retirement. A very conservative estimate for this is $1.50 per hour. In addition, you will have business expenses—copying costs, telephone calls, stationery, postage. These expenses will accumulate fast! It may be $2 for every billable hour. Now what does that leave you?

Looks like you're down to $5.50 per hour. Oh, and you wanted to purchase a laptop computer? On $5.50 per hour?!? That job at McDonald's is looking mighty good right now!

Actually it's not that bad. Although the realities of consulting are exaggerated and a number of calculation flaws exist in the example, you need to be fully aware of everything that goes into a consulting fee. A daily fee of $1,000 or more sounds good. Yet when you consider expenses, taxes, benefits, and nonbillable hours, a large chunk of that $1,000 disappears quickly.

Independent consultants may make a six-figure income. Then again, some consultants have trouble making any income. Some consultants make less than $50,000 a year doing the same thing as others who gross over $500,000. Statistics that identify the average consultant salaries vary considerably from source to source. It appears that, more than any other profession, consulting embodies the spirit of entrepreneurship. Free enterprise is alive and well! The potential is there. It depends on what you want out of it. It depends on how hard you want to work.

Myth 2: "External consulting means I will be able to avoid all the politics and paperwork that drive me crazy in my present internal job."

The politics at your present job can keep you from being productive and effective. Perhaps politics is a game you have seen your boss play. As an external consultant, you may be able to escape the politics of your present organization, but get ready to be involved in the politics of not one but 8 or 12 or 23 organizations, depending on the number of clients you have. As a consultant, you will have many bosses rather than just one. You will need to be acutely aware of their needs and shortfalls, and you may need to make some difficult decisions to ensure that you remain on the job.

The big difference is that instead of dealing with the same politics all week long, you will be able to go home at night knowing that you will have a fresh set to work around or through (depending on your project) later in the week.

No paperwork? You will most likely have *more* paperwork. Not only will you have more, but unless you are starting out with an administrative assistant, you will not have anyone to whom you can delegate some of the work. Some of your paper-work will have a higher degree of importance. As an employee, you may have been able to turn your expense report in late and then beg the bookkeeping department to slip it into the stack anyway. But if you file your quarterly taxes late, the IRS is not likely to slip it into the on-time stack.

You must track hours and work so that you know what to charge clients. You must bill your clients in a timely manner to avoid cash-flow problems. You must determine how you will track invoices to ensure that your clients are paying you. You must track all expenses to avoid paying a larger share of income taxes than you should. You must track and file all paperwork so that you can locate it for your attorney and accountant and banker when they request information.

Not only will you not be able to avoid politics and paperwork, but they will be multiplied as you open your consulting business. If you don't take care of your paperwork, you will be out of business faster than you got in it.

Myth 3: "I will be seen as an expert in my area."

You are probably seen as an expert in the job you now hold. People turn to you for answers; you are respected by your colleagues and praised by your bosses (some of them, anyway!). Enjoy that while you can. You will be required to build that repu-tation with every new client relationship. You are about to face a never-ending task of proving yourself.

Starting your business goes far beyond opening an office and introducing your-self to your local Chamber of Commerce. You will build your business one client at a time. You will build your expertise one project at a time.

---

*You will build your business
one client at a time.*

Myth 4: "Having my own consulting practice means more free time."

If you are looking forward to getting up at noon and being out on the golf course several times each week, you are in for a big disappointment. Being a consultant means that you will become a business owner—an entrepreneur. Like most entre-preneurs, you will spend 60 to 80 hours each week that first year getting your busi-ness up and running. You will be marketing your services and networking with everyone you know.

You will be working for others, most likely businesspeople who go to work early, have tight deadlines, and experience huge pressures. You will be there to work as a partner with them to meet the deadlines and to relieve some of their pressures. You may need to work nights and weekends to meet a client's critical deadline. All the while, you may be wondering when you are going to find the time to complete the marketing you must do to ensure that, after this project is completed, you will have another one waiting for you.

Myth 5: "Consulting is a respected profession."

I thought I had chosen a respected profession. I was shocked the first time I was called a "beltway bandit"—the term assigned to consulting firms in and around the Washington, D.C., beltway. Since then, I've been called a pest because I followed up too often with a client. I've also been called a con man, which really bothered me, even though the client couldn't tell he had the wrong gender! Jokes about consultants abound.

Some of the negativity is deserved. There are many charlatans in our business. Unfortunately, the profession lacks legal standards or legitimate certification. It is very easy to go into the consulting business. Go to your local printer and have business cards printed. You are magically transformed into a consultant before the ink is dry.

Often people who are temporarily out of work drift into consulting to pick up a few bucks. They are in the field long enough to make a mess and devalue the role of the consultant. One out of every 20 projects I accept requires me to build the reputation of the consulting profession in one of two ways: I may need to clean up a mess created by a wannabe consultant who lacked organization development knowledge, or I may find myself fighting a battle of trust due to poor ethics or overcharging by a consultant who worked with the client organization previously.

Myth 6: "It's easy to break into the consulting field. All you need to do is print some business cards."

This is actually true. It is easy to break in. Staying in the business is what's hard. You did want to make a living, too, didn't you?

Initially you will probably need to spend at least 50 percent of your time marketing your services. You will need to establish business systems; set up your computers and printers to do all the things you want them to do; and create tracking systems for money, clients, paper flow, projects, and dozens of other things identified throughout this book. You may feel exhausted, and we haven't even mentioned providing services to your clients.

Myth 7: "Deciding to grow your practice is an easy decision. Everyone wants to grow a business."

You would think that the business of consulting would become easier over time. Unfortunately it does not. If you are good, you will have more work than you can handle. At some point, you will question whether to grow your business and how to do it. Should you produce products? Take on a partner? Create a firm? Or stay solo?

This is not an easy decision. It requires risk and capital. The pressure will be on you to grow. You must remember that there are many ways to grow without adding people to your payroll.

The responses to these myths were not meant to disillusion you. They were meant to ensure that you had both sides of the story. Explore a few truths you might think are myths about consulting in the sidebar.

Truth, Not Myth

Sometimes you hear things and think, "That can't be true!" Here's a list of those very true truths.

- **First-time consultants rarely set their fees high enough.** Definitely. Your fees may be the first indication a client has that you can add value and that you have the confidence to get the job done. In Chapter Three, I ask you to put a price on your head; there is a 90 percent chance that I'll recommend you double it.
- **You can have clients immediately.** Affirmative. If you tap into your network, you'll learn how much need exists for consultants.
- **Other consultants are happy to help you.** Absolutely. The best consultants know there is more work than they can handle. Don't even ask those who won't share; they're probably not that good.
- **You may become friends with your clients.** Certainly. If you attend to building a relationship, this will happen. The downside is that you may need to give them up as clients if you want to keep them as friends. A good consultant must maintain objectivity.

- **Being a consultant can be a long-term career path.** Yep! You can make a great living and have a great life as a consultant. If you are good, you will receive job offers along the way.
- **You can be just as happy as a solopreneur as working for a growing business.** Sure, and maybe even happier. The great news is that you can design your own future and do what you like best.
- **Independent consultants are at an advantage for winning clients.** Yes. Over the years I've bid against the largest consulting firms and was chosen for reasons such as more flexibility, ease of customization, speed to market, innovative solution, and price.
- **Consultants have unlimited income.** Absolutely. With a handful of clients, as an independent consultant my small company has made as much as 20 times what I might have made in annual salary as a traditional employee. Keep in mind, your income may fluctuate annually; the key is to have a base income that you never dip below.

… and much, much more.

REALITIES AND REWARDS OF CONSULTING

I've listed some of the realities and rewards of consulting. Take them to heart as you make your decision about starting your own consulting business.

Realities

The rewards of consulting are wonderful, but, like everything in this world, there is a flip side—the reality. Consulting can be frustrating, too. Imagine it's your favorite aunt's birthday and you are sitting in an airport 1,300 miles away because your flight's been delayed. Imagine showing up at a client's office ready to work and discovering that they forgot to tell you that they had moved the start date out by two weeks. Imagine that you rack up a million frequent flyer miles, all for work domestically, many of them on red-eye flights. Imagine working with someone who despises consultants in general and is sure that they are all out to take advantage of the system. Imagine working all hours of the day and night, recognizing that you have just worked over 120 hours in a week. Imagine working on many weekends. Imagine investing 10 hours to write a proposal that you later learn never had a chance because the candidate was preselected. Imagine catching one of your favorite employees stealing from you. Imagine that one of your clients is six months late paying you. Imagine that the airline loses your luggage in which you packed your best suit that you intended to wear when you met the CEO of a Fortune 50 company.

Rewards

But wait. Read on. The rewards far outweigh a few irritations.

Consulting can be one of the most rewarding yet challenging careers out there. Imagine sitting at a desk looking out at the scene you have chosen. Imagine waking up every day knowing that you are going to do what you have chosen to do that day. Imagine not fighting rush-hour traffic. Imagine being able to select the projects you want. Imagine working with the people you want to work with. Imagine doing what you are best at and what you enjoy most. Imagine challenging yourself and living up to your potential. Imagine being paid well to do what you love. Imagine working your own hours. Imagine feeling the satisfaction of being a part of a project that you believe in. Imagine completing projects successfully and being genuinely appreciated. Imagine being able to make a difference. Imagine working in locations that you have selected. Imagine taking the day off without asking permission. Imagine getting up in the morning and not going to work … but going to play! These are the rewards of consulting.

What rewards and lessons in reality are in store for you as you enter the world of the consultant?

Yes, every one of these things describes events and feelings I can remember. Consulting is certainly a profession that produces the good, the bad, and the ugly. But then, it's all about your perspective and how you view it. You will definitely learn and grow from all kinds of situations.

JUST WHAT ARE YOU GETTING YOURSELF INTO?

As you can see, there are many pros and cons in the consulting field. The number-one reason that consultants love their jobs is the intellectual stimulation. Two key reasons consultants dislike their jobs are the long hours and the travel. Trying to decide whether to go it on your own can be confusing. Just as you would with any major decision, you will want to conduct your own research. You will want to discover whether consulting is a profession you want to pursue.

One of the best ways to do that is to talk to other consultants. Explore your concerns and confirm your hopes by interviewing people in the profession. Most of us enjoy talking shop, especially if we work alone. As professionals, we owe it to those entering the field to share our knowledge and insight. But what should you ask someone who has been in the business? Exhibit 1.1 provides a list of questions you can use to interview consultants. Also spend time thinking about the various aspects explored in this chapter and develop your own questions. How will a change affect your career path? How will it affect your personal life? Take your time in making a decision. Do your homework.

Exhibit 1.1. Questions to Ask a Consultant

You likely won't have time to ask all of these, so although they are in a logical sequence, you will probably have to prioritize what you ask.

1. How long have you been a consultant?
2. How did you start?
3. Why did you decide to become a consultant?
4. How would you describe your consulting practice?
5. How have you structured your business, and what are the advantages and drawbacks of that structure?
6. What do you do for clients?
7. What is a typical project like?
8. What do you consider the biggest lesson you've learned as a consultant?
9. Could you tell me about a time when you faced a difficult decision and how you handled it? What was your takeaway?
10. What is a typical day like?
11. What marketing activities do you conduct?
12. How do you determine pricing for projects?
13. What is the greatest challenge for you as a consultant?
14. What reason would you give me to avoid becoming a consultant?
15. What would you miss the most if you quit consulting?
16. What should I have asked you that I did not?

Exhibit 1.2 challenges you with several aspects of becoming an external consultant. Read the statements, checking all with which you agree.

Exhibit 1.2. Are You a Match for the Profession?

Quick Quiz

- ☐ I am willing to work 60 to 80 hours a week to achieve success.
- ☐ I love risk; I thrive on risk.
- ☐ I have a thick skin; being called a pest, "beltway bandit," or con man does not bother me.
- ☐ I am good at understanding and interpreting the big picture.
- ☐ I pay attention to details.
- ☐ I am an excellent communicator.
- ☐ I am a good writer.
- ☐ I like to promote myself.
- ☐ I can balance logic with intuition and the big picture with details.
- ☐ I know my limitations.
- ☐ I can say "no" easily.
- ☐ I am compulsively self-disciplined.
- ☐ I am comfortable speaking with people in all disciplines and at all levels of an organization.

Although the number of checks on the page is not significant, your willingness to face the reality of what it takes is *very* significant. Each time you are unable or unwilling to check a box, you show a disparate match to the profession.

Here's an Explanation of Each Statement

- *Are you willing to work 60 to 80 hours each week to achieve success?* You are about to enter the world of the entrepreneur. Perhaps you will be able to decrease the number of hours you work after your business is up and running, but until then it will be demanding. Most successful entrepreneurs require less than eight hours of sleep a night. Time is always a critical element to entrepreneurs. In his book *Entrepreneurs Are Made, Not Born,* Lloyd E. Shefsky (1994) teaches readers how to learn to get by with less sleep! By the way, I don't particularly recommend it. You will eventually become more disciplined about your use of time, learn to juggle many things at once, and identify priorities.

- *Do you love risk and thrive on it?* As a consultant you will live with constant uncertainty. The biggest risk is whether you find enough steady work to pay the mortgage. Even if you land a year-long project with an organization, the person who brought you in may not be there as long as you are. The possibility of a change in management through a promotion, transfer, or layoff could put the project, and thus your contract, in jeopardy.

- *Do you have a thick skin?* Does being called a pest, beltway bandit, or con man bother you? Consultants are not always respected. How will you react the first time your profession or your personality is criticized?

- *Are you good at understanding and interpreting the big picture?* Clients will often hire you because they believe that you will have a unique advantage and be able to see the organization from a different perspective. You will continually need to think outside the parameters that your client explains. You will often need to be a quick study in how the organization works, and you will need to be adept at asking the critical questions that will result in the insight your client needs.

- *Do you pay attention to details?* Although you must see the big picture for your client, you will also be running a business that will require you to focus on the details of accounting, proofreading, and scheduling, among others.

- *Are you an excellent communicator?* This is critical. I cannot think of a single consultant who does not need to be a superior communicator. If you did not check this box, I would seriously recommend that you obtain additional training and development in communication before you attempt a consulting profession. It is basic and it's required. You must be able to communicate clearly and completely. You must be a good listener.

- *Are you a good writer?* Writing is almost as important as verbal communication. You will write reports, marketing materials, letters, proposals, and client materials. In many cases your work will go before top management. If your writing is not as good as it should be, you may want to hire someone to proof-read your work or even complete the writing for you.

- *Do you like to promote yourself?* Knowing how to impress a client with your skills and expertise without bragging is an art form. It is often a matter of your attitude. You must believe in yourself and be able to convince a client that you can achieve what your client wants you to achieve.
- *Can you balance logic and intuition, the big picture, and details?* A consultant must be able to put on whatever hat is required to do the job. You may be buried in the details and logic of your cash-flow projections when a client calls and asks you to brainstorm the needs of the community in 2030. Your marketing plan will be a balance of logic and intuition. You must be flexible. You must be able to tap into all of your skills and expertise.

Tip: Puzzle practice.

I am one of those people who can get lost in the details. And yet the ability to attend to both the details and the big picture at the same time is one of the most important attributes I need when designing a project. I practice the skill of readily jumping back and forth by completing cryptograms that require the same dexterity.

- *Do you know your limitations?* Only you know what they are. Are they physical? Social? Financial? Might they prevent you from doing what needs to be done? We all have limitations. It's how we manage them that counts. One of my limitations is an inability to make small talk. I overcome that by planning ahead for situations in which I will be expected to make small talk. If you don't know what your limitations are, ask someone who knows you well.
- *Can you say no easily?* You will need to say no to some projects because they aren't right for you. (More about that in Chapter Five.) You must also stay focused on your strategy. It may be tempting to accept a project that's not right for you—especially if you don't have anything on the immediate horizon. You also must be realistic about the amount of work you can take on. Initially it will be better to overestimate the time a project will take than to have quality suffer because you spread yourself too thin.
- *Are you compulsively self-disciplined?* You must be a self-starter. You must be compulsive about your financial records. You must be compulsive about

planning and developing materials for your clients. You must be compulsive about billing your clients if you want to be paid.

Be compulsive about billing your clients if you want to be paid.

- *Are you comfortable speaking with people in all disciplines and at all levels of an organization?* Depending on the project you have accepted, you may find yourself talking to crane operators, secretaries, supervisors, janitors, teachers, presidents, welders, scientists, or cooks. You must feel comfortable with them so that they feel comfortable with you.

How are you doing? Ready to learn more about the skills of a consultant? You can read short first-year stories on Wiley's *The New Business of Consulting* website, www.wiley.com/go/newconsultingbiech, at Exhibit 1.3.

Clues You Are Ready

Is the thought of a consulting business exhilarating? Are you pumped? You have an opportunity to reimagine your life the way you have always wanted it. Consider these seven signs that you are ready to start your own consulting business. Mark each one red, yellow, and green: Red for "no way!" Yellow for "yeah, pretty close!" Green for "Yahoo! Let's go!" This should give you a push in one direction or another. And if you don't get seven green lights, stick with the book. It covers the rest.

- You feel the passion and you can define it.
- You are clear about the risks of starting a consulting business.
- Your job is boring or frustrating and you need to get out.
- You believe in you; you know you can do this and succeed.
- Failure isn't even in your vocabulary.
- You have the energy to make this happen.
- You can list at least 50 people to contact about your transition; some may provide you with projects, but all will be a part of your network.

For the Consummate Consultant

Exploring what you are getting yourself into is just the beginning. Do your research. Talk to people—lots of them. Ask them about their perspectives on consulting and listen to what they say. What resonates with you? Is consulting your dream job?

A Family Affair. Transitioning to be a consultant is truly a family event. Choosing to have your office in your home, for example, requires new ground rules. Have a chat with your family. Involve everyone. What are the upsides and the downsides of becoming a consultant?

Innovative Interviews. I mentioned interviewing other consultants. I think that is just common sense. But who else can you interview who will have insight for you? How about people who work inside organizations that hire consultants? What do they think works when they use consultants? What doesn't work? What surprised you?

Flawless Consulting. Have you read Peter Block's book *Flawless Consulting*? If not, you must get it. *The New Business of Consulting* informs you of how to run your consulting business so that you don't go bankrupt; Peter's book will inform you of how to be a consultant. Although you may know your subject matter well, *Flawless Consulting* shares a mindset, a perspective, and tools for being the best darn consultant anywhere.

Talents and Tolerance

2

Whether you believe you can or you can't, you will prove yourself correct.

Henry Ford

Shawn had been toying with the idea of retirement for a couple of years. Well, *retirement.* How did you define it these days? At least half the people he knew who had retired had gone back to work—part-time or freelancing. What were people calling it now? Hucksters? Hasslers? Side hustles! That was it. He'd always thought about being a consultant. But thinking about it was as far as it had gone. Yesterday he had learned that the company he worked for was offering early retirement. It was tempting to consider taking it. He'd been with the company long enough to qualify, and the daily grind of the same-ole, same-ole was getting tedious.

He rolled out of bed and staggered to the kitchen to start the coffee. One of these days he was going to figure out how to set the autobrew on this contraption his sister called a DeLonghi Nespresso. DeLonghi? Wasn't that the name of an expensive car? No, that was DeLorean. He just needed coffee to lift the fog. He glanced outside and saw there was fog outside his condo, too. And the leaves were turning colors. Autumn was here. Coffee. Finally.

Sipping his coffee, he sat at the window watching the leaves fall and realized that autumn represented where he was in life. He was nearing the end of his career. He gazed across the street, where the bright yellow chrysanthemums were blooming. He didn't feel like those falling leaves. He felt more like the sunny yellow chrysanthemums.

Resuming his earlier musings about retirement and consulting, he wondered whether he was too old to start consulting. He'd just read an article about second careers. What did it say? "It's not about how old you are but how much you believe in your dreams," or something like that. He had always believed in his ability to achieve. That's why he had done so well at the company. Too old? Maybe older was better. He had a healthy savings account. His kids had successful jobs. He had plenty of experience. He had the stamina. And his expertise in IT was in high demand.

He grabbed a pen and started to write on the back of his *Golf Digest*:

- What would it take to start consulting?
- What skills do I need?
- What are the legal ramifications?
- Where would I work from?
- What would I do?
- Who could I talk to?

He paused with his list and realized he was creating his dream, reimagining the next season in his life. There wasn't a single question on the list that he couldn't find the answer to right now. This is exciting, he thought. Jumping up from his chair he started yelling, "Gail! Gail! Wake up! I want to talk to you about something!"

■ ■ ■

The most important reason to become a consultant is because you want to. Whether you are new to the workforce or retiring, consulting is a good option. Whereas Chapter One focused on what it takes to *become* a consultant, this chapter focuses on the skills and the personal stamina you need to *remain* a consultant. It forces you to explore both sides of working out of your home and potential barriers to your success.

> *The most important reason to become
> a consultant is because you want to.*

You may be surprised to think of yourself as an entrepreneur, but you must examine this aspect of becoming a consultant. Your professional skills, abilities, knowledge, and experience provide the content. Your entrepreneurial abilities will determine how well you run your business. Both are required to be a successful consultant.

YOUR SKILLS FOR SUCCESS

As a consultant, you will possess skills that are valued and needed by clients who are willing to pay you for them. Naturally, many of the skills required will be dependent on the niche you carve out for yourself. Whether you work in the manufacturing or insurance sector, whether you focus on training or organization development, you will want to acquire the skills necessary to put you at the high end of the knowledge curve.

As a training consultant, for example, you may become certified by one of the larger training supplier companies, such as The Ken Blanchard Companies or DDI. In this case, you will need strong delivery skills. A training consultant who also designs training must have design skills. If you expect to broaden your consulting to working with clients on performance issues, you will need to add analytical, measurement, and process improvement skills to your list.

If you decide to be a consultant who coaches, you will need to be familiar with and certified to use a variety of assessment tools, be an excellent communicator, and know how to help another individual establish goals, among other skills and competencies.

In addition to these specific skills, there are general consulting skills that show that you are a professional. Exhibit 2.1 provides a self-evaluation to determine whether your general skills and characteristics are a match for the profession. Complete it by jotting comments in either the Strength or the Needs Improvement/Needs Attention column. Then read the following sections to determine which of the listed skills are important for you and your consulting plans.

Exhibit 2.1. Consultant Skills and Characteristics

Rate your strengths

Skills	Strength	Needs Improvement
Prospecting and marketing		
Promoting and selling results		
Diagnosing client needs		
Identifying mutual expectations		
Pricing projects		
Staying organized		
Understanding business data		
Designing solutions		
Developing talent		
Facilitating meetings		
Having a depth of experience		
Having a breadth of experience		

Characteristics	Natural	Needs Attention
Leader in many situations		
Team player		
People turn to me for decisions		
Enjoy competition		
Self-confident		
Enjoy working long, hard hours		
Always plan ahead		
Self-disciplined		
Sell myself with confidence		
Financial acumen		
Reasonable risk taking		
Family support		

Which skills and characteristics need the most improvement and attention?

How will you gain necessary skills or experience?

How will you adapt to necessary characteristics that are not naturally "you"?

Prospecting and Marketing. Prospecting, or looking for clients, will require much of your time when you first start. Having clients is the only thing that will keep you in business. You will find that you need to prove yourself over and over, and that is why referrals and repeat business are so valuable to a consultant. Your marketing efforts should clearly state what you have been able to achieve in the past and the kind of problems you want to solve for organizations. Your website is a start, but heed the advice from Donald Miller, CEO of StoryBrand, a company that helps businesses clarify their messages. He finds that most websites display five major mistakes. They don't present the customer's problems; they use too much copy; they don't have a clear offer; they don't provide a path to the solution; and they are focused too much on you the consultant (Miller 2017). Prospecting and marketing will ensure that the phone keeps ringing.

---

*Having clients is the only thing
that will keep you in business.*

Tip: Try StoryBrand.

Connect with StoryBrand on their website at www.StoryBrand.com.

Promoting and Selling Results. You can market your services, but people will be hiring you. You must feel comfortable discussing your successes. Few businesses will pay you for consulting if you don't have a track record that shows that you know what you are doing. Consulting gives you an opportunity to work with people at all levels of the organization. Promote yourself and your services to those at the top. They have the budget, the vision, and the ability to approve your proposals. Get others on your bandwagon. Obtain testimonials from CEOs or others you've worked with and post them on your website or add them to your proposals. It's important that you show confidence without cockiness.

Diagnosing Client Needs. You will be hired to provide solutions to the challenges that organizations face. In some cases you will meet with your clients and they will tell you exactly what they want you to do. Sometimes they will ask you what needs to be done. And sometimes what they say they want is not what they need! Your diagnostic skills will tell you what to do in all cases. If you are good at coaching, strategy development, operational improvement, technology implementation, identifying root causes, or general problem solving, you will likely have no trouble obtaining consulting gigs.

Identifying Mutual Expectations. The ability to lead a candid discussion with your client to reach agreement on what each of you needs, wants, and expects as a result of working together will ensure that your projects start on the right foot. Keeping these mutual expectations alive and healthy is valuable to you. To increase client retention and even to attract new clients, it is critical to satisfy your customers—always. It seems that there are two reasons why your client may not do business with you: a drop in quality and poor customer service. You might say, well, I would never let that happen. But imagine that you are really good and you take on more business than you can handle. Is there a possibility that the quality and client service might slip? Of course they might. Track your progress and results to always be ready to improve them. Finally, stay in touch with the client who hired you.

Pricing Projects. Both art and science are involved in pricing your projects. How long a project will take, how many on-site days are needed, how long it will take to design, develop, gather data, compile data, analyze what you learn, and how many trips you will make to the client's location will all affect the price tag you place on a project. Articulating the value to the client is not something many of us do naturally. A value proposition is not what you think you bring to the project. It is what your client needs to solve the problem. It is not about why you think you are special; it's about why your client thinks you're special! How much value will your client gain from your solution in increased profits, fewer accidents, or less turnover? What does that equate to in dollars and what percent do you earn, perhaps 5 percent? Ten percent? Be sure that you can succinctly and convincingly define the value proposition to your client.

Staying Organized. Organizing your office so that you will be able to locate everything that you file and developing processes to track clients, money, and work will be critical to your success. Keeping records is essential, and so is hiring a good accountant to ensure that you are always on time and in the good graces of the IRS or whatever the name of your tax agency might be. Developing standard documents, such as proposals or invoices, will help you stay organized and save time. In reality, however, you need to like being organized.

Understanding Business Data. You'll need a clear understanding of business data to take care of your business and to understand your client's business. This book offers numerous methods for tracking your data, such as expense records, profit-and-loss statements, and revenue-projection forms. Your ability to read them, analyze them, and know what they are telling you is important for your financial health. You also need to be able to read and understand numerous financial documents from your clients' perspective. They will share the financial health of their businesses with you, and you will need to comprehend the financial status and trends so that you can uncover the issues you've been hired to address.

Designing Solutions. Your clients will come to you to identify or solve their problems. You must be able to gather data to compare the pros and cons of different models. You may also be hired to be a catalyst for change. The client will count on you for your objectivity. No one inside an organization can tell the emperor that he has no clothes. Your fresh viewpoint can help an organization see that there is more underlying the issues they are facing.

Developing Talent. You may not bill yourself as a talent developer or a trainer, but you will train in many ways. You may coach a CEO, mentor a manager, or do some one-on-one training with superintendents on the floor. Often when employees know that you are competent and trustworthy, they will ask to talk to you. This happens to me a great deal. Employees meet me in the hall or pop their heads into my temporary space and ask, "Can I run something by you?" They might be asking for advice, a way to deal with a sticky problem, a recommendation for a resource, or 100 other things. Internalizing adult learning theory ensures that you are always ready for those teaching moments.

Facilitating Meetings. You very likely will be called on to facilitate meetings for your client. Brush up on meeting-management skills as well as facilitation skills. You know that all meeting leaders should:

- Start and end on time.
- Be sure the meeting is necessary, or cancel it if there is a better way to achieve the objective.
- Publish agendas in advance, with the most important items listed first.
- Use agendas that identify objectives, who's responsible, and time allowed.
- Restate action items at the end of each meeting.
- Only invite those who need to attend.
- Consider holding shorter, stand-up meetings whenever possible.

Be sure you practice all of these. You will be seen as a model in many situations. These skills will help you hold your own.

Having a Depth of Experience. How deep is your experience? If you are specializing in an area, you should know all you can about it. Read your professional journals and keep up with the latest books in your area. As a specialist, you have expertise in a particular field, industry, or focus area. See the sidebar to comprehend the wide variety of consulting opportunity. Whatever your specialty is, know all you can about it before calling yourself a consultant. Generally it is best to pick a narrow niche and stick with it.

Who's a Consultant?

Consulting covers a wide spectrum of specialties. How many of these have you heard of?

- Management Consulting
- IT Consulting
- Marketing Consulting
- Human Resource Consulting
- Training Consulting
- Talent Development Consulting
- Image Consulting
- Tax Consulting
- Publishing Consulting
- Auditing Consulting
- Cybersecurity Consulting
- Nutrition Consulting
- Financial Services Consulting
- Brand Consulting
- Insurance Consulting
- Retirement Consulting

Having a Breadth of Experience. How wide is your experience? You must be enough of a generalist to know what else applies in the situation you are dealing with. You should know where you can go for help when you need it. As a generalist, you will be expected to have a heavy dose of common sense to provide an outside perspective and to cut through internal politics. You will have a wide range of experience. If you need more experience in one area, you can always hire a subcontractor to work with you.

A balance of breadth and depth is a critical advantage your client will look for. It is also important to decide whether to present yourself as a specialist or a generalist. The more specialized you are, the more difficult it will be to obtain a wide variety of business; the more generalized you are, the less credible you may be in a potential client's eyes.

The more specialized you are, the more difficult it will be to obtain a wide variety of business; the more generalized you are, the less credible you may be in a potential client's eyes.

Consider the skills in the next section to be a starting point for your consulting talent.

PERSONAL CHARACTERISTICS OF SUCCESSFUL CONSULTANTS

Consulting is a profession of contrasts and high expectations. Not only will you need to be multiskilled, sensibly focused, knowledgeable, and widely experienced, but you will need to maintain a delicate balance of personal characteristics. Your clients expect you to be confident, but not arrogant; assertive, but not pushy; intelligent, but not a nerd; personable, but not overly friendly; candid, but not critical; understanding, but not too sensitive. In addition, they will want you to be creative and visionary, but at the same time logical and practical. You will need to see the big picture, but also watch out for the details that might trip you up.

This affords you quite a challenge! A client will be just as interested in your personal characteristics as in your skills. Although clients will ask you to discuss your skills, they will evaluate your characteristics. As unfair as it may seem, many contracts are awarded on personality. Clients may consciously (or unconsciously) realize that they will need to work with the consultant they are considering. I recently had a discussion with a vice president of a large Fortune 300 company who was emphatically telling me that he simply did not trust the last consultant he interviewed, but could not say specifically why. (I got the job.)

Although clients will ask you to discuss your skills, they will evaluate your characteristics.

ROLES YOU MAY PLAY

Although there are hundreds of roles you may play as a consultant, the following examples will give you an idea of what a client may expect of you. As a consultant, you may come in at any point in a situation facing a client. Although the examples here are somewhat oversimplified, they may help you decide the role that you can fill the best.

Identifying the Problem. You may enter when a client knows something is wrong in general, but just cannot identify what: morale is down, communication is poor, turnover is high, and profits are questionable. In this case, you may be asked to identify the problem. You will probably be required to gather data, interview people, study the bigger picture, recognize interfaces, and benchmark other organizations. The roles you will play include interviewer, analyzer, synthesizer, categorizer, and researcher.

Identifying the Cause. You may enter when a client knows there is a problem: sales are down, time from concept to market is too long, or defects are high. The client knows there is a problem but does not know the cause of it. You may be asked to identify the root cause of the problem. You will need to understand the basics of problem solving, how to uncover the root cause, how to communicate with process owners, and how to challenge the status quo. You may need to have a heavy dose of expertise in the area. The roles you will play include expert resource, auditor, devil's advocate, mediator, and problem solver.

Identifying the Solution. You may enter when a client knows there is a problem and has identified the cause: sales are down because the competition has introduced a new product, time from concept to market is too long because the staff doesn't work well together, or defects are high because the supplier is unreliable. In this case, you may be asked to identify a solution or solutions. You will probably need to research outside initiatives in the same or other industries. You may need to locate other resources or to coordinate and facilitate open discussion. You will need to help others identify potential ideas. The roles you will play include processor, idea generator, facilitator, and adaptor.

Implementing the Solution. You may enter when a client knows there is a problem, has identified the root cause, and has determined the solution: need to attract a new customer base, need to work better as a team, or need to improve supplier communication. In this case, you may be asked to create and implement the solution or change. You will be expected to make things happen. If you must install the new, you may also be required to dismantle the old. You will need to deliver information and assist others to communicate effectively. You may need to supervise installations and reconfigure the work force. The roles you will play include catalyst, implementer, change agent, mentor, communicator, and coordinator.

Each of these examples requires you to play different roles. Obviously, there is a lot of crossover, but think about your talents and which roles you could fill best. What are your strengths? What do you most enjoy doing?

The Ideal Consultant: The Top 10

What do other consultants think are critical consulting skills? Here's a list. Which ones do you think are most important?

- Knows how to methodically diagnose any problem, structure, or organization.
- Is always learning and growing.
- Never misses a deadline.
- Can prepare a compelling report with clear, helpful graphics.
- Knows how to tap the right and left sides of the brain.
- Admires the client and becomes a true friend.
- Understands how to use leverage for clients as well as in the consultant's practice.
- Is technologically competent.
- Knows how to run or participate in a meeting with equal effectiveness.
- Knows what's going on in the world and is generally well-read.

Tip: A Consulting Resource.

Check the consulting section of the Careers in Business website. It provides a variety of information, including skills and talent required, recommended books on jobs in consulting, facts and trends in consulting, and information about practice areas in consulting. Check it out at http://www.careers-in-business.com.

Being a Hired Gun. When support is needed or an organization senses that it doesn't have the expertise to complete a particular job, the company may hire an outside professional who comes in to bolster the marketing department or the sales department, especially to support a specific area or campaign. The outside objective analysis is valued by the hiring organization. In addition to consultants, the people taking on these projects might be called gig workers, contractors, or just part-time employees. Why "hired gun"? Although you won't be hired with that description, you will know once you get into the project. You might learn that projects are over budget or management has been lax in meeting goals. Often the root cause is a lack of accountability—but then, I won't spoil your fun as you try to figure these out. I try to avoid these kinds of gigs, but you can't always tell at the beginning that that's what they are.

Now that we've examined the skills and roles that may be required, let's look for signs that you may not be cut out to be a consultant.

SIGNS OF A MEDIOCRE CONSULTANT

In more than 30 years of consulting, I've observed hundreds of consultants. Many were very good and some were mediocre. You aren't starting your business to be mediocre, so here are some of the practices and characteristics that lead to mediocrity:

- A belief that being a consultant means that you can be just who you are without concern for what your clients expect and refusing to be flexible to fit their environment when necessary.
- An inability to identify practical marketing tactics or finding excuses to avoid implementing them.
- An inability to recognize an opportunity when it is slapping you in the face—for example, clients or potential clients saying, "Do you know anything about …" or "Something that is really bugging me is …" or "I'd like some help with …" These are all cries for help. Listen! Listen! Listen! Your next project may be speaking to you!
- An insistence on using a model or solution that you are familiar with rather than creating or identifying a new one that would be more appropriate.
- An insistence on doing the same things over and over, not creating new materials or trying new options.
- Limited desire to continue to grow and learn.
- No recognition that your consulting practice is a business.

Average is just average. Is that what you want to be?

YOUR PERSONAL SITUATION

Before you quit your job and buy your business license, take time to identify any personal situations that may make the profession difficult for you. I've listed five that are frequently identified. You may have others. The best way to discover these may be to discuss your own situation with a friend, your spouse, or a significant other.

Financing the Business

Even if you leave your present job with the promise of six months of consulting work, there is no guarantee that you will have your next projects lined up when that income stream ends.

You may become so tied up in the project that you don't take the time to prospect for new projects. Or you may decide that you deserve some time off before you plunge into your business. In either case, you may not have a steady income following your initial project.

What can you do? Do you have savings or other cash that you can draw from during your initial start-up or later if you have no income? Can you cut back on personal or business spending? Can you obtain a line of credit from your bank? Consulting has its ups and downs. Be sure to set some money aside in a liquid investment for times when things are not going as well as you would like. It may be difficult to adjust to the fact that consulting does not produce a regular paycheck.

Consulting does not produce a regular paycheck.

Working Alone

Leaving the hustle and bustle of an office sounds great initially, but once you spend several days in the same room without seeing anyone except the mail carrier, you may begin to go stir crazy. You may miss the opportunity to work as a team. You may miss the synergy that groups can create, and you may miss the social interactions.

What can you do? You can at least arrange to have lunch with someone once each week. You can plan to meet other consultants regularly. Even though discussion is likely to turn to work, you will still appreciate the camaraderie.

Working from Your Home

Does working from your home sounds like an ideal situation? Get up when you want to. No traffic to face. No time clock to punch. Work in your shorts and T-shirt. Listen to your favorite radio station. Brew fresh gourmet coffee in the morning. Eat a bagel while you're proofing a proposal. Walk outdoors at any time during the day. Flick the television on to hear the latest news. Pick up the kids from school. Read at your desk after everyone has gone to bed. Perfect day—right?

How about the day things don't go as well? The dog barks just as you are about to close an important sale. Your daughter spills milk on the proposal that's on its way to the post office. Your home-based office has spread to the living room. You need to leave for an important meeting and your son hasn't returned with the car. Your spouse is upset because you spend every waking hour in your office.

Both kinds of day are equally possible. You will need to face the reality of both. Think about how you can balance working at home and living at home.

Being a One-Person Company

Think about how you will feel when a client asks you how many people are in your company. Will you feel proud of being on your own or will you feel somehow inferior? How will you feel about doing your own typing, copying, errands, dusting, vacuuming?

An important factor to consider is backup support. What will you do when one of your clients is counting on you to facilitate a critical meeting and you are at home ill? Identify someone who could fill in for you. You could make a reciprocal agreement with several other consultants in your area.

Needing Family Support

Family support is critical. Starting your business will be difficult enough. You don't need your family saying, "We told you so!" when something goes wrong. Obtain 100 percent support from all immediate family members before you hang out your shingle.

Tip: Make a date.

Set a date with your spouse, partner, or significant other to review the 100 percent support agreement on a specific date. This could be three to six months into the future. Put it in writing and hang it someplace where you will both see it every day. This will give you time to figure things out.

The five personal situations described earlier are mentioned most frequently as interfering with consultants' ability to function. Each has its own solution. You must recognize the possibility of any of these problems coming up and plan your own solutions.

CAUTION: BUSINESS OWNER AHEAD

We have focused on what it takes to be a successful consultant, but it is bigger than that. You are headed for the entrepreneurial ranks. You are about to become a business owner.

Although there is no way I can prepare you psychologically for the long hours, the endless frustrations, the demands for patience and persistence, the multitude of ups and downs, and the desperate need for planning when there is no time for planning, I can provide some suggestions for success.

Estimates generally are that about 50 percent of all start-up businesses fail within five years. Responsibility for success or failure rests almost entirely with the person who started the business. What are some of these reasons?

- Mistaking a business for a hobby.
- Asking friends and relatives for advice.
- Borrowing money from friends and relatives.
- Mismanaging money.
- Lack of a business plan.
- Poor marketing.
- Lack of pricing knowledge.
- Inability to manage growth.
- Lack of commitment.
- Failure to set and revise goals.
- Inability to develop, monitor, and understand financial statements.
- Inability to balance business and family.
- Underestimation of time requirements.

You certainly do not want to be among the casualty statistics over the next year or two! The remaining chapters in this book provide you with the guidance to steer clear of each of these.

ENTREPRENEURIAL CHARACTERISTICS

Although all the experts do not agree about what makes a successful start-up business owner, the following seem to be mentioned most often.

First, you have to want to do it! Let's face it. You're tired of working for someone else and the idea of doing your own thing appeals to you—really appeals to you. You have already taken the first step. You've decided that you want to start a business, and, yes, you want to ensure that it is still around five years from now. What's next?

Self-confidence is on almost all lists. Be honest with yourself. If you don't believe in you, who will? Most consultants have a good dose of self-assurance—believing that they can do whatever they set their minds to. Before starting my business, I can remember thinking, "This is such a sure bet; I can't *not* succeed!"

Most entrepreneurs have a sense of urgency. They have places to go, things to do, people to see, and successes to pull off. They seem to have more energy than most people and a need to do things *now*. Interestingly enough, most require fewer than the usual eight hours of sleep each night.

> **Tip: Check this online magazine.**
>
> *Entrepreneur* magazine has a great website with all sorts of informative download-able articles, podcasts, advice for starting a business, and recommended books. Check it out at www.entrepreneur.com.

They have a willingness to work hard—to do what it takes to achieve success. Long hours don't scare them. They also play hard—and competitively!

Entrepreneurs have a need to control and direct. They want the responsibility and authority that comes with owning a business. They like making decisions; they do not like being told what to do.

They have the flexibility to think differently as the need arises. They can be either creative or analytical; they can be big-picture thinkers or detail-oriented.

Maintaining a positive attitude gets entrepreneurs through the ups and downs. They truly do look at problems as challenges. They are certain a solution exists and welcome the learning that accompanies identifying the problem and solving it.

They are good decision makers. They may rate high to medium in risk taking and are good at weighing the potential outcomes. They are decisive and move forward. They don't hesitate or procrastinate. They are also willing to change a course of action if the expectations for success are lower than they had hoped.

Entrepreneurs are creative problem solvers. They are conceptual thinkers and see relationships that others may not. They excel at creating order out of chaos.

They may be obsessed with quality—quality of service, quality of product, quality of a project. They are naturally committed to excellence and do not need the quality gurus to inspire them!

Good health is almost imperative, given the preceding list! I believe that health has a lot to do with positive thinking and the fact that entrepreneurs just don't have time to get sick.

Do you have what it takes to be a business owner? Can you cut it as an entrepreneur? Find out with the evaluation in Exhibit 2.2.

Exhibit 2.2. Entrepreneurs: Do You Have What It Takes?

Instructions: Rate yourself on the following qualities. They represent the thinking of several authors about the requirements of a successful business owner. Spend ample time pondering these questions and answer honestly. Although this survey can only give a general picture of what it takes to be a successful entrepreneur, only you can decide whether the move is right for you.

Rate yourself on the following scale from 1 to 4:

    1 = strongly disagree   3 = agree

    2 = disagree   4 = strongly agree

Circle your answer

1. I usually try to take charge when I'm with others.   1   2   3   4
2. I can do anything I set my mind to.   1   2   3   4
3. I have a high tolerance level.   1   2   3   4
4. I believe I can always influence results.   1   2   3   4
5. I am complimented on my ability to quickly analyze complex situations.   1   2   3   4
6. I prefer working with a difficult but highly competent person rather than a friendly, less competent one.   1   2   3   4
7. I can fire employees who are not producing.   1   2   3   4
8. I am willing to leave a high-paying secure job to start my own business.   1   2   3   4
9. I push myself to complete tasks.   1   2   3   4
10. I can work long, hard hours when necessary.   1   2   3   4

Exhibit 2.2. Entrepreneurs: Do You Have What It Takes?, Cont'd

11.	I need to be the best at whatever I do.	1	2	3	4
12.	I do not become frustrated easily.	1	2	3	4
13.	I thrive on challenges.	1	2	3	4
14.	I become bored easily with routine tasks.	1	2	3	4
15.	I dislike being told what to do.	1	2	3	4
16.	I have a higher energy level than most people.	1	2	3	4
17.	I have held numerous leadership positions.	1	2	3	4
18.	I have the skills and enjoy accomplishing a complex task by myself.	1	2	3	4
19.	I can change my course of action if something is not working.	1	2	3	4
20.	I am seen as a creative problem solver.	1	2	3	4
21.	I can balance the big picture and details of a business at the same time.	1	2	3	4
22.	I can predict how my actions today will affect business tomorrow and in the future.	1	2	3	4

23. I need at least _____ hours of
    sleep to function effectively.

1 = 8 hours	2 = 7 hours
3 = 6 hours	4 = 5 or fewer hours

24. I have at least _____ years'
    of experience in the business I
    will start.

1 = 1 year	2 = 2 years
3 = 4 years	4 = 5 years

25. Over the past three years I
    have missed a total of _____
    days of work due to illness.

1 = over 15 days	2 = 11–15 days
3 = 6–10 days	4 = 0–5 days

Scoring: Total the numbers you circled

90–100	Go for it!
82–89	Good chance of success
74–81	Pretty risky
73 and below	Better continue to collect a paycheck

Perhaps you completed the self-evaluation and you are still not sure. What descriptors identify someone who does not have the makings of an entrepreneur? Is there a way to identify specific characteristics of a nonentrepreneur? Check out the sidebar to compare.

Clues That Being an Entrepreneur Isn't Right for You

Not everyone is cut out for the entrepreneurial lifestyle. It's hard. These clues might suggest that it is not right for you:

- You are Mr. Nice Guy or Ms. Popular and want to get along with everyone.
- You love to plan but like to have others implement the plans.
- You are amazed at how creative and innovative others are.
- You avoid marketing and selling.
- You prefer to avoid mistakes by thinking and analyzing before making a decision.
- You believe you are at your best when you sleep the recommended eight hours.
- You are exhausted after a particularly challenging day.
- You like to follow a project through to the end as it was planned.

This chapter focused on the required talents and characteristics of consultants. You can begin to appreciate the multitalented person a client will expect. You probably have a better picture of the drawbacks now, as well as the rewards of consulting. If you are excited by the opportunity and challenged by the adventure, you are ready to begin thinking about what you need to do to start.

For the Consummate Consultant

Make certain that you are a fit for the profession. This requires you to examine your skills and passion. How do they match up to consulting? Consider who you are, your natural skills, and what you like to do when you have a choice. How well do you fit the requirements of consulting?

Where the Two Overlap. Make two lists. The first should be what you like to do—your passions, if you will. Be general, such as organize events or solve problems. Next make a list of what people would pay you to do. Is there a business potential where the two overlap?

Take a Test Drive. You may want to do your own trial run before taking the leap into consulting. Perhaps you could conduct a small project or team-building event for a local nonprofit or a community college. Be sure to tell your boss.

Pump Up Your Subconscious. Your brain isn't really smart. It only knows what you put into it. Are you telling your brain you will succeed in your consulting business? Or are you telling your brain that you will fail in your consulting business? Either way, it will become a self-fulfilling prophecy. You can train your subconscious mind to think more positively. Those positive messages will make it to your conscious being to ensure you achieve the results you desire.

Dollars and Sense

3

The harder I work the luckier I get!

Samuel Goldwyn

Another rainy day; another miserable commute home. Kelly had experienced this same drive from home to work and back again five days a week for more than 20 years. The trip that used to be a pleasant 20-minute jaunt had more than doubled to 40–60 minutes each way, every day. Daily she experienced gridlock and careless, angry drivers who darted in and out of congested traffic at more than 20 miles per hour over the speed limit. It was maddening and frustrating. Road rage was real.

Reaching her 20-year anniversary with the same company in northern Virginia, or NOVA, as the locals liked to call it, was a milestone for Kelly. The 20-year mark was significant because it meant that she was vested for retirement benefits. Although far from retirement age, she did not want to spend two hours every day on this busy and dangerous road. She had toyed with the idea of consulting for the past two years, knowing that her cybersecurity expertise was in demand.

But how could she switch careers? And what would she charge? She had tried a few calculations. "Let's see, my current salary is almost $120,000. When I divide that by 50 weeks and 40 hours per week, the answer is $60 per hour. Hey!" she thought, "I'll be the boss, so I'll give myself a raise! $75 per hour should do it!" Hooooonk!! "Great!" she thought, "Another crazy NOVA driver! I guess I'd better focus. The rush hour is at epic proportions today."

■　■　■

What should you charge clients? Determining your fee may be your most difficult decision as a first-time consultant. However, it is a decision that you must make before you can begin to solicit business. Your client will most likely want to know, "What will this project cost me?"

I moderate panels and speak at conferences about consulting. The two topics new consultants most want to discuss are salary and finding clients. We'll discuss several aspects of marketing in Chapters Four, Five, and Seven. But first let's address the emotion-filled topic of setting fees.

As the chapter title suggests, putting a price on your head is about dollars and how to make sense of your value. Figuring it out has two parts:

1. How much money do you require?
2. How much are clients willing to pay you?

Although the two questions are closely related, it is important to keep them separate in your mind. If the two amounts are relatively close or if clients are willing to pay you more than you require (what an exciting problem to have!), you'll find it easy to balance your budget. On the other hand, if you suspect that you require more than clients are willing to pay for your services, you may want to reconsider opening a consulting practice. Let's examine both of these questions and how they converge on a solution for you.

HOW MUCH INCOME DO YOU REQUIRE?

You can determine how much income you require as a consultant in one of two ways. The first is to calculate in detail your salary, taxes, benefits, and business expenses for one year. A second way, the "3 × Rule" (pronounced "three times rule"), will provide a quick estimate of your requirements.

Recognize that both of these calculations will be based on where you are today. Many consultants believe that you are limiting your potential income with these calculations. My thoughts are that you need to start someplace and starting from where you are today is as good as anywhere. And of course you should have a vision that takes you far beyond. For now, let's begin with today.

Calculation Method

Your perceived value is one way to start. What do you believe you should make in a year? Starting here makes sense because an annual salary is the way most of us think of our value. Don't forget benefits, including insurance, retirement contributions, self-employment taxes, and vacation time. You may identify each benefit individually or simply add on 25 to 33 percent as an estimate. After that, develop a budget for running your business. Exhibit 3.1 will help you remember most of your expenses. In addition to annual expenses, you will have some one-time start-up costs. Chapter Four provides more details about these. Use Exhibit 3.1 to estimate the amounts you will need to cover your salary, benefits, taxes, and business expenses. Remember to consider profit also. Ten percent is a good place to start. Total these to determine how much money you will require annually.

The 3 × Rule

If you don't want to take time now to identify your business expenses, the 3 × Rule will give you a close estimate. The 3 × Rule is used by many consulting firms to determine how much to bill clients (and in some cases how much business to generate as well) in order to pay salaries, taxes, and insurance; cover overhead; and contribute to profit for the company. For example, consultants with a salary of $100,000 are expected to bill at least $300,000 each year. Does this seem excessive?

Exhibit 3.1. Calculating What You Require

Your Salary for One Year	Total Salary _____

Your Benefits
- Health insurance _____
- Life insurance _____
- Disability insurance _____
- Retirement _____

Total Benefits _____

Taxes
- Self-employment _____
- Social Security and Medicare _____
- State income tax _____
- City tax _____
- Personal property tax _____

Total Taxes _____

Business Expenses
- Accounting, banking, and legal fees _____
- Advertising and marketing _____
- Automobile expenses _____
- Books and resources _____
- Clerical support _____
- Copying _____
- Donations _____
- Dues and subscriptions _____
- Entertainment _____
- Equipment _____
- Interest and loan repayments _____
- Liability insurance _____
- Licenses _____
- Lodging (nonbillable) _____
- Materials (nonbillable) _____
- Meals _____
- Office supplies _____
- Postage _____
- Professional development _____
- Rent _____
- Repairs and maintenance _____
- Telephone, Internet _____
- Travel (nonbillable) _____
- Utilities _____

Total Business Expenses _____
Planned Business Profit _____
Total Required _____

Do you wonder what happens to all that money? You already know that $100,000 is earmarked for your salary. The other two-thirds pays for fringe benefits, such as insurance, FICA, unemployment taxes, worker's compensation, and vacation time; overhead, such as marketing, advertising, electricity, professional development, telephone, supplies, clerical support, and management; downtime, those days when consultants are traveling, off for a holiday, or in training; and for development and preparation time. The additional money also covers days that cannot be billed due to an inability to match available consultants to client dates.

If you plan to work out of a home office and you do not plan to hire support staff the first year, you might be able to whittle your requirements down to a "2 × Rule," but your budget will be tight and you may experience cash-flow problems. (More about cash flow in Chapter Six.) Be cautious about playing a tight numbers game.

Consider Your Personal Situation

Consider what is unique to you as you decide how much income you require. Are you the primary breadwinner in your family? Can someone else pick up some of the slack as you are starting your business? What can you contribute from your savings as you start your own consulting practice? Many experienced consultants recommend that you have a 6- to 12-month cushion. What consulting projects can you count on immediately? How long will it take to generate additional consulting projects? Are you planning a life style change?

As the gig economy rolls on, many companies offer "consulting contracts" as a way to ensure continuity of completing current projects in progress. This may be an ideal scenario for you. It usually means that you are responsible for specific projects identified by your former employer for which you receive an amount that is likely a little more per hour than your former salary. You would not be expected to be on-site full time and you can use the rest of your time to generate and conduct other consulting projects. Generally these agreements extend for less than one year and are nonrenewable. Many budding consultants find this an ideal way to start.

If your company doesn't offer a consulting contract option to you, you could take the lead and suggest it to them. I had something similar happen when I started my consulting business. I was leaving a position where my department manager, two colleagues, the department administrative officer, and I were all leaving within a few months of each other. The organization asked me to stay on for six months to transition the five new people into the workplace. In exchange, they offered me a couple of consulting projects that they needed to pursue. It was a win/win. I received the starter consulting assignments required to provide instant cash flow; my former employer used my experience and corporate knowledge to quickly complete desired projects.

Okay, so now you have a ballpark figure of what you will need your consulting practice to generate the first year. Let's explore how you decide what to charge.

HOW MUCH SHOULD YOU CHARGE?

Deciding how much to charge is difficult because there is an emotional aspect to it. Sometimes it may feel as if it is tied to your value as a person. In addition, you may feel modest and not want to charge too much, but you also cannot afford to charge too little. Here is how to decide how much to charge for your services.

Determine Typical Charges

Charges are determined by many factors. The greatest determining factor is the client: the business or industry, the size and location, the demand, and the history of consultant use. The next determining factor is the consultant: the level of expertise, the amount of experience, and the person's stature. This unique supply-and-demand situation creates a wide price range. I've worked with consultants who have charged as little as $200 per day and as much as $75,000 for a one-hour speech! So what's realistic?

The type of client determines acceptable fee ranges. Generally, for-profit companies have more in their budgets for your services than do nonprofit organizations. Usually, the larger the company, the larger the discretionary funds available. Consultants tend to keep a close hold on what they charge. When discussing fees with my colleagues, I find that daily rates for consultants working in the corporate arena are the highest. In the past two years I haven't talked to anyone who is using less than a $1,000-per-day starting point. Another of my colleagues charges $6,500 per day for his Silicon Valley clients—of course, he has a unique expertise and many years of experience. In addition, he generally charges by the project. Government, nonprofit organizations, and associations are usually lower, in the $600 to $4,500 range. And, of course, it depends on what is included in your daily rate.

_____

The larger the company, the larger the discretionary funds available.

_____

Also check your market area for organizations offering services similar to yours that may be priced much lower. For example, a local health clinic or hospital may offer a stress-management class for $20. A community college may offer a time-management course for $35. If either of these is your specialty, you may have a difficult time convincing companies to pay $1,500 per day—even if you do customize the materials for them. We'll discuss the value you provide later.

The location of either the client or the consultant will also affect the fee charged. Ranges are different in different areas. It is natural to expect that consultants in large cities such as New York, Boston, or Frankfurt will charge more than consultants who work in smaller towns. In fact, in the United States, consultants on both coasts command a higher fee.

A wide variation exists internationally, too. In countries where it is difficult to find local experts, there is a willingness to pay the fee consultants request. However, as local citizens acquire skills and expertise to close the gaps, local consultants are taking on more of the consulting work—and charging lower fees proportionate to the local economy. This causes the demand for international consultants to decrease. I've experienced this in China and Peru. In general, the highest consulting rates occur in North America, Western Europe, Africa, and Australia/New Zealand. The lowest are in Eastern Europe and South/Central America (Hofferberth and Urich 2015).

Finally, your consulting foundation determines the fee. What expertise do you have? How long have you been in your specialty area? Is it unique or commonplace? How much experience do you have? With what type of clients? Do you work internationally? Nationally? Statewide? Locally? How well known are you? What perceived value do you add due to your stature in the business, authored books, or university affiliations? The answers to each of these will help to determine your rate.

Determine Your Fee

You probably realize that some consultants charge more for one day than you may presently make in a month. And that is, of course, where you'd like to be. How do you determine what you should charge? You'll want to do some benchmarking to understand the implications of your rates. Determine how you compare with others in your area of expertise and in the location of your primary client pool.

You can determine a fee in one of two ways. You can start with the requirements you compiled and plan toward that end or you can approach the problem from the standpoint of what the market will bear.

Plan with the End in Mind. To use this method, return to your calculations to obtain the amount that you need for living and business expenses for one year. Think in terms of how much billable time is actually available. There are 52 weeks in a year, and you will probably take off at least two of them. In addition, in the United States you must account for New Year's Day, Memorial Day, Independence Day, Labor Day, Thanksgiving, Christmas, and other holidays. If you live in another country, use those holidays. This leaves about 49 weeks or 245 days, assuming a five-day week. If you live in China or another country with a longer or shorter workweek, make those adjustments.

Generally, you will average between two and three billable days per week or a maximum of 120 days per year, for two reasons. The first is that the work you must do is not all client-facing. You will need time to run your business. You need to market, network, write proposals, travel, bill clients, and complete many other administrative details required to manage a business. In addition, you will need to develop your skills, learn new techniques, and keep up with the changes in your field as well as the industries in which you work. As a consultant you must maintain your professional edge.

The second reason it is highly unlikely that you will bill more than 120 days in one year is the difficulty of matching your clients' needs with your available days. You may find that all your clients need you the same week in September—a month that is notoriously busy in our field. You may need to turn down some of those billable days. Then again, you may find yourself with a week or two in December with no billable days. Exhibit 3.2 will help you to determine your actual billable days.

Exhibit 3.2. Actual Billable Days

Days in a Year	365
Weekend Days	– 104
	= 261
Time Off	
Vacation, personal (5–15 days per year)	– _____
Holidays (6–12 days per year)	– _____
	= _____
Marketing (1–2 days per week)	– _____
Administrative (2–4 days per month)	– _____
	= _____
Down time (15–30 percent)	– _____
Days you expect to work	☐

The New Business of Consulting

Let's return to Kelly and use her thought process. Kelly currently makes $120,000 per year and thought that if she charged $75 per hour she would be giving herself a raise. I stated that it would be highly unlikely that consultants can bill for more than 120 days in one year. Eight hours per day for 120 days equals 960 hours. Multiply that by the $75 "raise" Kelly gave herself and you see that she will make $72,000 and take a 40 percent cut in pay!

Let's take Kelly through a better scenario. Her $75 per hour is roughly $150,000 for a year. But she is now an employer and her salary is only a part of an employer's expense. Let's add $27,000 for self-employment taxes (about 18 percent). Kelly's company had a 5/10 contribution plan for her retirement. Kelly will now pay the full 15 percent or $22,500 for retirement. She will also pay for various kinds of insurance. This will vary greatly, but let's just add a rough $15,000 for health, disability, and life insurance. This brings Kelly's total to $214,000. Surprising, isn't it?

Let's suppose that Kelly will begin by working out of her home. That means she can expect overhead to be low for the first year, about $2,000 per month or $24,000 per year. Now the total amount that Kelly must bill is $238,000. Next Kelly divides the total dollar amount, $238,000, by the 120 days of consulting. This gives Kelly a daily rate of $1,983.33. Most consultants would round that figure to $2,000 for each billable day. Are you surprised?

You should consider one last thing. A successful business makes a profit each year. Don't confuse your salary with your business profit. A profit is your reward for business ownership and the risk that it incurs. A 10 percent profit is very respectable for a first year in business, so Kelly may want to set a goal of $20,000 as a profit margin. This, of course, increases what she will need to bill for her first year.

Of course, we don't know the details of Kelly's situation. For example, her spouse may have health insurance, so she would not need that expense. Or she may want to have an office, which increases her expenses. Although we used the average of 120 billable days, she will have to hustle to bill that many days. Few consultants bill that many days the first year, unless their present employer will retain them to complete existing projects or they have client agreements before quitting their current jobs.

Tip: Try a rate calculator.

Nation1099 has produced an online rate calculator where you can plug in the numbers of your own situation to estimate your minimum requirements. I recommend that you try the advanced version for increased reliability. You can try it at nation1099.com/freelance-rate-calculator.

Does $2,000 per day sound high for Kelly's first year in the field? It may be. She may need to return to her original budget. Can she cut expenses? Could she do all her own design work instead of using a temporary service? Can she forego her "raise" this first year? Can she decrease the amount required to live? For example, she could skip the expensive vacation she's always taken. Perhaps she could use some of her savings for living expenses? Think about Kelly's situation. Any of these will change the equation to lower her billable rate. Use Exhibit 3.3 to calculate your consulting fee.

Exhibit 3.3. Calculating Your Fee

Daily Fee:
What You Require / Days You Expect to Work = Daily Fee
$ _____ / _____ days = $ _____ per day

Hourly Fee:
Daily Fee / 8 Hours = Hourly Fee
$ _____ / 8 Hours = $ _____ per hour

Although this exercise is an excellent way to determine your billable rate, you must also consider what a client will be willing to pay for your services. You certainly do not want to price yourself out of the market your first year!

By the way, we'll explore why daily or hourly rates may not be the best pricing strategy, but for now it gives us a way to make equitable comparisons for how to determine a billable rate. In addition, it gives you a basic unit of measure for other calculations.

Determine What the Market Will Bear. An easy way to establish your fee is to emulate your competition. Place a price on your head by determining what you believe the market will bear—that is, how much you believe your targeted clients will pay for your services. Realize that you are not charging what you are "worth" but what clients are willing to pay. In his classic book *The Consultant's Calling*, Geoff Bellman (2002) says, "We are not talking about what you and I are worth; we are talking about what you and I can get. ... Your ultimate value as a consultant or as a human being is not being put on the line in this negotiation." This is an important distinction. Your fee does not measure your actual worth, but only what clients are willing to pay for your services. Geoff goes on to say, "You can't put a financial value on who you are, so don't mix up your struggles about personal worth with your efforts to sell your services."

As a new consultant, you may want to collect as much information as you can about what clients are paying for services and what consultants are charging for services. Don't be surprised if this information is difficult to obtain. If you are still employed, perhaps you could to do some covert data gathering before you leave to learn what your company pays for their consultants. I have found most consultants to be quite private about what they charge. Of course, you need to pay attention to the Sherman Anti-Trust Act to ensure that you will not be accused of price fixing!

Tip: What are you worth?

You may feel better about your value if you find out what you are worth at payscale.com. You can input information about yourself, for example, where you live, where you graduated, your certification and degrees, and number of years of experience to calculate a current compensation analysis. You will get the basic information for free or a more detailed salary report for a six-month membership fee. Two other sites you may wish to visit for insight are salary.com or indeed.com.

If you decide to follow what the market will bear, you will want to explore some other issues to help you determine your fee. Ask yourself these questions: What's your specialty? How common is your expertise? How many alternatives does the client have? What is unique about your experience? What industry are you targeting? What size organization will you serve? What constitutes a typical consulting fee for companies in this industry? Where is your market? What is the range of fees organizations pay in this market? Who else offers similar services? What do they charge? Use Exhibit 3.4 to help you sort through the factors that will determine your rate. The more Xs in the left column, the higher rate you will be able to charge.

Exhibit 3.4. How Much Will Clients Pay?

Place an X in either the left or right column next to the item that most closely describes you and your potential clients.

My Consulting

___ Expertise in high demand	___ Minimal demand for expertise
___ Stand out; a specialized niche	___ Lots of competition in my area
___ More than 20 years in the industry	___ Fewer than 10 years in industry
___ High name recognition	___ Little name recognition
___ Rare area of specialty	___ Specialty readily available
___ Published work is well known	___ No published work
___ My confidence level is high	___ Hey! I'm just starting this!
___ Offer customized solutions	___ Offer content with minor tailoring

My Clients

___ High-operating-margin industry	___ Low-operating-margin industry
___ For-profit organizations	___ Nonprofit or government
___ Large organizations	___ Small organizations
___ Large cities	___ Small city
___ U.S. coast locations	___ U.S. Midwest
___ High use of consultants	___ Minimal use of consultants
___ Urgent; burning issues	___ Not time-sensitive

Total _____   _____

The 1% Rule. Like the 3 × Rule, the 1% Rule will give you a quick and dirty estimate—but in this case for what to charge. The rule, popularized in Marion McGovern's (2017) book *Thriving in the Gig Economy,* states that taking 1 percent of your salary gets you quite close to an estimated daily rate. So in Kelly's scenario, she was aiming at a salary of $150,000. One percent would be a $1,500 daily fee. I've always found this formula to come up a bit short, which means Kelly would need to work more than the 120 average number of days each year in order to pay for insurance, taxes, overhead, and so forth. The 1% Rule is just another way to gauge what you may want to charge.

Pricing Strategy

Whether you decide to plan with the end in mind, go with what the market will bear, or use a combination of the two methods, you must still select a pricing strategy. Your figures will result in a range, so you will have to determine whether to charge closer to the high end or the low end of the range. Experience shows that most new consultants select the lower price. They feel that if they price low, they will find more contracts to start out. I did that. Worried that I wouldn't have enough work and basing my fee only on my current salary, I started by charging $350 per day. I was busy! I felt as if I were in a revolving door, doing something different for a new client every day. I had no time between clients to prepare.

Pricing services too low is the biggest mistake new consultants make. Besides a lack of time, it opens up other issues. You may work long hours and not make the amount of money you deserve for the job. Your long hours to scrape by may not allow enough time for you to grow your business or to develop yourself. A low bid may help you acquire some early projects, but may also be a reason that clients are uncomfortable hiring you again—especially if the project was not large enough to develop a solid relationship.

If your price is too low, you may be inadvertently telling clients that you are not as good as other consultants. You want your clients focused on the value for the services that you will provide. Adding all these together means that your attitude will eventually suffer. Achieving the reputation of being the cheapest consultant in town means only that you are "the cheapest consultant in town"! The only thing a low rate should provide for you is a walkaway rate, that is, the rate below which you will not work.

Choose the high end of the range—for several reasons. First, the higher price means that you will need to accept fewer contracts. This allows you to manage your time better, giving you the flexibility to deal with all those unforeseeable things that crop up when starting a business. It also allows you to spend more time with your clients, giving them better service, rather than worrying about your next contract. You may experience a longer buying cycle, but the wait will be worth it. Charge a price that allows you to do the job with superior quality.

Charge a price that allows you to do the job with superior quality.

Second, your consulting rate sends a message. True or not, a higher price often is equated with higher quality. A low price may send a message that you are not worthy of important projects. At one point in my career I was overwhelmed with requests from clients. I thought that if I increased my rates I'd have fewer clients. It didn't work. The message I sent with a higher rate was that I produced higher quality! My plan backfired! And more clients wanted to work with me.

> **Tip: A message in your rates.**
>
> If your consulting time is booked solid, you may be charging too little. You may need a new strategy that defines who you won't work with and what you won't do.

Third, unless your price is radically different, clients care less about your price than you may imagine. If you are stressing out over pricing, stop. In most cases, if you offer what clients need, they will most likely pay the price you request without questioning it. They want you to solve their problem. Don't let pricing detain you from moving forward.

SELECTING A PRICING STRUCTURE

The discussion so far has focused primarily on a daily fee. There are other possible pricing structures. Often the industry you serve or the kind of consulting you do will determine the pricing structure you choose.

Daily Rate

Training, organization development, or management development consultants typically charge by the day. That day may be 6 to 12 hours long, depending on the task at hand. If you are conducting training that begins at 8 a.m., you will probably need to arrive before 7 a.m. to set up the room—or even set it up the night before the session. The session may last until 4:30 p.m., but participants may stay around to discuss the day with you. After they leave, you may still want to organize the room and your materials for the next day, study your notes, or examine work that was generated by the participants during the day. It may be 6 p.m. before you leave for the day. An 11-hour day may be the norm, and you do not charge overtime for the additional hours.

Billing by the day may make you seize as many days of work as possible—even when they don't fit into your schedule well. When a day has passed without a billable client, you have lost that income potential forever. Billing by the day limits your earning power to the number of days in a year. This puts strong emphasis on days worked as opposed to results achieved. Remember that a billable day is a billable day; once it's gone, it is lost forever.

A billable day is a billable day; once it's gone, it is lost forever.

Hourly Rate

Consulting fees charged by the hour are standard in some industries, such as computer programming, accounting, legal, and engineering. It is also often required in government projects that require proposals priced for auditing purposes. In some cases, you may provide a range of hours (minimum and maximum) you expect the job to require. Travel time is not generally billed in any of the other methods of charging; it often is in the hourly rate structure.

Jenn Labin, a consulting colleague, offered this advice in a recent email to me: "The work we do as consultants is valued more highly than just the number of hours we put in. I prefer to bill on a project basis; however, I may bill on an hourly basis when it's the organization's preference and I clearly understand the context of the project, I am confident of the process and technology that will be used, and I am certain that the scope boundaries are stable."

Both a daily rate and an hourly rate require the client to assume the risk for the total cost of the project. Thus, they are more typically used for training or tasks that have clearly defined time parameters and outcomes. Depending on your consulting projects, hourly rates can be the most limiting in how much you can earn. If not, clients are penalized if the consultant is slow and consultants are penalized if they are efficient! It's important to communicate clearly and regularly about the number of hours that are accumulating.

Fixed-Price Projects

Establishing a firm price for a complete project is how I prefer to bill. Specific results are identified for the completion of a project. Although some consultants resist this method of pricing, due to the risk involved if the price is too low, my experience shows that this is the trend. Tom Peters says, "It's a project-based world. If you're not spending at least 70 percent of your time on projects, you're living in the past" (Peters 1997).

You may have to bid on a fixed-price basis if you work for government agencies. Responding to a Request for Proposal (RFP) from any organization may also require you to determine a fixed price for an entire project. But it may also require you to break the work down to show how much you are charging per hour. An RFP is often used when several consultants are competing for a job.

I prefer this pricing structure for several reasons. First and most important, the client's employees can call at any time for assistance and, unlike my attorney, I won't start the timer. Second, the method is performance- and results-oriented. We are paid for what we accomplish. Third, this method is the best match for a custom design. Fourth, this method is better for larger contracts. Several large contracts are easier to manage than dozens of little ones.

How can you determine a price? First, estimate how much time you expect the project to require. If this is your first time with this method, you may still want to use a daily rate to find a ballpark price. With this method, you assume the risk of the total cost of the project. Ethically, you cannot charge more than the original quoted price—even if you lose money. We have lost money on a couple of projects due to poor estimating. In these situations, we have always continued to provide the highest-quality work and have not disclosed our predicament to the client. This would be unprofessional. It certainly taught us good estimating skills quickly!

The one drawback is scope creep. That's when your client asks you to do more than what was agreed upon. These things happen because neither you nor the client will be able to predict everything. This can be managed easily, as long as you bring each of these additional client requests that go beyond your original agreement to your client's attention. At that point, you can both decide how to manage the new requests. They may be included in the project at an additional fee or they may be left for a later time.

Per Person

Charging by the number of participants who attend a session is another way to look at pricing for a training consultant. It is typically used by trainers offering public seminars, although there may be a few nonprofits that like to contract this way, too. Government agencies may want you to use this type of fee structure because it more closely matches their budgeting structure. If you do choose this method, consider an up-front agreement that you will be paid for a minimum number of participants. In other words, if you require payment for a minimum of 18 and only 16 people attend, you will still be paid for 18.

Of course you should also specify a maximum number of participants. I deliver training for talent development professionals in China, where it is critical to specify the exact maximum number you will accept. I remember conducting a two-day session that was supposed to be for 35 participants. As I was setting up, I thought we had a very large room for 35 participants. And then I learned why. As the session began, 50 additional people started to stream into the room, standing against walls and sitting on the floor around the perimeter! My contract had been interpreted as "35 official participants" who would be seated at tables and as many unofficial spectators as would fit in the room!

Retainers

I see more and more retainer arrangements. A retainer establishes a set fee that the consultant receives on a regular basis, generally monthly. A retainer works best if you've already completed one or more initial projects with your client, because it allows both of you to get to know each other and the business culture. A retainer, or pay for access, typically covers a span of 12 months. The client is assured that the consultant is available on an as-needed basis. The client and consultant determine an approximate amount of time that will be required monthly. Given enough advance warning, the consultant is expected to respond. The work may be on-site, on the phone, or both. The advantage to the consultant is a regular income; the drawback is that the consultant must plan around the needs of the client. I charge my coaching clients this way.

Conditional Fee

Some organizations pay a fixed price to a consultant on the completion of a clearly defined task. This method may be used by search firms in executive recruiting, where the conditional fee is paid only after the recruiting consultant provides the organization with four qualified candidates for a specific position.

Performance Percent Fee

Pay for performance fees are used when the financial outcome of the project is easily and clearly measurable. The consultant agrees to a percentage of the financial success of the project. This method works well for sales or marketing consultants. The client and the consultant agree that a percentage of the financial gain or savings will be paid to the consultant. A consultant can do very well with this arrangement, and the client is assured that the consultant will focus on the bottom line. There are a few drawbacks. First, the consultant will not have insight into whether the client is manipulating results. A client may not implement everything that you recommend, thus compromising your ability to reach a maximum payout. Finally, the results may not be measurable until some time after the project has been completed. In this case, you can require a start-up fee prior to beginning the project.

Value-Based Fees

Some consulting gurus may lead you to believe that if you are not using value-based fees, you are a dimwitted amateur. Value-based fees are based on the value you contribute to the results of a project. So if you agree to a 10 percent value-based contract, your fee is 10 percent of the success of the project. You are paid for the value you create. For example, you might convince a client that you can generate $5 million in savings, or profits, or new revenue. If you have agreed to be paid 10 percent of the success of the project, you would receive $500,000. Plus, you probably will agree to annualize the results and be paid into the future, too. It's an advantageous arrangement in which you act as a true partner with your client. Sound too good to be true? Unfortunately, economics isn't that simple or most consultants would be using value-based fees. Yes, there are a few successful consultants who have a unique skill set or capability that most in the market do not have—and, of course, that the client needs. Most of us must admit that there are others in the profession who can provide the same services to our client, and some at a lower price.

No matter which pricing structure you choose, your fees must be based on how much you require as well as how much the market will bear.

OTHER PRICING DECISIONS

Many other decisions must be made around pricing. You must be clear about what you think about the following before you can discuss costs with a client.

Definition of a Day

If you have decided to charge by the day, you must determine what constitutes a day. If you attend meetings at your client's business from 10 a.m. until 3 p.m., is that one day? If you work on a project in your office from 7 a.m. until 7 p.m., is that one day? Do you count hours? Do you count calendar days? How will you define one day? Although we typically charge by the project, when we use daily rates we charge for one calendar day no matter how many hours beyond eight we work. No matter how you determine the length of a day, be sure to decide prior to working with clients.

Half-Day Events

What if a client needs you on-site for four hours and you are basing your charges on full-day rates? Should you charge half your regular rate? We recommend that you charge more than half. Why? First, you will spend the same amount of time going to and from the site. Second, you will probably spend the same amount of time in preparation. And, third, this billable day is spent! You have little chance of using the rest of the day in billable work. So what can you do? You may wish to bill for something more than half a day's rate but less than a full-day rate. Or you may wish to do as I do, which is to charge a full-day rate, even for a half-day event.

Perceived Value

Your price may send a message to potential clients about your expertise. I notice consistently that new consultants tend to establish fees that are lower than the market would bear. An astute client will question whether you can successfully complete the project at the rate that you have quoted.

Proposals or Sales Meetings

We do not charge for writing proposals. We see it as a cost of doing business. If we initiate a sales call, we do not charge for the time or expenses. Nor do we charge if the client requests a visit and it is local (within a two-hour drive). However, if the client initiates a sales call that will require an overnight stay or airfare, we do request payment for out-of-pocket expenses. To open this discussion in a professional manner, I usually say, "Would you like us to make travel arrangements and bill you at cost? Or would you like to make the travel arrangements and let me know what they are?"

Pro Bono

Work that you complete for free is good for your business, good for the community, and good for your soul. I set aside at least 15 days each year to do pro bono work for professional organizations such as the Association of Talent Development, volunteer groups such as the American Red Cross, or schools and government agencies that cannot afford to pay. In these cases I do not charge a reduced fee. I tell them that I have only two fees: my client fee and free. The more you give, the more you get. Try it.

OTHER CHARGES

Besides your billing rate, you will incur extra charges that will be reimbursed by the client.

Travel Expenses

Travel, lodging, and meals are generally an additional charge to the client. Bill your client for the same amount you paid. It may be a common practice in other professions to tack on a "handling fee" for expenses, but it is not accepted in consulting. You will be expected to provide receipts for your expenses. If you work for government agencies, you will hear the term *per diem*, which refers to a preestablished daily rate that has been determined for the city in which you are working. This fee, allowed by the Joint Travel Regulations, is expected to cover your lodging, meals, tips, and sometimes local travel. If you are traveling on a per diem basis, find out what it is prior to making your travel arrangements so that you can stay within the maximum amount allowed.

Materials

There are three possible ways to handle charges for materials that will be used during the consulting project: (1) materials can be included in your daily fee; (2) materials can be an additional charge to the client and can appear as an additional line item on the invoice; or (3) materials can be provided or produced by the client. When a contract includes many repeat sessions, you may help clients to save money by providing them with masters for the materials and allowing them to make their own copies. This saves you time and eliminates your need to transport materials for each session.

Overhead

Most consultants' fees include the cost of overhead. However, some larger firms itemize the charges for administrative tasks, data entry, editing, data analysis, and other off-site activities. Some firms also track and charge for telephone calls and other correspondence. Although it is unlikely that a start-up consultant will do that, you should be aware of this practice. If you ever find yourself competing on a daily or hourly rate basis with one of the large consulting firms, and you wonder how they can charge less than you, dig deeper. You will find that the firm's total sum will most likely be greater than yours due to all the additional charges.

Cost to Hire

Given most organizations' greater emphasis on part-time, contingency, and free-lance work, some consultant groups suggest that clients should also bear the cost to hire. Within the organization, this includes all the expenses for recruiting, hiring, onboarding, and training employees. I am not advocating this for now, because this "savings" is one of the advantages that consultants can use to sell their services to organizations. Let's keep an eye on the future to see what occurs.

Travel Time

Will you charge for travel time? A very small portion of consultants itemize travel time as billable to the client at a reduced rate. Most consultants simply consider it a cost of doing business.

FEE INCREASES

If you believe setting your initial fees is difficult, wait until you are faced with increasing your fees. You will have many questions on your mind: "Will they pay more?" "Will I lose some of my clients?" "How do I tell them?" First, remember that an annual increase is normal and expected. It just makes good business sense.

When I first started, I charged a daily rate because that was the kind of work I was getting. I remember sitting next to the Elizabeth River with a friend, trying to decide whether I should increase my fees from $750 to $800 or $900. In the end my friend convinced me to go for $1,000! Turned out to be easier than I thought.

Although I've never experienced a negative reaction to fee increases, I know that some consultants have. An increase in your fees may result in a loss of clients. However, if you give your clients enough time to adjust their budgets and you're not increasing your rate by an astronomical figure, your clients will most likely understand. A six-month notice is generally considered fair, ethical, and appropriate. We tell our clients about an increase verbally, then follow up with a written note. In addition, we include a reminder with the first invoice at the new rate.

This is one time that you cannot overcommunicate. And, by the way, don't apologize for a rate increase. Instead, tell your clients how much you appreciate working with them and that you would be happy to answer their questions. This is a critical time when you need to be clear about your pricing strategy.

How do you know that it's time to increase your fees? You'll know when you are so busy you don't have time to increase your fees! It's a simple matter of supply and demand—or so I once thought. As I mentioned earlier, at one point in my career I had about twice the work I could handle, so I increased my fees. In fact, I doubled them, thinking that my projects would be cut in half and that I would break even financially with less work. That didn't happen. My plan failed! Instead, when I raised my fees it created a perception that I was more valuable! Raising my fees actually *increased* business.

Are you too busy to have lunch with a friend or working on proposals every weekend? Then it is time to evaluate your fees. Yes, you may lose a couple of clients—but then, isn't that the point? To free up some of your time? It is noteworthy that in today's gig economy, many consultants try it for the lifestyle, but stick around for the money.

Are you too busy to market to a better client base? Increasing your rates may force you to market to clients who can pay more. Review your business plan. Are you really working with your dream clients? Those who can pay your new rates and who have the ability and the need to hire you again and again?

Let's pause for a moment here. This conversation isn't simply about your fee, increasing your fee, or even what you are going to do for the client. You should not focus on the tools, the processes, your services, and what you do. Instead, focus your discussion on the value you bring to them. This helps your client to see the results they will achieve when they hire you, such as reduced cost, increased profits, a competitive advantage, or many others. Focus on the benefits and the value they want.

Sometimes when you increase your rates, your proposals are bumped into a new category, requiring approval by a higher level of management. This is good, because higher levels in any organization generally have larger budgets and more discretionary funds. A difference of $13,000 one way or another is not as critical to a vice president as it is to a line manager. Lesson learned? Don't underestimate yourself. If you add value, the work will be there.

If you add value, the work will be there.

For another perspective, be sure to read Geoff Bellman's book *The Consultant's Calling*. I'd like to be able to tell you to read just one chapter, but I can't do that. The book represents a philosophy, and to appreciate its holistic nature, you need to read the entire book.

ETHICS OF PRICING

Although Chapter Nine is dedicated to the ethics of consulting, three issues about pricing ethics deserve to be mentioned here.

Determine Your Market Pricing Strategy

The highest compliment that I can receive from a client is to hear that we are trusted and ethical. The fastest way to undermine that trust is to price inconsistently for different clients. To ensure that this does not happen, identify a clear and consistent pricing structure for all of your clients. Charging one client $1,000 for one day of training and another on the other side of town $1,500 for the same type of training will cause problems. Clients get together at their industry professional meetings and share what they are doing. You do not want them to discover a difference in your pricing.

Some situations do exist in which you might not charge the same for all clients or for all work, but be certain that these occasions are clearly spelled out in your pricing strategy. Be certain that you adhere to your own strategy. Three situations in which you might charge different prices follow:

1. *The work is different.* You might use a different pricing strategy for different kinds of work—one price for work done on-site and another for work done at your office. You might have a consulting fee and a training fee and perhaps a design fee that is less than either of them. You may charge a different fee for speaking engagements than for training. And, of course, if you are subcontracting with other consultants, you will always charge less, as they have the burden of risk and acquired the contract with their marketing investment.

2. *The organizations are different.* You may also choose to discount your rate for nonprofit organizations, associations, government agencies, church or school groups, or even your favorite charity, but always identify a measurable reduction and be consistent. Why would you give one nonprofit group a 10 percent discount and another 50 percent? You may have a good reason, but being clear about your pricing strategy will help you to maintain an ethical image.

Remember that your discount strategy is something that you have determined ahead of time. It is not something you negotiate with a client.

3. *The time period is different.* You may have a situation where the client asks you to do the work in a shorter than normal time. If your client's project is urgent, you might need to work weekends or bring in additional people to help with the project. In this case you would be justified in raising your typical rates, and I am guessing that the client will be happy to pay a premium to complete the task. The time period might also be different because it is a long-term contract—say over a year. In this case you might be justified in providing a discounted rate for repeat or prepaid business because you will not need the time to get up to speed as you would if you were starting with a new client each month.

The point in each of these three examples is that there is something different—something unique that justifies a different pricing strategy. The key word here is *strategy.* Know your strategy and stick with it.

Save Bargains for Department Stores

Although we all love a sale, consulting is not a postseasonal business. It is unethical for you to lower your rates simply because clients do not have adequate funds in their budgets to cover the amount you first quoted. How could this happen? You determine that your rates for the project will be $15,500. The client responds that there is only $10,500 in the budget for the project. It is very tempting (especially if you don't have any work lined up for the next few weeks) to say, "Okay, I'll do it for $10,500." This is one of the ways that consultants gain a bad reputation. If you can do it for $10,500, why did you ask for $15,500? Does that mean that you had $5,000 worth of fat in the proposal? It will make a client question your ethics and the ethics of all consultants.

The only way that you can lower the price of an original quote is to eliminate some of the services, so that there is a true trade-off for the services you offer. For example, you might say, "We could do it at the lower price if you print the training materials there, compile the evaluations yourself, and provide all the equipment." Or you might eliminate a more valuable service, saying, "We could do it at the lower price, but it would mean that I would not spend a day at your company interviewing people in order to customize the participant materials." When I take this approach, two things usually happen. First, I feel good about myself when I do not succumb to the monetary temptation. Second, the client usually does not want to give up the service and most often says that the money will be found someplace.

If neither of these types of suggestions works, be prepared to walk away from the project. I have walked on at least a dozen occasions. Every time, the clients called me back to say they could "scrape up the money" somehow. I'd like to believe that something greater occurred. I believe that I was educating the client about appropriate consulting ethics.

Don't sell yourself short. If you find that new clients often ask you to reduce your rates, you may want to research the marketplace in which you are working. Have you priced yourself above what the market will bear? If yes, you have at least two choices. First, you may want to lower your prices. To do this, you may need to decrease the services you presently provide to clients or decrease your cost of doing business. Second, you may want to locate another market in which your fees are more competitive.

Charge Higher Rates for a Unique Project

The ethics of increasing your rates are even fuzzier than those for reducing your rates. If you are up-front and candid with your client, it's probably okay. Why would you raise your rates? I can think of at least two reasons: The client wants the task completed in a ridiculously short amount of time, or the client insists on using you for a project that you dislike.

In either case, you are most likely justified in quoting an increased fee— especially if you are candid in your explanation to your client.

MONEY DISCUSSIONS

During discussions with your clients, you may want to take the responsibility for bringing up the topic of cost. Talking about money is difficult for some people. Take the lead by saying, "You probably want to know how much this will cost." When I open the discussion, I often see relief on the client's face—grateful that I brought up the subject.

Sometimes during that first discussion, you may see potential complications with the project, an unusual timeline, or something unique that you haven't done before. This may make it difficult to price the project on the spot. In this case, you can say, "I'm not sure of the price at this time. Let me go back to my office and put a proposal together that will outline a work plan and the cost. I will have the proposal on your desk tomorrow." This buys you time to plan the project and to price it appropriately. Don't allow yourself to be forced into providing a "rough estimate." An exact figure the next day is better for both you and the client. Naturally, you must live up to your promise to deliver the proposal and price quote when you say you will.

VALUE OF A GUARANTEE

If you are just starting your consulting practice, you might consider offering a 100 percent satisfaction guarantee. If the client is not satisfied with your work, you will return the full amount. Sound risky? It shouldn't. If you don't believe in yourself, who will? If you don't believe in your ability to meet and exceed clients' needs, perhaps you are considering the wrong profession. You should not be practicing on clients. You should know your abilities and be able to guarantee the job.

If you don't believe in yourself, who will?

I've offered a 100 percent money-back guarantee from my first day in the profession. Many of my first clients gave me a chance because the guarantee provided reassurance that I was confident in my ability to complete the project successfully. If I wasn't successful, they wouldn't have to pay. Since that time, many have said the guarantee made the choice easy. As one of my clients from NASA said, "It was a win no matter how we looked at it!"

A guarantee does two things for you and your business. First, it makes it easier for the clients to say "yes" to you. They have nothing to lose. Either you accomplish the task that needs to be done or it doesn't cost them a thing. Second, it tells the client that you are confident and competent at what you do. What better way to begin a consulting relationship?

A guarantee tells the client that you are confident and competent at what you do.

Establishing your fee and pricing structure may be the most difficult decisions you must make in the business of consulting, but it's not impossible. Don't let it prevent you from moving forward.

For the Consummate Consultant

Putting a price on your head is one of the most difficult decisions that you'll make as you transition to consulting. Consider these thoughts to increase your pricing confidence and to help you make sense of the dollars.

Set a Rate You Deserve with Confidence. Price your work commensurate with the value you bring to your clients. The emotional stakes are seldom as high as we may imagine. Your clients are less concerned about your consulting fee than about whether you have a solution for them.

Don't Discount. Working from home does not justify a discount. You are still as smart, as experienced, as reliable, and as results-oriented as you were when you worked in a cubicle. You deserve a sufficient salary, the ability to pay your bills, and a profit for your risk. Your clients are not doing you a favor by hiring you. You provide them with value and they pay you a commensurate sum.

Scout About. Learn as much as you can in as many ways as you can by asking other consultants about their fees and fee structure, obtaining feedback about your pricing when you lose a proposed contract, checking out what companies pay for consultants in your area of expertise, and reviewing research results about other consultants and consultant practices.

Starting . . .

4

If you put everything off till you're sure of it, you'll get nothing done.

Norman Vincent Peale

Vivian looked gingerly around the little coffee shop. Andrea had been shouting for more than 20 minutes—and her voice carried so far! Vivian was hoping no one else from the office was in the café, but it was unlikely anyone was. After all, it was 6:30 p.m. on a Friday night and everyone else was probably home preparing dinner. She looked at Andrea, who was yelling, "Why tonight, too? He knew I was going to the concert. I told him about it last week! Besides, it's Friday night! Doesn't he have a life? All these long work days! I'll tell you, I can't take it anymore! I can't work for him. The entire department depends on me to solve every crisis! My skills are not appreciated and I want to do something for me!"

Trying to think of a way to calm her friend, Vivian said, "Well, maybe it's time you did."

"What do you mean?" Andrea shook her head slightly as if trying to refocus.

"Well, you've been talking about consulting for years. Maybe it's time to do something besides talk about it. Maybe you should spend time thinking about what that would look like. You know—create a plan."

"But I wouldn't know where to start! What do I do first? How do I know I'll make any money? What kind of consulting would I do? How do I find clients? What do I charge them?" asked Andrea in a more moderate voice.

Thankful that she'd been able to redirect her friend's attention, Vivian chided her, "Oh, come on! You do all the strategic planning for your department and your division. You created the process to write the vision and mission. You even created a more efficient way to track the budget. You've been doing this for 13 years. Don't say you don't know how. You should be able to transfer some of your skills to your own consulting endeavor. Right?"

"Well, maybe …" Andrea replied hesitantly.

"Maybe?! Are you crazy? I'll tell you what. I have another 40 minutes before I need to leave to meet Gil for dinner. Let's brainstorm some of the things you know you'd need to do, the questions you need to answer and who you could tap for more information. Are you willing to try that?"

■ ■ ■

Are you excited to start your consulting practice, but have no idea how? Sometimes starting can be so overwhelming it becomes debilitating. You may be excited about tackling all the things necessary to begin your business but, like Andrea, you need a push to start. Making a list of all those questions is a good place to begin.

- How much will it cost to start a consulting practice? Surprisingly less than you may think.
- What shall I call my company?
- Who can help me with the financial aspects?
- What do I need to do legally as a start-up?
- Do I need to incorporate?
- Do I need a business plan?
- What's the best way to define what I'll do?
- How do I project a professional image? Consultants always seem so together.
- How do I gain experience?
- How do I land my first client?

This chapter explores each of these questions and wraps up with a checklist that you can use to start your consulting firm. You may be surprised that starting a consulting firm can be easier and cheaper than you might expect. Even so, let's review why start-up companies fail and why they succeed.

WHY SOME START-UPS SUCCEED AND SO MANY FAIL

You've probably read the statistics of high failure rates for start-up companies. I've always thought they were just out there to scare people like you and me who want to start our own companies. It seems that Shikhar Ghosh of the Harvard Business School has nailed down actual numbers, stating that the failure rate of all U.S. companies is 50 percent after five years, and 70 percent after 10 years (Henry 2017).

But why? A *FastCompany* magazine (Linamagi 2015) survey of 100 start-up companies that failed cited many reasons for the failures. I was surprised that several were things that seem to be practical common sense. It would seem that they don't have a chance without some of the basics in place. Several related to consulting include:

- Lack of motivation, commitment, and passion
- Lack of market need
- Running out of cash
- Pricing and cost issues
- Lack of knowledge about the competition
- Ignoring customers

It would seem that if you pay attention to these logical items you will be in a better place than most start-ups. But there is more.

Why do start-ups succeed? Well, let's start by saying there is no silver bullet, no guarantee of success for any entrepreneur. It seems that commitment to plans is critical—and that, of course, means that you have a plan. It also means that you are not so inflexible that you cannot adjust as changes come your way. Commitment also implies that there is passion and the founders believe in what they are doing. According to Henry (2017), "You need a plan, persistence, perseverance, a willingness to be flexible, and a world-class team. You also need to be frugal, bright, and cultivate strong mentors." Is that you? Then success is in your future.

Let's get started with naming your successful business.

WHAT'S IN A NAME?

When selecting a name, consider two important aspects: It should project the image you desire, and it should be easy to remember. Your business name is not something you will want to change. It will identify you for many years, and changing it is an expensive proposition. So choose carefully.

What do I mean by projecting the image you desire? Think in terms of who you are and what guides you every day. What values are important to you? What message should your business name portray? What do you want others to think and feel when they hear your business name? Credibility? Reliability? Authority? Excitement? Think about the image that the name Big Sky Bold Consulting conjures up for you.

The name of your company might tell a prospective client something about what you do. Halelly Azulay and I recently started an online business and wanted the name to clearly define our niche. We chose Building Your Training Consulting Business. In our situation, we definitely know that is all we will do; however, do take care that the name of your company is not too restrictive. For example, using the words "Strategic Planning" or "Talent Management" may not allow for expansion at a later time.

If your name does not explicitly state what you do, like ebb associates inc, you may want to add a tag line. A tag line is three or four words that explain what you do. My tagline is "consulting, training, design" to better define the work we do.

The name you select will have implications for how your clients view you and your business. The name can also project size. For example, you might choose to use your name. "Connie Sultant, Inc." is clearly a one-person shop. It says who you are and the nature of your business. It does, however, limit your clients' perception to one person. Even if you have a dozen employees, the name does not project that fact.

What plans do you have for changes in your company's future? Will they include more people than you? Associates? Partners? "Connie Sultant and Associates" suggests that there are more consultants than Connie (you don't really have to have those consultants when you start). However, the name also suggests that Connie is the owner. This may be a problem for those who work for her now or if someone joins her firm in the future. Since all clients want the best, they will assume that Connie is the one they want without even knowing the skills of other people in the firm. On the other hand, if you have strong name recognition, such as "The Ken Blanchard Companies," you may want to take advantage of it.

"Sultant Associates" or "CSS Consulting" conjures up a group of people working together with less emphasis on Connie. Another consideration is that the second one tells you what the company does. "Sultant Website Designers" or "Sultant Marine Engineers" clearly defines each company's area of expertise. Be sure that the names do not limit you for future growth. For example, if "Sultant Website Designers" wants to branch out to software design, computer security, or general computer graphics, the name will no longer be inclusive of the work they perform.

Also remember that your business name will be a marketing tool and, even though you want something that is easy to remember, you do not want it to be too cute. Select a name and add a graphic that adds to your marketing image, rather than detracts from it. For example, "Get Better" for a wellness training company or "Bank On Us" for a financial management consulting firm might project a less than professional image than either of the companies desire—especially if they intend to provide services to Fortune 500 companies. And, of course, there are always exceptions to the rule. Higher Grounds is a great name for a coffee shop. Can you think of anything similar for a consulting group?

Your image may be as important as the name. McDonald's golden arches is a great example. You don't need to be as big as McDonald's to have name recognition through your brand. I have had people say, "the consultant with the three little letters," referring to my lowercase name, "ebb associates inc," which is an important part of my image. And, although they did not remember the company, they remembered the brand image and knew whom they wanted to work with.

It is never too late to change your company name if you are not satisfied with it. After being in business for four years, I was less than satisfied with the name of my company. At the time, I thought I could not change it since I had a client list and a good reputation. Now, after being in business for more than a quarter of a century, I look back in amazement about how small the reach of that reputation actually was and how much easier it would have been to change it then, rather than now. In fact, although I am not contemplating a name change, I now see it as a potential marketing opportunity!

How can you generate possible names? You can brainstorm with friends, search the Internet, hire a professional, or use one of the business name generators online. There seem to be hundreds of tools to generate a name, including Anadea Business Name Generator, Business Name Generator, NameMesh, and Namesmith.

Once you have generated a list of possibilities, allow plenty of time to sort through your results. You may want to share them with others to get their thoughts. After you have a short list, put them away for a couple of days before making your final decision.

Tip: Check availability.

Before you decide on your business name, check to make sure it's not already trademarked. The federal database of the U.S. Patent and Trademark Office, Trademark Electronic Search System (TESS) will be helpful. In addition, search Google to make sure it is not being used.

You want a business name that grabs attention and hangs on. Your name will be a marketing tool, and even though you want something that is easy to remember, be careful of names that have double meanings. A business name that I thought was very creative was "Bank @Lantec." Unfortunately, the company is no longer around. Another name that I like is "Team Up," because these consultants are very clear that building teams is all they will ever specialize in.

Think about all the ways that your business name will be used: website, email address, stationery, business cards, pens, T-shirts, even coffee mugs! Consider the length of the name. Long names will not fit on computer-generated labels. If you are thinking about working internationally, research the translation of your name into other languages. Also be aware that if your company name begins with "The," such as "The Schmidt Group," it will be alphabetized under "The" in most directories unless you specify differently. Who would think to look under "The"? By the way, just for fun, check your local business directory under the word "the."

Although they may seem minor, here are a few other questions before you make the final decision. Will your business structure dictate the use of an abbreviation such as Inc. or LLC? How might the length of the name matter? Will it be easy to pronounce? Should it be directly related to your services, such as consulting? Does the name you select limit you in any way if you change your focus in the future?

Tip: Get a domain name now.

While you're at it, search for a domain name. This is a simple process, but finding a good one that works for you and has not already been taken can be challenging and frustrating. To date, over 150 million domain names have been registered, so it may require some creativity to find one that will meet your needs. Even if it is not available exactly, you may be able to use an abbreviation, hyphens, or an alternate top-level domain (such as .net). Just because a domain name is available does not mean that you can use it without incurring liability for trademark infringement. The least expensive way to obtain a domain name is to be the first one to register it by contacting one of the authorized issuers of domain names, known as a "registrar."

By the way, if your business name is anything besides your own, you may be required to register your business name with the Secretary of State's office in the state in which you intend to do business. In addition, if you use any name in addition to the one you've chosen, you must file a Certificate of Trade Name or a Doing Business As (DBA) certificate. For example, your corporation may be Greene Ventures, Inc., and you may name your consulting practice Corporate Computer Consulting. This practice allows you to do business in states where someone else is already known as Greene Ventures, Inc. In addition, this practice allows you to incorporate once and have flexibility for various new start-ups. Contact your local city or state officials for more information. Finally, if you want to trademark your company's name, you will need your attorney's assistance.

If you have a limited liability company, a corporation, or a limited partnership in the United States, you will need to register your business with your state authorities. This is when your business name will also be registered. If your business is a sole proprietorship or a general partnership, you probably won't need to register your business entity with the state, but instead through the county and/or city where your business is located. It's not required, but you may also want to register your business name for a trademark.

Avoid These Naming Mistakes

Deciding on a name is hard enough. Don't interject more problems. Here are a few to avoid:

- Don't confuse your clients by using a K instead of a Q or a Ph for an F. Make it user-friendly.
- Don't use overused clichés, such as those that mean you are at the top of the industry, like apex, pinnacle, or peak.
- Don't use words that will not stand out, such as General Electric.
- Don't box yourself into a location. "Midwest Marketing" may have a certain ring to it in Madison, Wisconsin, but when you gain a reputation, will the name encourage a store on Madison Avenue to hire you?

Choosing a business name can be a lengthy process, but it is well worth the time you put in. Once you have chosen your business name, not only have you made a significant step toward officially launching your new venture, but you have also started branding your business and carving out your own niche in the small business world.

Finally, make sure you love the name. You're going to say it over and over again!

SELECTING AN ACCOUNTANT

Your first task is to select an accountant. You're thinking, "Hey! Why do I need an accountant? I haven't made any money yet!" That may be true, but you have many decisions to make that will be dependent on good advice.

How do you find a good accountant? I do not recommend that you use your second cousin Joey. You are making life-changing decisions and need someone who is knowledgeable (Joey probably is), experienced (Joey may be), impartial (Joey will have difficulty), and not personally involved with you (not Joey!).

You will find a good accountant the same way you have probably found the best employees, restaurants, and barbers—by networking and asking others. Start by asking successful people, preferably other consultants, who they use for accounting. Try to identify the qualities you are looking for so that you can describe your *ideal* accountant. First, you want someone who understands what you want—even if *you're* not sure yet. Ideally you will find someone who has experience with small consulting start-ups. Interview a few accountants before you select one with whom you will work. This relationship is one of the most important to your business. It is worth the time to look for someone with whom you can partner on your most intimate business matters—money.

It is worth the time to look for someone with whom you can partner on your most intimate business matters—money.

I tried several accountants before I found one who met my needs. I wanted someone who would challenge me, keep me abreast of new tax and investment laws, and would take risks with me. I finally found the right person because I was able to describe what I was looking for in one phrase. I wanted a "creative accountant." That may seem like an oxymoron, but when I used this phrase while interviewing accountants, I could tell by their immediate response whether they understood what I was looking for. Stephanie did. She keeps me informed, suggests options, challenges my reasoning, looks for creative alternatives, and allows me to take risks within legal boundaries. Stephanie practices in Virginia Beach, but that did not stop me from working with her for the 10 years that I lived in Wisconsin. The relationship works—even from a distance. It continues to be a successful partnership.

How do you know whether you've found a good accountant? The accountant should ask you about your business. Listen carefully to determine how he or she perceives your needs. Look for someone who knows something about your business and the issues you'll face. If the person hasn't had experience with consulting, has he completed some research prior to your meeting? How well does she communicate with you? As a business owner, you're going to need to understand some legalese; will this accountant be able to clarify the jargon for you? Can the accountant provide referrals? How does the accountant calculate fees? Will you work with the accountant you are interviewing or a junior staff member?

A good accountant may offer to review your financial documents and present suggestions. After your initial meeting, follow up with questions. It will be a good test to determine how quickly you receive a response. Do you feel as if the accountant is going the extra mile to land you as a client? If not, he probably won't once you hire him, either. And it probably is a given, but be certain any accountant you hire is a CPA.

The first decision your accountant can help you with is determining the business structure that will be best for you. Many of your other decisions will be based on your business structure.

SELECTING A LEGAL ENTITY

Selecting a legal entity or business structure is one of the first and most fundamental decisions you must make. This is more critical than you might initially think, as it influences nearly every aspect of operations, such as how much you pay in taxes, the extent of your personal liability if anything goes wrong, and your ability to raise money for business expansion. There are four basic types of business structures: sole proprietorships, partnerships, corporations, and limited liability companies.

Note that some of the following information may only be valid in the United States. Check into your country's business structures and tax laws.

> **Tip: Check with the IRS.**
>
> The IRS can provide you with tax information online. Go to the IRS website at IRS.gov and click on "Tax Stats, Facts & Figures," at the bottom of the page." You will be able to access information on tax considerations based on the legal structure you choose and download tax worksheets and forms.

Sole Proprietorships

A sole proprietorship is the simplest form and creates no separate legal entity. Usually your Social Security number will serve as your company's federal taxpayer-identification number. Federal tax reporting for sole proprietorships is the easiest of the four structures, requiring only the addition of a Schedule C on which you list business income and take deductions for expenses. The structure incurs no additional tax liabilities beyond yours. Although the fact that no separate legal entity is created is usually considered an advantage, it also poses a concern. It means that any legal or tax liabilities that transpire become your personal liabilities. For example, if a client sues you for business reasons, you are personally liable and your personal assets are at risk.

I do not recommend remaining a sole proprietorship. You need an entity, like an LLC or a corporation, to insulate your personal assets from litigation.

Partnerships

Like sole proprietorships, a partnership is not a separate legal entity. The difference is that you will need to obtain a separate federal employer-identification number, known as your FEIN. Your partnership will file a partnership return, even though it pays no separate federal tax. The business losses and income are reported on the partners' personal tax returns. The division of profits will be governed by a partnership agreement. The decision to share equally or on a percentage basis is usually dependent on contributions of cash, experience, property, labor, and perhaps even reputation or earning power of each partner. Legally you and your partners are all personally responsible for liabilities incurred by any of the other partners or the partnership as a whole. Because so many terms must be spelled out in the partnership agreement—for example, the rights and obligations of each partner or what happens if one partner dies—a partnership can be more complicated than it may initially appear.

Limited Liability Companies

A limited liability company (LLC) is the most flexible and may provide the best of both worlds. It has the limited liability of a corporation, but the flexibility and tax status of a partnership. An LLC files articles of organization and an operating agreement with state authorities. Tax reporting is similar to a partnership, but liability is limited to the assets of the LLC.

You can establish an LLC online in a couple of hours. Start by checking with the Secretary of State offices. LLCs are best if you plan to have mostly a side hustle that brings in less than $100,000.

Corporations

Corporations differ from the first two structures in that they are separate legal and tax entities. Your personal liability is limited if the corporation is sued. Corporations are formed when individuals invest assets to create equity. To incorporate you must file articles of incorporation, create corporate bylaws, and fulfill other state requirements. Stock must be issued, even if you are the sole shareholder. The corporate structure that you are most familiar with is the "C" corporation, which is required to pay income taxes separate from you and the other shareholders.

A subchapter-S corporation (commonly called an S corp) is an option for smaller businesses. This special structure is available to U.S. organizations of 35 or fewer shareholders. There are other guidelines, which your accountant will explain to you. One of the advantages of the S corp is that you will avoid double taxation on income to the corporation and dividends to you. The income is passed through to the shareholder (you), which you report on your personal return. By the way, both corporate structures require you to submit annual paperwork.

I usually recommend the S corp for a start-up consulting business. It has all the legal protection without much added expense. If you later decide to bring others into your business, the documentation is in place. If you anticipate that your company will take in $100,000 or more, choose an S corp. On the other hand, current tax law allows you to switch tax-free from an LLC to an S corp but not the reverse. Because choosing the right business structure is essential for maximizing your success, it is a choice you will want to make with the expert advice of your accountant.

A BUSINESS PLAN TO GUIDE YOU

A business plan is a fabulous tool to help you think about your future and as a place to gather all your ideas. Unless you will try to woo investors, it can be quite simple. Your business plan allows you to put everything that is in your head on paper in an organized way. This will help you stay focused on what is important to you. View your business plan as a working document that you refer to regularly. Make it work for you. Later, as you make new business decisions, you can return to your plan to identify what you might change, how to go about changing, and how those changes might affect the rest of your business.

View your business plan as a working document that you refer to regularly.

Business plans generally follow a similar format, as described here. Exhibit 4.1 will provide a guide for you.

Exhibit 4.1. Sample Business Plan

Cover Page
Table of Contents
Executive Summary
Business Description
   Purpose
   Plans for the Business
   Business Activities
   Demographics of the Business
Market Analysis
   Estimated Market Size
   Estimated Market Dollar Value
Competitive Analysis
   Geographic Competition
   Competition's Strengths and Weaknesses
Organization and Management
   Key Players
   Resources Available
Marketing and Sales
   Market Niche
   Pricing Strategy
   Marketing Tactics
   Literature
Service or Product Line
   Description
   Benefits
Financial Projections
Appendices
   Financial Statement
   Supporting Documents

Tip: Check with the SBA.

The Small Business Administration's website at sba.gov is an excellent source of business information. You will find resources to plan, launch, manage, and grow your business. You will also find a template for a business plan.

Cover Page

The cover page includes the company name and logo, date, owner, address, telephone, email, and website.

Table of Contents

The table of contents provides an opportunity for you to impress your business plan reader by showing your organizational skills.

Executive Summary

Your executive summary is a snapshot of your business plan as a whole and briefly describes your company profile and goals.

Business Description

Begin the actual narrative with an introduction that states the purpose of the business plan. Follow this with a description of your consulting business. Use the following questions to guide you. You may divide the description into your plans for the business, the work you will conduct, and the business's demographics. This will most likely be the longest and the most important section of your business plan.

- Introduction that states the purpose of the business plan
- Your plans for the business
  - What are the mission, vision, and purpose of your consulting business?
  - What are your goals for the business? (Your goals should be specific, measurable, and time-bound.)
- Business activities
  - What specific activities does the business do to raise revenue?
  - What services and/or products will it provide? What is the mission of your business?
  - Why do you believe your business will succeed?
  - What relevant experience do you bring to the business of consulting?
- Demographics
  - What's the name of the business? The address? Telephone and fax numbers? What's the email address? What's the website?
  - Who is the owner(s)?
  - What's the business structure and, if incorporated, where?
  - What information is important about the start of this business? For example, is it a new business or an expansion of an existing business? What was the start-up date?

Market Analysis

Before launching your business, it is essential for you to research your business industry and the market. Your market analysis will be most beneficial if you can quote statistics about consulting, your consulting specialty, or the industry you have chosen. You may find some of this data in industry journals or on the Internet.

- What industry or industries are you targeting?
- Are you in a stable, growing, or declining industry?
- What is occurring now or is expected to occur in the future that will affect your business either negatively or positively?
- Who are your current customers?
- Who are your potential customers?
- What are the demographics of your current and potential client base?
- What is the size of your potential market? What percent do you expect to penetrate?
- What's the estimated total market in dollar value?

Competitive Analysis

Spend some time examining the competition you expect to face. Answer the questions that are most unique to your business.

- Who is your competition?
- How would you describe your competition in the geographical and specialty areas you have targeted?
- How do your consulting products and/or services differ from your competitors'?
- How do your competitors' pricing structures compare to yours?
- What experience do your competitors have?
- How strong is each competitor's name recognition?
- What share of the market do these targeted competitors have?
- Are competitors' businesses increasing, decreasing, or remaining steady?
- Why would someone buy from them instead of you?
- How do your competitors market themselves?
- What are your comparative strengths and weaknesses in sales or marketing?
- What differentiates you from your competitors?

Organization and Management

Every business is structured differently. Decide on the best organization and management structure for your business. Answer these questions about how you intend to manage your consulting business.

- Who are the key players in your business? What are their duties, compensations, and benefits?
- If you are the sole employee, how will you manage all that needs to be completed? What is your starting salary?
- What resources are available if you need assistance?
- When do you expect to hire additional personnel—if ever?
- What experience do you bring to the business in marketing, sales, managing a business, and other supporting roles?
- What is your education level?
- What professional support will you use, such as an attorney, accountant, or banker?
- What banking services will you use and where? What process will you use to establish credit?

Marketing and Sales

How do you plan to market your business? What is your sales strategy? You can use the following questions to develop a simple marketing plan. Remember, however, that you will develop a more in-depth plan in Chapter Five.

- Describe your market niche in detail:
  - What size company will you serve?
  - What specific geographic area will you serve?
  - What kind of organizations will you serve?
  - Will you serve special situations, such as start-ups or mergers?
- What is your pricing strategy and structure? How do your pricing strategy and structure differ from your competitors'?
- What marketing tactics will you pursue? What advertising? What promotion?
- How will you implement tactics throughout the year?
- What expertise will you use to develop your marketing plan?

Service or Product Line

What do you sell? How does it benefit your customers? What is the product lifecycle? Tell the story about your product or service.

Financial Projections

Provide financial projections for the income and expenses you anticipate. Use these questions to write a narrative. Support your narrative with financial statements in the appendix of your plan.

- What assumptions are you making as a basis of the plan, such as market health, start-up date, gross profit margin, required overhead, payroll, and other expenses?
- What expenditures will you require for start-up?
- What are your cash-flow projections for each month of your first year? What are your three-year cash-flow projections?
- Do you have a line of credit? How much?
- What is your personal net worth as displayed in a financial statement?
- Where do you expect to find financing and under what terms? How will the money be used, for example, overhead, supplies, marketing?

Appendices

An appendix is optional, but it is a useful place to include information and documents such as resumes, permits, and leases. Your appendices will include documents that support your narrative. It may be divided into two sections or more. You may wish to include some of these listed here.

Financial Statements
- Start-up expenses
- Budget
- First-year cash-flow projections
- Three-year projections
- Personal financial statement
- If you are already operating, an income statement from the past year

Supporting Documents
- Testimonials from satisfied clients
- References
- Demographic information
- Your resume
- Biographical sketches of your accountant, attorney, and others
- Industry data or demographics

Print Your Business Plan

Once you've completed your plan, have it proofed and edited. You may wish to give it to several people: some who know the consulting business well, and others who can edit for typos, spelling, and grammatical errors. Make the corrections and print out a clean copy of your business plan on high-quality paper. You may wish to put it in a clear-front document binder.

Tip: Sample plan.

You can see over 500 sample business plans, including those for consulting, at bplans.com/sample_business_plans.

Whatever you do with the plan, do not put it on a shelf. It should become a working document that you refer to regularly.

PLAN TO USE YOUR BUSINESS PLAN

Keep your business plan handy and use it to help you make decisions. Check your business progress against the plan at least quarterly. Your business plan will keep you focused. Of course, if something is not working, you will change your direction. Staying focused does not mean staying the course even when something is not working. You will modify your strategies if they are not as effective as you originally envisioned. Keep your long-term vision in mind and continue to move in that direction. Consider the following to ensure that your business plan serves its purpose.

- Check the data from which you are operating to ensure they are still current.
- Read the *Wall Street Journal* daily to be knowledgeable of the industries in which you work.
- Subscribe to *Harvard Business Review* and *Fortune* magazine (at least) to stay on top of business and management trends.
- Read biographies of the leaders you respect to inspire new ideas for your consulting business.
- Attend conferences that focus on improving your skills and knowledge in the areas you have designated as needing improvement.
- Learn as much as you can from customers about their present needs, but also become adept at predicting their needs.

- Never hesitate to pick up the phone and call someone in your networking sphere to discuss something in your plan that doesn't seem to be working.
- Use all of the information from the previous seven suggestions to update your business plan and ensure that you are focused on an appropriate vision.

Plan a Review with Yourself

After you complete your business plan, and before you leave this chapter, schedule a date with yourself in your calendar to review your business plan. Schedule that date for six to 12 weeks out, depending on where you are in the process of establishing your consulting business. If you're just starting out, "meet" in six weeks; if you have been consulting for some time, you could wait as long as 12 weeks. You decide. What seems appropriate to you?

> **Tip: Entrepreneurial resource.**
>
> During your planning, bookmark sites that you find helpful. One that will be useful is a site maintained by *Entrepreneur* magazine, entrepreneur.com.

Financial Supporting Documents

Exhibits 4.2 through 4.5 provide the answers and supporting documentation for the financial section in the business plan. You will complete them and include them in the appendices.

Exhibit 4.2. Start-Up Expenses

	Estimated Cost
Furniture	
Desk and chair	$ _____
Filing cabinet	$ _____
Bookcases	$ _____
Table and chairs	$ _____
_____	$ _____
_____	$ _____

The New Business of Consulting

Exhibit 4.2. Start-Up Expenses, Cont'd.

Equipment

    Computer $ _____

    Software: _____

              _____

              _____ $ _____

    Printer $ _____

    Copier $ _____

    Telephone system $ _____

    Mobile business phone $ _____

    _____ $ _____

    _____ $ _____

Office Supplies

    Stationery $ _____

    Paper $ _____

    Pens, pencils $ _____

    Tape, glue, other adhesives $ _____

    Scissors, rulers, miscellaneous $ _____

Marketing

    Website $ _____

    Business cards $ _____

    Brochures $ _____

    _____ $ _____

    _____ $ _____

Corporate Set-Up Fees

    Professional fees $ _____

    Legal fees (incorporation) $ _____

    Business name search $ _____

    Accounting fees $ _____

    Banking start-up $ _____

    Insurance $ _____

    Licenses/permits $ _____

Remodeling to accommodate office $ _____

Unanticipated Expenses $ _____

Exhibit 4.3. Budget Format

Net Salary for One Year   _____
Benefits
    Health insurance   _____
    Life insurance   _____
    Disability insurance   _____
    Retirement   _____   **Total Benefits**   _____

Taxes
    Self-employment   _____
    Social Security and Medicare   _____
    State income tax   _____
    City tax   _____
    Personal property tax   _____   **Total Taxes**   _____

Business Expenses
    Accounting, banking, legal fees _____
    Advertising and marketing   _____
    Automobile expenses   _____
    Books and resources   _____
    Clerical support   _____
    Copying and printing   _____
    Donations   _____
    Dues and subscriptions   _____
    Entertainment   _____
    Equipment leases   _____
    Insurance   _____
    Interest and loans   _____
    Licenses   _____
    Meals   _____
    Office supplies   _____
    Postage   _____
    Professional development   _____
    Professional fees   _____
    Rent   _____
    Repairs and maintenance   _____
    Salaries (employees)   _____
    Seminar expenses   _____
    Telephone   _____
    Travel   _____
    Utilities   _____

Total Business Expenses _____
Planned Profit   _____
Annual Total   _____

Exhibit 4.4. First-Year Cash-Flow Projection

	Jan.	Feb.	March	April	May	June	July	Aug.	Sept.	Oct.	Nov.	Dec.
Revenue												
Total Revenues												
Expenses												
Accounting/banking/legal												
Advertising/marketing												
Automobile												
Benefits												
Books/resources												
Clerical support												
Copying												
Donations												
Dues/subscriptions												
Entertainment												
Equipment leases												
Interest												
Insurance												
Licenses												
Lodging												
Materials												
Meals												
Office supplies												
Postage												
Professional dev.												
Rent												
Salaries												
Taxes												
Telephone												
Travel												
Utilities												
Total Expenses												
Monthly Cash Flow												
Cumulative Cash Flow												

Exhibit 4.5. Three-Year Projection

	Year 1	Year 2	Year 3
Total Revenue	————	————	————
Expenses:			
Salaries	————	————	————
Benefits	————	————	————
Taxes	————	————	————
Marketing	————	————	————
Administrative	————	————	————
Total Expenses	————	————	————
5 Percent Inflation	————	————	————
Contribution After Inflation	————	————	————

Your business plan will keep you focused.

START-UP COSTS

Now you will need to determine whether you have the money to start or to expand what you are already doing.

Start-Up May Cost Less Than You Think

Consulting start-ups usually fit into the low-cost category because starting a consulting practice can be surprisingly inexpensive. Exhibit 4.2 lists everything you need to start. As you review the list you might be thinking, "I already have a computer. It can't be that expensive to have stationery and business cards printed. And I could work out of my home office initially." As you total the expenses on Exhibit 4.2, you may find that you could start with as little as $10,000.

As you think about start-up money, consider your personal wealth. You have likely created a personal financial statement at some point. If not, you can find a simple financial statement on the website at www.wiley.com/go/newconsultingbiech. You may want to include it in your business plan; it is also a good place to identify what you might use as cash to start or expand your consulting business.

Where Will the Money Come From?

You have several options for raising funds to start your consulting practice. You could:

- Save the money required before you take the leap.
- Take money from your savings account.
- Borrow against your retirement account.
- Obtain a loan on the equity in your house.
- Borrow against your life insurance policy.
- Go on margin against your stocks.
- Obtain a line of credit from your bank.
- Ask your spouse to increase his or her contribution.
- Sell something—for example, a motor home or sailboat.
- Cut back on some of your spending—for example, forego a vacation.
- Obtain a business bank loan.
- Get a loan from the Small Business Administration (SBA).
- Ask a friend, relative, or colleague to sponsor you.
- Create a fundraising campaign on a crowdfunding platform.
- Borrow against your credit card. (Don't do this unless you have an immediate and very good opportunity in hand.)

These are all possible ways to raise money to start your business. I'd like to add some precautions to one of the suggestions. When you ask friends, relatives, or colleagues for start-up funds, take care that you do not jeopardize your relationships. Turning to family and friends is common when banks resist extending loans to companies without a proven track record; however, be thoughtful about this option. First, be clear about what you are asking. Are you requesting a loan or offering part ownership of the business? Second, be transparent about the risks and spell them out on a business plan. Third, record your agreement in writing and make sure that everyone signs and receives a copy. And finally, keep everyone informed about progress, setbacks, and expectations. The best way to maintain the relationship is to pay back the loan on time and in full. Just because the lender is your dad does not mean he should be the last person to get paid.

Home Office Advantage

Because few clients will visit you at your office, working out of your home is a practical option. Just remember that it will take discipline to stay focused on writing your marketing letters instead of watching television, to continue to pay the bills rather than visit the refrigerator. A home office offers financial advantages because you will be able to deduct a proportionate amount of your home's utility costs, taxes, or rent. Keep in mind that the IRS may require proof that your home office is used exclusively for business. Also, a home office is sometimes a red flag that alerts the IRS to an audit, with potential tax implications. Your accountant will provide you with advice about your home office.

Tip: Tap the IRS.

Download IRS Publication 587 to gain comprehensive information about working from your home. The publication addresses depreciating your home, business furniture, and equipment, qualifying for a deduction, calculating expenses, and, of course, record keeping. It supplies you with worksheets and instructions so that you can calculate your own deductions.

Given all the ways that you can reduce start-up expenses, the cost of starting a consulting business should not deter you. My only caution is this: Do not cut corners. Your professional image is at stake right from the start.

FINDING YOUR NICHE

The opportunities available to you as a consultant are so broad that you must narrow the choices. Narrowing your choices will help you be more efficient and will ensure that you can achieve depth in an area. Some of this will come naturally due to your skills and the experiences you have had. And you should not forget where you have passion. Other decisions may be dependent on the kind of lifestyle you have chosen—for example, whether you wish to travel.

The terms *niche market* and *target market* are often interchanged, but there is a difference between them. A target market is the group of people you will serve. It is the "who." A niche adds another dimension by combining your target market, who, with the "what" you are helping your clients with. For example, if you are a coach, you might be helping senior executives utilize their talent to create a more agile company. It is important to understand that your clients don't buy a service or product. They want to buy solutions. The solution can help them solve problems or achieve goals. So your niche might be that you work with senior executives to create a more agile workforce to increase their competitiveness.

As you narrow your choices, you will define your niche or what service you will offer and to whom. A niche is a specific subset of a larger market where a customer has been identified with a specific problem. And the more specific, the better. There are many ways to define your niche. Let's create a simple niche with three components: (1) who your client is, (2) what you will do, and (3) why clients will work with you (what result you will produce).

Who Your Ideal Client Is

This is your first choice. You may define your ideal or dream clients by their level in the organization—that is, front-line employees, first-level supervisors, managers, or executives. Or at times your ideal might be the structure of the groups with whom you work—for example, teams, intact work groups, or individuals. You could also add your preference of location such as local, statewide, regional, national, or international.

Decide whether you want to work in the for-profit or nonprofit organizational category. Within the for-profit sector you can consider manufacturing, service, and so on. Within the nonprofit sector you can consider associations; educational institutions; local, state, or federal government agencies; or others in the public sector.

You can further narrow your niche by focusing on a specific industry. If you have decided to work in the for-profit service sector, you may narrow that down even more by selecting healthcare, hospitality, or finance. Focusing on a small number of industries can build your credibility in each.

You may choose to work with organizations that have special situations. These could include small, family-owned businesses, start-up businesses, multinational businesses, merged organizations, or high-growth businesses.

The size of the organization on which you focus gives you credibility with other organizations of like size. You may decide to work only with Fortune 500 firms. You may decide to work only with small organizations. I consider a small organization as one with 100 or fewer employees, a medium organization as one with 100 to 2,000 employees, and a large organization as one with over 2,000 employees. You may also consider the organization's revenue. In some cases, the size measurement is industry-specific. Hospitals, for example, measure their size by number of beds.

Define who can benefit the most from your expertise. Who might be looking for your solution and is willing to pay for it? Consider also who you are passionate about helping.

What You Will Do

You may define your work by the role that you play—for example, trainer, facilitator, coach, technical advisor, process consultant, cybersecurity guide, content expert, or resource. You might also define your work by your topic expertise—for example, team building, time management, leadership, computer programming, mergers, investing, or regulatory laws. You might also consider the processes you will use, such as surveys, interviews, research, or coaching. What is it you have the expertise to implement?

Why Clients Will Work with You

Decide why clients would want your solution. What problem can you help them solve? Increase profits? Decrease expenses? Increase employee engagement? Reduce turnover? Reduce rework? Increase customer satisfaction? Eliminate accidents? Increase a competitive advantage? Each of these is a reason a client would hire you. Ask, "What problem am I solving for my clients?"

However you define your niche, ensure that it is broad enough to have enough clients, yet narrow enough to provide focus for you. Once you decide, you can capture your niche value proposition in this format:

I help (who) to (what) so that (why). For example, "I help midsized manufacturing organizations to increase employee satisfaction in order to reduce turnover.

It can be difficult to narrow your niche before you even begin providing services. Yet this is another important element of your start-up. Don't fret about it. Do the best you can. Have a *now plan* and a *forever plan*. Your now plan defines the best possible given the data you have as you begin. Six months into your business, you can redefine your niche based on what you know at that time. Don't procrastinate. You can adjust as you go. It's one of the benefits of being your own boss!

By the way, many consultants think that if they define a broader expertise and niche, they will appeal to a wider audience and be hired by more clients. That isn't always true. The less specific you are in your definition, the less likely clients will be to think of you when they need assistance.

Don't Buy In to These No-Niche Excuses

New consultants may not want to be pinned down with a specific niche, so they make any number of excuses. Don't let this be you.

- I want to remain flexible to be available to more clients.
- I don't have time to do the research necessary.
- I don't have a large enough client base yet.
- I don't know what my clients need.
- There may be too much competition if I am too narrowly focused.
- I'm afraid I'll choose the wrong niche.
- I don't want to turn away business.
- It's too soon to box myself in.

YOUR IMAGE IS EVERYTHING

Your image is the most important marketing asset you have. In fact, as you start, your image is a critical attribute of your business as a whole. You do not have products to display; you do not have clients who brag about you; you do not have experiences to discuss. All that you have is *you* and the image you present. Therefore, it is imperative that you invest in making it all that it can be. Your name, your logo, your visual look, the public's recognition and affection are all vital to your success. Your corporate identify is your most valuable possession.

Here's some good news: You can look like a million on a shoestring budget right from day one! The secret? Ensure that everything you do reeks of quality. Nothing should leave your office unless it looks impeccable, sounds professional, and feels flawless. Quality should touch all the senses.

You can look like a million on a shoestring budget right from day one!

If you send a letter, it should exude quality in how it looks, sounds, and feels.

Looks. It should be aligned on the paper correctly. The type should be dark black, printed with a fresh cartridge. The stamp and envelope label should be affixed straight.

Sounds. The letter should be error-free. It should be written using correct grammar. The tone should send the message you desire. It should be written for the interest of the reader. If possible, the letter should begin with the word *you*.

Feels. The letter should be printed on the highest-grade paper money can buy. The reader should feel the quality in the paper. If you need to save money, do it somewhere else; the pennies you will save by buying second-grade paper will not be worth the harm you may do to your image.

Create a brand image for your business. Invest in a logo. A logo is an important image builder, but it is also an important marketing tool, as it provides a recognizable identify for your consulting business. Keep these in mind when designing a logo:

- It should have immediate impact. Instead of receiving a passing glance, will it attract and hold attention?
- The logo should accurately represent what you do. Is the logo specific enough to tell an uninformed person what you do, yet broad enough so that it will grow with you?
- As the cornerstone of your brand, a logo should represent your image positively. Do you want to project a serious and professional image, an optimistic and whimsical image, or something else?
- The best logos are memorable. Is the logo pleasing to look at and unique enough so that someone will remember it?
- A good logo is also practical. Will it copy well? Does it lend itself to stationery, business cards, brochures, websites, and promotional materials? It should be as effective on a business card as it is on a billboard.

Tip: Looking for a logo.

A traditional design firm will charge $2,000 to $10,000 for a corporate logo. Instead, you can use one of the online firms. Check the websites of these three firms online: www.LogoDesignPros.com, www.Logojeez.com, or www.LogoWorks. com. I like all three because they have samples you can view, guarantee your satisfaction, provide fast turnaround (three to four days), and most important, offer reasonable pricing (packages from $199 to $599).

Printed materials that represent your business should also be created with quality in mind. If you own a copier, buy the best that you can afford. When you make copies, be certain that they don't pick up the dirt specks from your copier's glass. What's the secret? Clean your copier glass often with a copier glass cleaner. If you use the services of a local copy shop, build a relationship with the manager and employees. Let them know how important it is that your copies be clean, straight, and on high-quality paper.

What else can you do to look like a million? The following quick ideas will help. Keep your eyes open for other ideas and add them to your list.

- Review your LinkedIn and other social media profiles. How well do you show-case your brand? Are you a results-oriented professional? Motivated self-starter? Superior communicator? Of course you are, and so is everyone else on LinkedIn! How can you set yourself apart? What changes will you make as a consultant?
- Design stationery and business cards. The investment may seem high at this time, but it will pay off very quickly. Your paper products speak first for you. A professional design says, "I'm serious about my profession!" The logo companies listed earlier also design these products at a reasonable price.
- Use overnight express carriers to send proposals and important communication to clients when urgency is important and email simply won't do.
- Secure all paper documents with gold paper clips.
- Ensure that your invoices are complete, correct, and businesslike. Help your business appear bigger by using a numbering system that begins with a number that is greater than one. You could simply start with 301. Or you could present a series of numbers such as 13-076-20. The middle number is the sequential number of the invoices; the last number is the year; and the first number is just for luck!
- Take the time to record a professional message on your phone. You may even want to change your message daily to encourage callers to leave a message. Smile when recording your message; the feeling comes through. Say something like, "Hello! You've reached the voice mail of Annie Trainer. Today is Thursday, October 30, and I will be away from the office. I will check for messages today, so please leave your name and telephone number. I look forward to speaking with you and hope yours is a great day!"

In addition to these ideas, you will want to think about the image you project in general. When I first went into business, I wanted to project a subtle professional image. I wanted to speak quietly, but professionally. To express this image, I chose to use all lowercase letters in the corporate name. I carried out the theme further by printing gray on gray. Since that time, my business has changed, as has my outlook on the world. I decided to shout a little. The corporate name, ebb associates inc, is still in all lowercase, and we shout with happiness using red, white and metallic gold—again on high-quality paper.

What image do you want to project? Many things complement this: the name of your company, the graphics you choose, the tone of your website, your title, the color and style of paper, the color of the ink, the style of brochure you distribute, the content of your marketing pieces, and the tone of your correspondence. Every interaction you have with your clients will express your image. Make sure it's the one you want.

EXPERIENCING THE EXPERIENCE MAZE

Remember when you were looking for your first job? It seemed that every job required experience, but how could you get experience without a job? It was a crazy circle: You needed experience to get a job, and you needed a job to get experience. Well, you may feel as if you are in that same place as you look for your first consulting project, and you may be asking yourself: "I need experience to get a project, but how do I get a project to get experience?" Landing your first client can be easier than you think if you plan ahead, expand your networking, and identify creative options.

Plan Ahead

It may take one to six months from the day you first speak with an organization until the day you begin the project. This means that you must decide to either maintain an income while you are establishing yourself or live off money you have saved for the start-up period of your business.

Your planning should include your present employer. A common way to transfer from your present job to consulting is to have your current employer become your client. You must plan this carefully. Identify which projects you could complete, list the benefits for your employer of utilizing your services, and allow enough time for your employer to accept this idea. Of course, the risk you run is that your employer may not agree with your plan, which may put you in an uncomfortable situation until your final employment date.

Another way your present employer could assist with your transition is to allow you to work part-time while you use the rest of your time for business start-up. If your employer is gracious enough to allow this to happen, make certain that you give your part-time work your full attention. It may be very difficult to focus on the same old job when you are starting an exciting new adventure. Remember, your employer is doing you a favor; you owe the company 110 percent in return.

Expand Your Networking

Before you leap into a start-up, examine your network. Have you maintained an active network of professional contacts? If not, give yourself at least six months to build this network before starting your consulting practice.

Join professional associations and attend their meetings to identify organizations that might use your services. A word of caution, however. There is no greater turn-off to a corporate manager than to be accosted by a wannabe consultant at a professional meeting. Do not ask for work or make appointments at the meeting. So what's the point of the suggestion to attend these events?

Attend meetings with plans to meet people who may use your services. Most people are attending for business-related reasons, so it will be appropriate for you to initiate conversations about the projects in which they are involved. Find topics about which you both enjoy talking. Share your business card. The next day, follow up with a note expressing a common interest, your pleasure at meeting the individual, or some other theme that was a result of your discussion. *Be sincere.* If you cannot be sincere, forget it. You will appear pushy and hungry. A test of your sincerity is whether you want to follow up even when you sense that there is no potential project at the present time. The key phrase here is "at the present time." True networking is an investment in the future. Follow your note with a phone call to set a date for lunch or a meeting to explore opportunities or simply to learn more about the organization.

Identify other networking opportunities that can move you toward your goal, including the following:

- Make a list of everyone you know who could lead to business opportunities. Then follow up with a telephone call or a note. Many of the recent articles I've read about starting a consultant practice recommend that you not stop making the list until you have at least 100 names.
- Volunteer to make presentations at local, state, and national conferences and meetings.
- Identify organizations that might use your services. Request exploratory meetings with some of the decision makers. These meetings are more about them, what problems they need to solve, and less about you and what you can do—at least for now.
- Take other consultants to lunch to gather ideas for identifying business contacts.
- Search your local newspapers for people you would like to meet.

Chapter Five covers the topic of marketing once you are in business; however, many of the ideas in the chapter can be used as you network prior to starting your business. But be sure to expand your networking list before you begin to count on a full-time salary from consulting.

Identify Creative Options

The most creative tactic I used to break into the consulting business was to work part-time for a small consulting company for three months without pay. I agreed not to contact their clients and to work as an employee under their corporate name. It was a true win-win for both of us. I was able to observe the business generation (finding clients) and billable (serving clients) processes in action and to gain experience with actual clients whom I could use as references. They acquired a skilled trainer who added value to their business, worked without pay, and would not pirate their clients. Because I worked part-time, I could implement what I learned to build my own business during my off hours.

If you don't want a long-term arrangement like mine, you can provide pro bono work for community, government, or nonprofit organizations. These organizations usually have limited funds and appreciate the services that you can provide. This can be the beginning of your list of clients served.

You could also subcontract full- or part-time with a large training firm that certifies trainers, or you could subcontract with other consulting firms. The first could be an easy route, especially if you have been certified to conduct training programs for the organization while employed at your present company. The drawback, however, will be conducting repetitive training material. The second approach may provide more options in projects or actual consulting. The drawback here is that you must suppress your own ego to represent the prime firm's name. Drawbacks for both are that you will bill about one-third to two-thirds of your typical billable rate. The advantages are that you will have an income and will be able to build your own business while working part-time in the field.

If you're looking for something more full-time, you could join an existing firm to gain experience. The obvious drawback is that it continues to put off even longer the opportunity to begin your own consulting business.

Although any of these ideas can serve as quick starts to becoming a consultant, some may also slow the process of starting your own business. Only you can weigh the pros and cons of each start-up tactic. Only you can weigh the advantages of finding work versus finding the work you want. Only you can make the final decisions. The sidebar will help you think of everything you need to make decisions for a successful start-up.

Start-Up Checklist

The items on this list are in a relative sequential order. I've suggested a general order, but you may have other circumstances that you want to take advantage of for timing or opportunity reasons. If so, do it! The key is to just start.

- ❑ Take responsibility to start—no one can do that except you.
- ❑ Gauge your family's support of your decision.
- ❑ Research your chosen market to determine what problems need to be solved.
- ❑ Conduct a Internet search of key words related to your intended industry.
- ❑ When you are ready, conduct a couple of exploratory meetings with people you know in the market.
- ❑ Describe your business, its services, and products.
- ❑ Analyze your competition.
- ❑ Conduct a self-assessment: What are you passionate about? What are you good at?
- ❑ Take two or three busy consultants out for coffee to tap into their knowledge about consulting and the market.
- ❑ Make a list of at least 100 people you will want to contact when you launch your business: friends, family, and professional colleagues.
- ❑ Determine your niche and what sets you apart.
- ❑ Name your company.
- ❑ Identify your dream clients.
- ❑ Determine your budget and your pricing structure.
- ❑ Confirm that potential clients can support your pricing plan.
- ❑ Identify your start-up costs.
- ❑ Find a mentor.
- ❑ Create a business plan.
- ❑ Interview potential accountants; select the best one.

Start-Up Checklist, Cont'd.

❑ Determine your business structure.

❑ Meet with your supervisor to share your plans and to determine whether your company will be interested in supporting you with project work (don't expect them to pay your desired fee).

❑ Check on zoning laws, licenses, taxes.

❑ Select a location and address.

❑ Select a banker, attorney, and insurance agent.

❑ File legal documents to register your business.

❑ Obtain a tax identification number from the IRS.

❑ Open business banking accounts: checking and savings.

❑ Arrange for a line of credit.

❑ Apply for a city business license or home occupation permit if needed.

❑ Set up your financial records.

❑ Select a logo.

❑ Order business cards and stationery.

❑ Create a website.

❑ Create your plan for future watercooler discussions (consulting can be lonely).

❑ Don't procrastinate; start now, be flexible, and adjust as you go.

If you really want to start your own consulting firm, do it now. If you don't, a year from now you will wish you had started today.

A year from now you will wish you had started today.

For the Consummate Consultant

Getting started is the biggest step you take. It certainly can be daunting, but if you create a transition plan and find the right people to help, it can be smooth and fun. On the other hand, procrastination can lead to lots of regrets. Start with these suggestions to, well, *start*!

Hire the Best. You need the best accountant you can find on your team, and hiring one needs to be one of the first steps you take. Your accountant will provide advice as you make decisions about your business structure, accounting procedures, growth plans, and profitability. A great accountant will keep you in the black and out of trouble with the IRS (or whoever collects taxes in your country). Hire an accountant who educates, advises, and helps you grow your business.

Find Your Passion. The most successful consultants find that it is not just about making a living. It is about making a difference. That difference comes when you find your passion and you add a plan, perseverance, and persistence. Sprinkling in a bit of flexibility and agility ensures success.

It's Really You. It's never too soon to begin thinking about the image you wish to project. Of course, you know how to dress and groom professionally. That's not it. Also consider how you align with the business you are starting. That would include your attitude, behavior, and conversation. Exhibit a positive, respectful attitude. Be confident but not cocky, polite but not compliant, friendly but not annoying. Of course, you need to be authentic. Your image is not about being something that you aren't. However, you are now something that you haven't been before—a business owner. You want to be viewed as one.

. . . And Staying in Business

5

It is not necessary to change. Survival is not mandatory.

W. Edwards Deming

Heinrich stared at his calendar in disbelief. It was October 30 and there was not one client for the month of November—or, for that matter, for any other month!

Just four hours ago, Heinrich had been celebrating the final work with his ship-building client. It had been a huge project—almost too big for his first six months in business. But he'd bid on the job and won out over two other consulting firms that were much larger. Of course, the truth be known, he probably underbid that project. He didn't have his project pricing down pat yet, which caused him to work many more hours than he'd anticipated. His family was not pleased with his long hours and absence during weekends. But the project was done and he would be paid. The client was ecstatic with the results and promised him a testimonial he could add to his website.

But now he faced another problem. He had no billable work on the schedule. How did this happen? He thought back. He'd started out with a bang! He'd had too much work to do, but didn't feel he could turn it down. He sent out postcards to 125 people, just as his mentor had suggested, a month before leaving his job. His colleagues in other companies recommended him to their supervisors; his golf buddies introduced him to a couple of department heads; his old boss asked him to finish up a project during the first month. Oh, most of the projects were small, but he was busy. Boy, was he busy! There was no doubt about it. Now what?

What was that his mentor said? Something about "sales funnels and pipelines" and "The most important time to market is when you are too busy to market"? Yes, indeed, he had just experienced that.

Well, Heinrich wondered how his family would react to the exact opposite of what they'd experienced the past few months. Not only was he going to be home every weekend, but it was likely that he'd be home every weekday, too!

■ ■ ■

Starting your business is the first difficult step. The second is staying in business. Staying in business as a consultant means that you have a continuous flow of clients. Heinrich experienced what many new consultants experience. He tapped into his network and was flooded with requests from people interested in helping him get off to a good start. New consultants are often overwhelmed with all that they need to learn and do. For many, this is likely to be the first time that they have been responsible for every aspect of business: selling, marketing, customer relations, invoicing, banking, paying the bills, replenishing office supplies, communication, and everything else. They are likely implementing new processes, working with new software, and feeling their way through what it means to be an entrepreneur.

Heinrich is headed for a couple of rough months. His address book has likely been exhausted and can't continue to sustain his consulting practice. His immediate network leads have dried up. It's been half a year since he sent his original message out, so it may be a little uncomfortable to reconnect. He probably has a very sketchy marketing plan in place—if he has one at all. And if he does have a marketing plan, it is unlikely that he has completed anything on it that he originally targeted. What should Heinrich have done—or, a better question—what will Heinrich do next time?

Obviously, you cannot just sit back with your stack of business cards on your desk and wait for the phone to ring! You may be the best consultant in the world, produce the best materials, know the most innovative solutions, provide the best service, and be the most knowledgeable in your field. However, if no one knows about you, what are your chances of having clients? Slim to none! So you must let people know that you are available for consulting. You must market your products and services. You must promote yourself.

A successful business can be measured by an adequate supply of clients, a professional image, and an ethical reputation. Each requires your attention and energy. All three will happen at the same time, and they will all happen all of the time. Everything you do will affect your business success, as measured by your clients, your image, and your reputation.

Chapter Four addressed your image. Chapter Nine addresses building an ethical reputation. This chapter addresses how marketing will ensure that you have an adequate flow of clients to stay in business.

Consultants must be marketing-oriented. In the beginning you may need to market yourself tirelessly, using every tactic that is at your disposal. If the term *marketing* scares you, think in terms of simply putting the word out that you are in business. Unlike Heinrich, you must get the word out. You *must* promote yourself.

You must promote yourself.

This chapter helps you prepare a simplified marketing plan and explores marketing with little or no money. Some of the ideas will stimulate your creativity as you explore your own ideas to keep yourself in front of your clients. The chapter will help you plan the most efficient and effective networking activities and show you how the dreaded "cold call" can be fun when you warm it up and refocus your attitude. Prepared consultants start marketing before they start their businesses.

MARKETING FROM DAY ONE

The most successful consultants recognize the importance of marketing and started marketing activities long before they had their business cards printed—in fact, long before they became consultants. Actions you have probably taken since starting your consulting practice will be helpful now as you develop a solid marketing plan. From the start, from day one, you can begin to market.

Start a Mailing List. Every person you come in contact with who has the potential of being a client or knowing someone who could be a client should be on this list. As the list grows, you can organize it so that you can easily use it for specialty mailings—for example, CEOs, personal contacts, female executives, petroleum industry, or retail contacts. I have both an email list and a mailing address for special mailings, thank-you notes, and greeting cards.

Start a File of Marketing Ideas. If you see an AT&T ad, a Dilbert cartoon, an item in a catalog, or hundreds of other things that suggest marketing ideas, file them in one place. You will be busy with other things, and you will forget the idea if you don't have one place you can go to be inspired. We use an accordion file because not everything can be reduced to a URL or a PDF. The extra space gives us room to add small items that we can physically ship.

Print Business Cards Early. The least costly, high-impact marketing tool you have is your business card. It may take a couple months to work with a designer to create a logo and design for your stationery. Therefore, print a few hundred cards to start. However, do not let these cards be a substitute for high quality for very long. Business cards send a message and project your image. Ensure that they are as professional looking as possible and start working with a designer as soon as you can.

Begin a Testimonial File. Your clients will begin to rave about your work. Collect those statements. You may receive unsolicited thank-you letters or notes. Place them in a file. If clients compliment your work verbally, ask them to put it in writing. You will use these testimonials for brochure copy, in prospecting letters, or in proposals.

Initiating these activities from the first day you are in business ensures that you will be better prepared to implement many of the marketing tools presented.

So what's marketing all about? It's about getting your name in front of clients and keeping it there. It's about keeping work flowing and your consulting practice growing. It's all about staying in business. This chapter gives you advice and suggestions for staying in business once you've started.

CREATING YOUR MARKETING PLAN

More books have been written about marketing than about any other business topic. The topic of marketing can be pretty complicated. You may find yourself reading about marketing goals, objectives, strategies, tactics, promotions, and practices. You may read about the marketing mix. Some marketing experts discuss the "four P's" of the marketing mix: product, price, place, and promotion. Other experts discuss the "eight P's and an S": product, price, place, promotion, positioning, people, profits, politics, and service. You will read about advertising, public relations, and media. Then there are discussions about personal versus impersonal promotion or direct versus indirect marketing. How does social marketing support consulting? How do content marketing and blogging fit? You can read about personal selling, client-centered marketing, leveraging your clients—well, you get the idea.

No, you do not need a degree in marketing. You must find out how to put the word out that you have consulting services to offer. Although this may seem like an overwhelming task, and one you would rather skip, don't be tempted. Developing a marketing plan is critical if you are to stay in business.

You may say, "What? Another plan?" The answer is yes. Your marketing plan will convert your ideas and intentions into commitment and action. Your marketing plan will guide you through the year so that the important task of marketing is never pushed to the back burner, or, as in Heinrich's case, forgotten completely.

You will put your plan in writing. A written plan helps to add discipline to your ideas, enables you to measure success, and provides data for future use. Note that a marketing plan must follow a few guidelines in order to be useful. The sidebar lists several mistakes that consultants make with their marketing plans.

Common Marketing Plan Mistakes

Creating a marketing plan requires you to make sound decisions based on data. You need to know your market. Consultants frequently make these mistakes when they develop a marketing plan.

- Doesn't align with demand (What are the current needs?)
- Isn't differentiated in an overcrowded space (What distinguishes you?)
- Doesn't target the ideal client (How well have you defined your dream client?)
- Insufficient investment (Are you reinvesting 10 percent of revenue on marketing?)
- Lack of focus on list building (Are you tracking in LinkedIn or by another means?)
- Lack of nurturing inbound leads (What is your response plan and how quickly?)

We touched on a marketing plan in Chapter Four when you prepared a business plan. You have two choices: (1) If you went through that exercise and have the information, you can now use it as input to this more specific marketing plan or (2) If you did not spend time yet, you can use this process to develop a more specific marketing plan and slip it into your business plan.

Formatting Your Marketing Plan

A marketing plan can become quite complex. If you have never written one before, the format presented here is a simplified version. Exhibit 5.1 will take you through the eight easy steps. You will find that marketing is a combination of intuition and logic. The eight-step format will move you through the process comfortably. It will ensure that your resulting marketing plan does what it is supposed to do—put your name out there!

Marketing is a combination of intuition and logic.

---

1. Analyze the Present. Because you're just starting, there may not be much to analyze. However, a year from now when you make comparisons, you will want to ask these questions:

- How am I perceived in the marketplace?
- How do I compare to my competition?
- What's happening to revenue and profits?
- How satisfied are my customers?
- How do customers, colleagues, and competitors describe me, my performance, and my results?

Responses to these questions will guide you as you focus on whether you project the image you desire, whether you have the competitive edge you desire, whether you are as financially successful as you desire, whether you meet your clients' expectations, and whether you have the reputation you desire.

If you have been in business for more than a year, complete this subjective analysis. If you are just starting, imagine your future. Alan Kay often says in his

Exhibit 5.1. Marketing Plan

1. Analyze the present.

2. Clarify your strategy.

3. Set measurable 6- to 12-month goals.

4. Select marketing tactics to accomplish your goals.

5. Identify resources.

6. Develop an annual marketing plan.

7. Implement your plan.

8. Monitor your results and adjust as needed.

speeches, "The best way to predict the future is to invent it." Next year, you will have something to analyze. Today, each of your answers may still be described as your preferred future—the one you are inventing!

2. Clarify Your Strategy. First, of course, you need to be certain that you have one. Clarify your position and how it differs from your competition. Clearly state the niche that you have selected. You must have a strategy for several reasons. The first is so that you know where to focus your energy. If you have decided to focus on large businesses as your niche and you continue to work with the federal government, you may work the same number of days but may not reach the financial goals you set. Even with a strategy, many consultants stray from it and get their business into trouble. So it's not enough to have a strategy; you must also pay attention to it. Besides, if you don't have a strategy, how will you know when you stray from it?

Determine the targeted client base on which you will focus, what size companies, what type of organizations, and in what industry. What skills will you promote, what services will you provide? And in response to the previous section, describe what you will offer these clients and identify what you will tell your clients about these services.

Determine whether you will target your current clients or new clients and whether you will market current services or new services. That means four combinations. Exhibit 5.2 shows you the risk, cost, and potential growth of each combination. Obviously, marketing the same services to the same clients has little or no risk or cost, but also results in little growth. Marketing new services to new clients is the highest in risk and cost, and results in slow growth. Marketing current services to new clients is moderate in risk and cost, and results in moderate growth. Marketing new services to current clients has a low risk and moderate cost with significant growth potential. These decisions should fall out of the research you completed in Chapters Two and Three.

What increases the risk in two of the four combinations? It is the potential of new clients. In general, new clients also require more marketing dollars and result in slower immediate growth.

Exhibit 5.2. Client Strategy Choices

	Current	**New**
New	Risk: Little Cost: Moderate Result: Significant Growth Potential	Risk: High Cost: High Result: Probable Slow Growth
Current	Risk: Little Cost: Little Result: Little Growth	Risk: Moderate Cost: Moderate Result: Moderate Growth

Services (vertical axis) **Clients** (horizontal axis)

It may take months—even years—of marketing to acquire a new client. That is why a client in hand is worth 10 in your marketing plan. Where is your business heading? Some questions you might ask now include:

- What size company do I want to serve?
- What geographical area will I serve?
- Will I work for government, nonprofit, or for-profit organizations?
- In what industry will I specialize?
- Will I serve groups or individuals?
- Will I serve special situations such as start-ups or mergers?
- What projects do I want to conduct?

Your answers will reflect the kind of business you wish to develop. These questions will help you generate a list of potential customers with whom you want to do business.

Your strategy might be to focus on medium- to large-size financial institutions located along the East Coast that are facing mergers and need assistance working toward efficient, shared visions of the future.

3. Set Measurable 6- to 12-Month Goals. You know how important goal setting is. Be specific. Make sure you can measure yours and add time limits to them. Go ahead and establish longer-range goals if you choose. No matter what your timeline is, make certain that you believe all are achievable. Here are some examples:

- Generate $100,000 in repeat business from July 1 to January 31.
- Generate $140,000 in new business from July 1 to January 31.
- Acquire three new clients by February 28.
- Acquire one new client in the banking industry by February 28.
- Present at one new conference in the next calendar year.

4. Select Marketing Tactics to Accomplish Your Goals. Generally, advertising and direct mail do not work very well for promoting consulting, but there are hundreds of other things you can do.

This is where the fun begins. We have listed several self-promotional tactics in this chapter. Use some of them or, if you prefer, use the list to spark your own tactics. Tactics are actions, including anything from cold calls to hot presentations, that put your name in front of potential clients. The marketing tools you select should have your client in mind first and foremost. Where does your client expect to see your name? In what medium will your client expect to see your services? The marketing climate is changing for professionals, so don't be too conservative. Examples include actions such as these:

- Make 25 contacts in the banking industry.
- Submit proposals to at least three new conferences.
- Begin a podcast series for leadership.
- Submit an article to the *Journal of Engineering*.

5. Identify Resources. There is a cost to marketing. Whether you speak at conferences, write letters to the local newspaper, make calls to potential customers, purchase magazine advertising, publish a newsletter, or rent a booth at a trade show, there is a cost. You must weigh the cost and the benefits to determine whether a particular marketing strategy makes sense for you.

As you make plans, take care that you do not commit yourself to one medium too soon. Most print media (newspapers, journals, magazines), for example, will sign you up for a series of ads. You might commit to a year of advertising at $450 per month, only to find out that the ad does not garner one phone call after five months. You are still committed to the last seven months and the payments that equal $3,150. Try to maintain as much flexibility as possible in your plans.

But resources mean more than money. Resources can also mean people who can provide you with information or assistance. For example, you may have targeted a certain industry on which you would like to concentrate. You could publish an ad in one of the industry's trade journals. Or you could go to lunch with someone you know in the industry to brainstorm ideas for approaching organizations within the industry.

6. Develop an Annual Marketing Plan. This is the step where it all comes together on several pages. You will lay out your plan for the year on an annual marketing planning calendar, like the one in the exhibit. Each of your goals will be broken down into substeps using the activities you chose and listed on the calendar. You will, of course, need more detail for some of the activities, but this format will help you see everything at a glance: how time will be expended each month and what the anticipated marketing will cost for the month.

Your marketing activities will be more appealing if you break them down into small steps. For example, if you want to break into the banking industry to acquire two new banking clients this year, part of your plan might look like this.

• Contact my banker for ideas	January 15
• Speak at a banking conference	February 8
• Make 25 contacts at the conference	February 7–9
• Conduct additional research on contacts	February 10–11
• Follow up with all conference contacts	February 14
• Brainstorm special mailing to contacts	February 16
• Send special mailing to contacts	March 1
• Follow-up calls to contacts	March 8
• Include banking contacts in spring mailing	March 21
• Submit article (presentation) to *Banking Today*	March 28
• Send brochures to 25 contacts with personal note	April 22

Exhibit 5.3 provides a layout for your marketing calendar. Notice that you can track the dates and the expected costs each month. You can tell at a glance what you intend to do each month, where your focus is, and which months are heavy or light in activities.

7. Implement Your Plan. There is not much to say here. You've planned the work; now work the plan. This step is really the reason you put the plan together in the first place. You are ready to implement what you decided to do. Stay on top of your marketing activities. Your marketing may not yield any results for several months. Start now. Don't fall behind. You cannot go back to fix anything that was not implemented six months ago.

> **Tip: Action over planning.**
> Even though we've been examining a marketing plan, your emphasis should be on the actions you will take. A plan without action is useless.

8. Monitor Your Results and Adjust as Needed. Although a plan provides you with your best guess at the moment, you may need to adjust at times. For example,

Exhibit 5.3. Annual Marketing Planning Calendar

Marketing Activity for 20XX		Jan	Feb	Mar	April	May	June	July	Aug	Sept	Oct	Nov	Dec
	Dates												
	Cost												
Total Budgeted Costs													

you may have focused your business on small companies. After you start, you may find that the demand was there but the revenue was not sufficient. Perhaps you will need to refocus your client mix. You may add some medium-size companies to boost the revenue. This will be a portion of your analysis before you develop your next marketing plan.

There is lots of churn around a one-page marketing plan. If you can create a meaningful plan on one page, definitely do it. The key, though, is to make sure you have all you need to know in one place and that in the end you know what you will do.

Develop a Marketing Plan for Free

Most business schools require their marketing majors to develop full marketing plans. Students usually write plans for the school itself or for nonprofit agencies connected to it. Most would rather write a marketing plan for a real business.

Two things will make this a successful experience for you. First, allow enough time. Writing the plan will probably be a long process occurring over a full semester. You will want to speak with the professor the semester before. Second, stay involved. Your input will be critical. You will need to provide the correct data so that the plan will be based on accurate assumptions. In addition, your involvement will increase the enthusiasm of the students and the professor. Even if the plan is less than perfect due to the students' inexperience, you may receive good advice from the professor.

USING THE INTERNET

Take time to decide how your website and social media fit into your marketing plans.

Creating Your Website

You will use the web to help attract new clients. Your website is a credibility statement. Most potential clients will either ask for your website or visit it before meeting you. Your website is today's brochure. (That does not mean that you do not also need a brochure—you do for your clients' convenience and for folks who like print material.) The business world assumes that, if you are in business, you have a website. You need one. It is a self-serve marketing tool that is open 24/7. I am always surprised when I meet a potential client for the first time and they tell me they have already been on my website. Websites are good for generating more leads as well as qualifying those leads.

In Chapter Four I mentioned that you needed to obtain a domain name. You can either design your website yourself or hire someone to design it for you. You can have lots of bells and whistles for $10,000 or more, or you can hire a freelancer to design a very simple website for you for under $1,000, or you can design it yourself. Heck, if you have children in junior high or high school, they probably have a pal who would design it for you for less. Keep in mind that you still need to know what you want and need on your site. Be sure you are very clear about the purpose.

Donald Miller is my go-to guy for clarifying messages in general, but specifically through websites. In his book *Building a Story Brand* (2017), Miller suggests that your website should include five things: an offer (above the fold), obvious calls to action, images of success, a bite-size breakdown of what you do, and very few words. I know this doesn't tell you what you need to do, but it gives you some focus as you are building your website. You can incorporate these concepts in your own words as you sketch out the important pieces and create the pages.

Once it is up, keep your website up-to-date and refresh it with something new at least monthly. How do you generate traffic to your website? The primary way to promote your website is to create valuable content. Search Engine Optimization (SEO) is the process of modifying web page content to improve the search engine ranking of the page. Since more than 70 percent of people who are looking for products and services use search engines, SEO will increase the number of visitors. Be sure that the signature on all your emails has the powerful tagline that invites the recipient to click on the link and visit your site. Be sure that your website address is on all of your documents, brochures, newsletters, business cards, and promotional materials. You may also wish to write web articles and submit them to article directories. And finally, if you want to bring more traffic and keep people returning, give something of value away, such as free ebooks, articles, games, self-assessments, or podcasts.

Using Social Media

Since there are no barriers to entry into social media networks, many consultants join all of them. Don't join every social media network unless you first determine what your customers use. No matter which you use, they will require time and even money at some point.

Check out the data first. Who is purchasing your services and where are they likely found? I'd say to go with LinkedIn and Twitter to start out. Part of your marketing plan should include the use of social media. Don't get caught publishing often at the beginning and then running out of ideas at a later time. It is probably better to keep a list of potential blogs, for example, and post them on a regular basis.

Experiment to determine what your audience responds to best: stories, humor, solid content, case studies, or practical tips. Last, but certainly not least, is to determine your goal for using social media. Are you just trying to get a hundred likes or are you trying to generate leads by driving traffic to your website? Identify the influencers in your industry and follow them. Share their content and comment without self-promotion on posts. Be careful of investing too much time. You aren't likely to seal a $20,000 contract using social media, but you should be able to turn your likes into leads and, when done well, enhance your presence. Include a social media strategy in your marketing plan.

Turn likes into leads.

Blog Ideas

Keep an open list of blog topics so that you always have a fresh idea.

- A list of positive actions to take
- A case study summary
- Views on the future of the industry
- A recent experience you've had
- A controversial topic
- How to do anything
- What you are doing, such as a speaking event
- Research results
- A review of someone's exciting content

Need a formula for a blog? Michael Hyatt (2018a) shares his six-step template for writing blogs: choose a compelling title; write a short lead paragraph; insert a relevant image; share a personal experience; write a scannable body; and pose a discussion question. He keeps the posts short, uses simple words, and provides internal links. Using a formula like this to start with can save you some time.

SURPRISING BUT PRACTICAL THOUGHTS ON MARKETING

You may not feel comfortable about marketing, but the following thoughts will put you at ease and help you think of more ideas on your own.

Market All the Time

The drawback of a calendar of marketing activities is that it suggests that there are certain days of the month that you will be marketing and that there are certain days that you won't. The truth is that you are marketing all the time. Every experience with every client, every conversation with a colleague, every visit to a professional meeting, every comment to a friend is a marketing event. You are selling yourself. As a consultant, you represent your product or service. People around you are making decisions (subconsciously at least) about whether they can or will use your services.

The time to market is all the time.

"The time to market is all the time" also means that you must religiously complete the marketing activities on your calendar. You may find yourself too busy with a current project to complete the marketing event that you had planned (for example, contacting two organizations in the next city or going to lunch with a colleague). Yes, you must complete the project, but if you tell yourself that you are too busy to complete the marketing as well, you will come to the end of the busy project and not have another project to be busy on! Yes, the time to market is all the time. And the most important time to market is when you are too busy to market!

The most important time to market
is when you are too busy to market!

Keep Yourself in Front of Your Clients

You can do this in three ways. First, you can physically be in their presence. When working on-site, I frequently pop in on the CEO, president, HR director, or the person who hired me with a favorite Starbucks order, even if we were not scheduled to meet. I'm sure some of you shudder at my lack of formality, but it represents who I am. I can get away with this. You may need to schedule meetings. The point is, make time for them. And the other point is that I know what each of their Starbucks brew is—I've created a relationship with each of them.

Second, you can keep yourself in front of your clients with permanent, practical year-end gifts. We always look for something unique, something special. We have gained a reputation for creative gifts. For example, one year we sent miniature mugs filled with gold paper clips. They were high quality, useful, and put our logo on everyone's desk every day.

Third, you can keep yourself in front of your clients by ensuring that things periodically go across their desks—for example, articles, notes of interest, books, announcements, cards, seasonal greetings, or even cartoons! Find a reason. When someone joins our firm, we send a special announcement. For example, when Garland joined our firm, we sent a miniature chalkboard and chalk with the message, "Chalk another one up for ebb associates, Garland has joined the ebb team."

Have a Strategy

Well, that certainly isn't rocket science! True! You must determine the kind of client on whom you will focus. The second step of your marketing plan is critical. Do not skip it!

The purpose of a strategy is to keep you focused. Know what you want and where you are going. And that means that you must also pay attention to it.

Go for the Big Fish; You'll Spend the Same Time Baiting the Hook

When I started my business, I decided to focus on medium- to large-size businesses. This strategy is one of the best decisions I ever made. Many new consultants focus on small businesses as their first targets, perhaps because large organizations are more intimidating. In general, small businesses have smaller training and consulting budgets. Because the decision to hire a consultant may be a small business's one and only budgeted consulting expense for the year, it may take longer to make the decision.

On the other hand, large businesses make numerous training and consulting purchases in a year. They may feel more comfortable taking a risk on a new consultant. Because this is not their one and only decision for the year, they can make hiring decisions faster. In addition, if you do a great job, you will have a better chance at repeat business with a larger organization. Small organizations may want to have you return, but may not have the budget.

Go for the big fish; you'll spend the same time baiting the hook.

Don't let the size of the organization scare you. The people who manage organizations need good consulting, no matter what the size. You will invest the same amount of time marketing your services to a large organization as to a small one. Your payoff, however, may be much greater.

Keep an Eye on Your Competition

One of the difficulties of being a consultant is being alone and outside the employment loop. Although it is psychologically difficult, it can be financially devastating if you do not keep up with what is going on in your field. What your competition does will affect your marketing plans.

Although you may have a specialty, be aware of the trends around you. How will a surge in downsizing affect what you provide? How will the latest management fad affect your philosophy? How will the changes in technology affect your service delivery?

Keep an eye on your competition. Read your professional journals: Who's advertising? What are they selling? Who's writing articles? Attend conferences: Who's presenting? What are they expounding? What's the buzz in the hallways? Visit bookstores: Who's writing? What topics are being published?

If you are not going to lead the profession, you must at the very least stay in touch. Your clients expect that of you.

Wallow in Your Junk Mail

Junk mail and spam are marketing research gifts. Read them! You can spend thousands to find out what your competition is doing or you can acknowledge the free research delivered to you every day. I often hear consultants complain about the piles of advertising they receive, especially in conjunction with conferences for which they have registered. Instead, welcome your junk mail as the gift it is.

What can you gain from your junk mail and spam? You can develop a sense of the trends in the field. Trends are always changing. Is stress management "in" this year or "out"? Junk mail can spark ideas for your own marketing. Notice that I said spark ideas—not steal them. Spam can keep you informed of new companies that have entered the field.

Don't bemoan your junk mail delivery. Instead, be grateful for all the competitive information that has just been dumped in your lap. I have been working on a plan for developing consultants online. I registered for one free class on how to develop an online course and now I am inundated by others in the same arena. The first thing I learned is the overwhelming number of people who are out there with a similar gig. It seems to be the latest fad everyone is buying into. The other thing I learned is that the trainers who are promoting how to create online courses are the ones making most of the money! Even better, I am learning all about their marketing ploys! I am amazed! Don't throw it away! Read it. Study it. Wallow in your junk mail—whether it arrives in your mailbox or your inbox!

Wallow in your junk mail!

Mail a Lumpy Envelope

The idea is to capture the recipient's attention so that the envelope is opened. First, just getting an envelope is attention-getting, since we've become a society of texts. But when the envelope is lumpy and obviously has a surprise inside, it gains even more attention. You certainly don't want to think that your envelopes could be placed in someone's junk mail stack!

Over the years we have mailed dozens of lumpy envelopes. We've mailed typical things such as staple removers and holiday ornaments, but we've mailed the unusual, too, such as:

- Tree-shaped pasta in January to send greetings for a "tree-mendous" new year with many "pasta-bilities."
- Light-up yo-yos at the end of 2001 stating that "it's been a year of ups and downs."
- Tape measures asking the recipients how they measure up.
- Crayons to complete an interactive creativity brochure.
- Pewter sea shells that spoke of uniqueness and beauty.
- Light up stemmed glasses to send special congratulations.
- And this winter we are sending a make-your-own-snow kit.

When there is nothing to make a large lump, we may add confetti to celebrate a business success or tiny stars to say congratulations. We have acquired a reputation for our lumpy envelopes. Some clients will only open our envelopes over a wastebasket. This marketing tactic has gained us a reputation for being creative and fun. In fact, deciding what the next lump could be is one of the most delightful things I do.

Mail a lumpy envelope.

Personalize Your Marketing

One of the rules of consulting states that a consultant should not be too close to the client because it prevents objectivity. I intentionally and completely ignore that rule. I want to get to know our clients as people and in doing so celebrate their humanness as well as their professionalism.

I do not do this as a marketing tactic. In fact, when I first started the business, most of my exchanges with clients were very informal and personal. I claimed that we did no marketing, until Ian, one of my clients, asked what I thought I was doing when I sent him a handmade thank-you card. Whether it's marketing or not, I do believe it builds a strong relationship with my clients and potential clients.

How do we personalize marketing? We send cards filled with confetti to congratulate clients on job promotions. We send birthday cards. We send custom-designed cards to celebrate graduations, births, engagements, weddings, anniversaries, new cars, trips, a new life focus, a new house, a move. Most recently we have discovered singing cards—a bargain at less than $5. We send lots of cards—always with a handwritten message.

We send articles of interest about a favorite subject, hobby, child's college, vacation site, competitor, or mutual friend. We may send items that have a special meaning, such as Georgia O'Keeffe stamps, job ads, special coffee, music CDs, books (lots of books), pens, photos, good-luck tokens, or stones.

We send many handwritten notes to follow up on conversations. Sometimes items are added. I once had a conversation with a vice president of a large New York City bank about the best training activity he ever saw: analysis of the task of eating a piece of pie. Following that conversation, I sent him a piece of pie to tell him how much I enjoyed our conversation. Another time I had a discussion with a publisher in which we both marveled at the magic of television. I followed up by sending her a children's book, *How Things Work,* including the magic of television.

Remember that I do these things because I like people and I enjoy it! Although my approach may be seen as a marketing tool, I see it as a people tool. This may not work for everyone. I do it because it's who I am and I enjoy it. If it's not sincere, this kind of contact will backfire. If you are doing it "just to market your services," do not do it.

Know How to Acquire a New Client

Acquiring a new client requires 10 times the effort as acquiring repeat business. There is a saying that "the best way to get clients is to have clients." This is true for two main reasons: first, if you are producing results, your clients will recommend you to other clients; second, if you are producing results, your clients will invite you back for additional projects.

Acquiring a new client requires 10 times
the effort as acquiring repeat business.

Many books written by successful consultants state that you will spend 25 to 40 percent of your time in marketing activities. I probably spent 80 percent of my time during the first months of start-up, but since then I have spent no more than 15 percent of my time marketing, and most of that is of a very personal nature.

Use Your Clients to Market Your Services

The ideal situation for you as a consultant is to find that your clients speak highly of you and recommend you to other clients. Nothing—absolutely *nothing*—is more valuable to you than a client's recommendation. You earn that by exceeding your customers' expectations, adding value at every point, producing the highest-quality results, building trusting relationships, and modeling the highest ethics. In other words, doing a good job. Do good consulting!

Our vision statement says, "Our clients are so satisfied that they market for us." Although it has taken a long time to achieve that vision, we have. We can trace more than 80 percent of our business back to three of our original clients.

TACTICS FOR LOW-BUDGET MARKETING

You need business. You need marketing tactics. You want to make a name for yourself, promote yourself, enhance your image, and build your reputation. But you have little money! What can you do? The following ideas will help you start. All will give you visibility and ensure that you stay in business. Some of these are common sense, and you may already have thought of them. Others, on the other hand, may be too unusual for you. All of them should spark your creative thought process. All of them are tactics we have used.

Networking to Market

- Attend professional conferences to network.
- Join local civic organizations.
- Join organizations that represent the industries you serve.
- Join your professional organizations.

- Attend local chapter meetings for the professional, civic, and social organizations to which you belong. Network! The greater the number of follow-up notes you write, the greater your success!
- Plan to meet three new people in every networking situation.
- Following a presentation, have everyone toss a business card in a hat for a drawing. After drawing for the prizes, send a personal note to all who submitted business cards thanking the individuals for their attendance.
- Contact your college roommate and ask for an introduction to an organization.
- Serve on a board for your community college, a local company, an association, or a charity.

Basic Marketing

- Submit press releases to the media regarding your major consulting engagements, awards, published articles or books, or appointments.
- Publish an electronic newsletter, but heed the cautions of experts. Your newsletter should be filled with useful information, resources, and helpful ideas. It should not be filled with advertisements or rewritten old press releases.
- Agree to be interviewed on a podcast. Share it with potential clients.
- Conduct a survey. Publish the results. Share the results with clients.
- Share your expertise freely with clients and other consultants: advice, ideas, materials, instruments. It will come back to you.
- Write articles for your professional journal. Contact the editor to obtain a calendar of topics for the year.
- Purchase professional-looking reprints of your article or others' articles and send them to present and potential clients.
- Write a book. It is really not as difficult as you might think. You need to start it.
- Ask your clients for referrals.
- Create a mailing list and an email list. They should include everyone you meet in the line of business every day.
- Blog regularly.

Some Budget Required

- Invite potential clients to a mini-presentation to get an idea of your expertise and services. Sometimes called showcases, these are often held in local hotels where food and beverages are served to encourage a more social atmosphere.

- Start your own cable show.
- Host a summer picnic.
- Sponsor a community event, such as a 10K run.
- Buy T-shirts for your employees, colleagues, or even clients.
- Sponsor an offbeat memorable event. Perhaps you could rent your local theater for an afternoon and invite clients' children for a free showing.
- Give an award to one of your suppliers. This becomes a marketing tool for both of you.
- Trade show booths are generally very expensive, but you may be able to share one with another organization, or you could trade the cost of the booth for services to the association. Creativity, bedsheets, and lots of action can make up for the lack of the glitz and glamour of the more typical booths.
- Sponsor a roundtable breakfast for members of a specific industry in one locale.
- Host a webinar series; you may be able to volunteer to work with an association in your industry.

Common Sense
- Find a reason to call special clients.
- Every time you meet a potential client, even a remotely potential client, follow up with a personal note.
- Scan your newspaper for awards local business people have received and send a note congratulating them. I like to include the article as well.
- Speak at civic and professional organizations' meetings and conferences.
- Talk to a client about a new idea.
- Meet with other consultants. If they are offered a project outside their scope of work, they may pass it on to you.
- Collect testimonials from customers, experts, or celebrities and use them to spice up your marketing.
- Practice a perfect handshake—not too firm, not too weak.
- Create a list of success stories you have had with past clients, such as an effort that resulted in a savings of $3 million each year and shortened the time from concept to catalog by 11 months. Perhaps they could be used as case studies on your website.

- Send targeted geographic mailings before you visit a city. Send a note to several people letting them know you will be in their city. Follow up with a phone call to set a meeting time.
- Use your signature line to promote a new service or a book you've just published.

The Personal Touch

- When you are not given a project, send a thank-you note saying you appreciated being considered. Compliment them on their choice—your competition.
- Send articles that will interest your present and potential clients.
- Send a card for atypical holidays: Thanksgiving, Valentine's Day, St. Patrick's Day, Groundhog Day, or Independence Day.
- Tie a client message to a holiday—for example, "We're thankful to have you as a client" (Thanksgiving Day), "We're lucky to have you as a client" (St. Patrick's Day).
- Send a lumpy envelope for a holiday: a gourd for Thanksgiving, candy hearts for Valentine's Day, a four-leaf clover for St. Patrick's Day, a sparkler for Independence Day.
- Send birthday cards for both people and companies.
- Send "congratulations" cards for promotions.
- Send personal, handwritten thank-you notes.
- Start all emails with "you," followed by a compliment.

Above and Beyond

- Pass your extra work on to a trusted colleague. It will come back to you.
- Help your client locate other consultants who can do work you are not qualified to do.
- Send any book your client would appreciate.
- Enter your projects in industry award competitions.
- Page through a corporate specialty catalog to locate something around which you could build a theme. You will be surprised at some of the creative items you can purchase for under $2.00.
- Do things that make people feel special, such as using their names in the middle of the notes you write to them, sending pictures that you took at their team-building session, tracking down a special request they mentioned, or attributing an idea to them.

- Visit an industry trade show to compile a list of potential clients in an industry. You can visit their booths, speak with their employees, and pick up their literature. Keep a supply of business cards with you. Hand them out freely.
- Offer a full money-back guarantee.
- Offer a finder's fee to colleagues who generate a project for you.
- Use Google Hangouts, Zoom, Facebook Live, or YouTube Live to create and deliver free how-to-do-something videos.

These marketing tactics are just a start. You can think of others. The key is to find ways to promote who you are and what you do—and to have fun in the process! Looking for more in-depth marketing information? *Marketing Your Consulting Services* (Biech 2003) is another *Business of Consulting* resource that will answer all your questions.

Marketing to Local Clients

If you are planning to work within your city or other local surroundings, you can focus on a few "locals only" ideas to inform organizations that you provide consulting.

- Register your consulting practice with local directories.
- Claim your Google My Business page and ensure your information is listed correctly.
- Ask your current clients to leave a review on your Google My Business page.
- Be sure your name, phone number, and address are visible on all your web pages.
- Include some location-specific content on your website.
- Identify a local network of business owners, such as social networking meetups. We have a social event called Wine Down Wednesday, where participants are expected to bring business cards and talk business.
- Join local association chapters, but here you meet and greet at the meeting; specific marketing or selling is frowned upon, so you schedule a meeting with a follow-up email and an invitation for coffee.
- Get involved in your local community as a volunteer for something such as a fundraiser.

CONTACTING POTENTIAL CLIENTS

Many people assume that contacting clients will be difficult and should therefore be avoided. It is easier than you might think.

Cold Calls

What is a person's greatest fear about making cold calls? Rejection. What can positively be guaranteed about making cold calls? Rejection. So create a positive cold-call attitude. I have a friend in sales who lives by cold calls. The numbers he works with are daunting. He says he must make 100 cold calls to find 10 people who will talk to him. Of those 10 people, 2 will agree to meet with him and 1 will purchase his product.

So what if someone says "No," hangs up, or is rude? Don't let it ruin your day. You must refocus your attitude. You were not rejected; your services were rejected. The person did not need your services at this time. When you run into someone who frankly cannot use your services and he or she cuts the phone call short, you should *silently thank the person for not wasting your valuable time*. Rather than feeling rejected, you can feel thankful. Say "Thank you for your candor and have a great day!" Create your own cold-call attitude.

Cold Call Warm-Ups

Quite honestly, I have made only a few cold calls in my life. I prefer to make warm calls. Although this takes more preparation time, I believe I have better results, and I enjoy the process more. To start, I warm up the client with a letter—not just any old letter, but one that I have written specifically for the client. This requires research.

Tip: It's on the web.

Begin your research on the web. Identify a list of 20 to 30 potential clients with whom you would like to do business. Use your favorite search engine to gather as much data as you can.

I target 12 to 16 companies at a time. I start to gather content on the Internet. If I still need more information, I visit the local library. I use the library's resources, including local business magazines, journals and periodicals, local business newsletters, the newspaper, the city directory, manufacturer and business directories, and any other resources available. Each of these has an index that makes it easy to research the list of clients. I use Exhibit 5.4, the company profile, to synthesize the information I find.

Exhibit 5.4. Company Profile

Company Name _____

Address _____

_____

Telephone _____   Website _____

Employees _____

Management Positions

_____   _____

_____   _____

_____   _____

_____   _____

_____   _____

Products and Services _____

_____

History _____

_____

Future Plans _____

_____

Financial Information _____

_____

Organizational Philosophy _____

_____

_____

Relationship to My Consulting Services

_____

_____

Additional Relevant Information _____

_____

Resources Used _____

_____

Enlist your librarian to help in your search. Librarians are a wealth of knowledge. If possible, I also copy articles that I find. I gather information for two key purposes: first, to learn as much as I can about the organization and, second, to have enough information to compose a unique letter that will grab the reader's attention. An example of a letter is displayed in Exhibit 5.5.

Begin by making sure you are sending the letter to the right person. Double-check the spelling of the person's name and the person's title. Focus on the recipient in the first paragraph. Demonstrate that you know what is important to him or her. The second and third paragraphs should connect the recipient's organization to the need for consulting services in some way and establish your qualifications. Both of these paragraphs must be customized. For example, when referring to past clients, select only those who are related to the recipient by industry, location, or size. If that is not possible, select only a couple of your most impressive clients. In the last paragraph tell the recipient what to expect next. I developed this format over 30 years ago and continue to obtain remarkable results.

I usually find information for 30 to 50 percent of clients on the initial list. After I return from the library, I compose the marketing letters and mail them. I follow the letter with a telephone call on the date that is stated in the letter.

Ninety-five percent of all recipients are interested in speaking with me, and more than half of them agree to a meeting within a month. Of those, about half become clients in less than one year. The rest become contacts, resources, or clients in the future. These odds are much better than for cold calls, and the process is more fun. I enjoy the challenge of the research and the creativity of the letter composition. I particularly like beginning a relationship in this positive way. And a secondary benefit is that I always learn a great deal in the process.

I usually send the correspondence in a letter. However, I know that email can work equally as well.

Exhibit 5.5. Sample Introductory Marketing Letter

July 12, 20XX

Carl Hansen, President
Pizza Place, Inc.
2100 Allentown Avenue
Madison, WI 53704

Dear Mr. Hansen:

Free, fast, hot delivery has placed Pizza Place a step ahead of the rest. In 14 years you have turned this unique idea into a successful business with over $26 million in sales. Pizza Place has grown from one location to a chain of nine Dane County stores and a successful franchising business. One hundred franchised units in five years is an ambitious goal—one we're sure you will achieve as one of the most awarded pizza chains in the Midwest.

At ebb associates we recognize the important role employees play in the successful growth of any company. Further, we have found that improving employees' communication skills results in improved productivity and increased profit. Your anticipated rate of growth will require you to be on top of the communication needs of your staff for a smoother expansion.

ebb associates presents workshops and seminars that focus on communication for supervisory training, management development, sales training, and customer relations. Our clients, including Land O' Lakes, McDonald's Corporation, International Food and Beverage Suppliers, and other food service chains, recognize us for our commitment to excellence in training, customizing to fit individual company needs, and obtaining results.

With your plans for expansive growth, talent development is a part of your future plans. Enclosed is a list of the course titles that we will customize to meet your needs. I will call you within the week to schedule an appointment to discuss how we can assist you to meet your expansion goals at Pizza Place. I promise a free, fast, hot delivery!

Sincerely,

Elaine Biech
ebb associates inc

Exhibit 5.6 provides a list of questions to ask potential clients. You can use these to guide your discussions on the telephone or in person. Do not—I repeat, do not—ask the amateur's question, "What keeps you up at night?"

Exhibit 5.6. Questions to Ask Potential Clients

1. What does your company (division, department) value most?
2. What are your company's (division's, department's) vision and mission?
3. What is your strategy to achieve your vision and mission?
4. What are your company's (division's, department's, leadership team's) strengths?
5. What's going well for your company (division, department, team)?
6. What are the greatest challenges you will face over the next two years?
7. What prevents you from achieving your goals (objectives, mission)?
8. What do you see as the greatest need for improvement?
9. Considering that improvement, by what percent do you need (sales to increase, profits to increase, turnover to decrease, productivity to increase, and so forth)?
10. What prevents you from making that improvement?
11. How would the results impact the bottom line?
12. If you had one message to give your company president (CEO, board of directors, manager), what would it be?
13. What should I have asked you, but did not?

Ways to Track Client Contacts

After you begin to contact clients, you will want to track who you called when, what they said, what you sent them, and when they have asked you to call again. Exhibit 5.7 will help you keep this information organized.

Exhibit 5.7. Client Contact Log

Organization/ Phone Number	Contact Person	Date	First Contact	FUP*	Date	Second Contact	FUP	Date	Third Contact	FUP

*FUP = Follow-Up

146

Questions Clients Will Ask

Clients who have used consultants in the past will ask many of the same questions. Most will want to know what you do. Know how to tell your story in a 60-second sound bite. I experience the following variations repeatedly.

---

*Know how to tell your story in a
60-second sound bite.*

- What are the deliverables? What will the final product look like?
- What are the critical milestones? At what point will progress, quality, quantity be checked? How?
- How much will this cost me? (Answer this one using the word "investment"— for example, "Your investment for completing this project will be $13,900.")
- What are your billing practices? How often will you invoice me?
- How can you help me with the kickoff of this project?
- Whom do I contact if there are problems or concerns?
- How can we stay in contact?
- How can you help me communicate with my boss?
- What is our responsibility at each phase? How will you involve our employees?
- How will you evaluate the success of this project?

If Your Clients Don't Ask

What if the client does not ask questions? Perhaps your client has little experience working with consultants. You will still want to ensure that certain basics have been covered in your discussion. If your client does not ask, introduce the topic by saying, "You probably want to know. ..." This puts the topic on the table in an efficient way. The previous list of questions can be adapted for this purpose.

If you have read Peter Block's (2011) *Flawless Consulting* (and you should if you are considering a consulting career), you undoubtedly recognize that you are moving into the contracting phase of the consulting process. Contracting is ensuring that both you and your client are as explicit as possible about your needs, wants, and expectations of one another. Contracting is covered more completely in Chapter Seven. The contracting discussion is an important link to writing a good proposal.

PROPOSALS LEAD TO CONTRACTS

Proposals and contracts are two written documents that you will probably use at some point in your career. Each serves a purpose for staying in business.

Proposals

I use proposals frequently and like them. Often I am asked to submit a proposal as a step in competing for a project. At other times I am asked to submit a proposal to clarify a previous discussion. The proposal will identify *who* will do *what* by *when* and for *how much.* I actually like to write proposals. It clarifies the project in my mind, and I find myself developing creative possibilities during the process.

A proposal typically includes a purpose statement; a description of the situation as it now exists; a proposed approach that the consultant will take (this may include data gathering, design of materials, content relationships, delivery of services, and implementation); a timeline; the consultant's qualifications; and the investment required to complete the plan.

I guarantee that you will write the best proposal if you listen to what your client says and take good notes. Do not take this statement lightly. In fact, reread it. Take it in. After reading our proposals, clients often say complimentary things about the proposal, such as, "This is exactly what we need! How did you know?" We knew because we listened and we fed back their exact words. Consultants make a big mistake by putting things in their own words. If the client has requested an attitude survey, identify it that way in your proposal. An "employee engagement survey" may be more meaningful to you and the resulting surveys may have the identical words on paper. Unfortunately, your client will not know that.

You will write the best proposal if you listen to what your client says and take good notes.

Specify an effective date—for example, "The terms of this proposal are effective through April 30, 20XX." You do not want to get caught by a client who has a proposal that is two years old and for which the budget was just approved. Why is this a problem? First, the fee you quoted may be lower than what you presently charge. In addition, you have most likely grown and improved your skills, so the process you have proposed may be outdated. Finally, an effective date reduces the amount of time a client will keep you dangling.

We like to use the word "investment" (as opposed to cost or price) when we write proposals. It echoes our philosophy that we believe what we do adds value and that it does not just cost money.

Proposals are often written in competition with other consultants. They may range in length from 1 to 50 pages. I've written some that are even longer; however, length does not always equate to better. A one-page proposal may be considered a letter of agreement. An informed client will be as interested in the content of the proposal as in the price. You can find an example of a proposal online at www.wiley.com/go/newconsultingbiech.

Tip: Special delivery proposal.

Don't just send your proposal as an attachment to an email. That's so ho-hum! Send a memory stick that incorporates a video clip. Perhaps it is of you in action leading a team-building session. It could be you delivering a message about how you work with the client. It could be endorsement statements from some of your clients.

Contracts

Contracts are legal documents that bind both parties to the content stated. I personally do not like them because I believe they start the relationship on a trust-questioning level. Contracts usually involve the legal department, which usually holds the project up for a time. Except for our government work, most of our work is conducted on the basis of a clarifying proposal and a handshake.

What should contracts look like? What should they say? No matter how complete we have been or what we have written in contracts, legal departments have always slashed them apart. I recommend that you have the client's legal department initiate the contract. It will save you a great deal of time and frustration. If you believe a contract will provide you with security or clarity, use it. Quite honestly, I believe a well-written proposal meets our needs better. We use contracts when it makes the client feel more comfortable with the new relationship.

Contracts frequently include terms (effective dates), project scope, deliverables, confidentiality statements, communication expectations, staffing requirements, supervision of the consultant, scheduling, payment schedule, incentives and penalties, termination terms, the cancellation policy, arbitration arrangements, transfer of responsibilities, taxes, and modifications to the contract. Go to www.wiley.com/go/newconsultingbiech to check out a simple version of a contract drawn up by a client.

WHY WOULD YOU REFUSE AN ASSIGNMENT?

There will be times when it is better to walk away from an assignment than to accept it. I was once called to conduct a team building for a manager for whom I had completed some previous work. During our second planning discussion, he began to make some unusual requests—all directed toward one employee. It turned out that he really was not looking for a team-building session, but for evidence and documentation that could be used to fire someone on his staff! Needless to say, I turned the job down.

In another situation, our firm was selected based on our proposal and interviews to coordinate a major change effort that would occur over an 18-month time frame. One of our contingencies was a satisfactory meeting with the CEO. When I met with him, I found that he supported the change for all the wrong reasons and that it was unlikely that his support would continue when the going got tough. I ended our conversation with, "It doesn't seem that you are ready for this change. We will be unable to accept this challenge until you can guarantee your full support." There was a lot of sputtering and disbelief. He had never heard of a consultant turning down work. I left saying that if he wanted me to help him prepare for what was ahead, I would do so, but otherwise we would not accept the project. He called that same afternoon and I spent several sessions with him explaining exactly what he was getting himself into.

Yes, there are times when you will refuse an assignment, including some of the following:

- The client asks you to do something unethical or clandestine or you just feel uncomfortable about the project.
- The project lacks support from the right levels of management.
- The project is doomed for failure. It is unethical to take the client's money in that situation.
- The scope is too large for the money available.
- The project requires a steep learning curve for you, but the time is not available for the learning to occur.
- You do not have the time to do the project with your usual high quality.
- The chemistry is missing between you and the client.

If a prospect seems to be a bad fit, move on. Be honest early with the potential client when the project isn't a match to your strategy. You need to be brave enough to say no. the prospect will appreciate your candor. Remember, this is probably one of the reasons you started your own consulting business—so that you didn't have to complete work that you really did not want to do. You can simply say, "I'm sorry. I don't think we will be able to meet your needs on this project.

For the Consummate Consultant

Many things can happen to ensure that you stay in business. Only one thing will ensure that you go out of business—lack of client work. If staying in business is critical, the key will be found in your marketing plan. If you don't like to market, it's not necessary. To paraphrase W. Edwards Deming, "It is not necessary to 'market.' Survival is not mandatory."

Diversify Your Client Base. Yes, it is really exciting to get those first few clients—the ones that helped you get started. If you don't want to become one of the statistics of small businesses that close within five years, you need to expand your client base. It is not only a smart thing to do; it is dangerous if you don't. Your current work will eventually dry up. Be prepared with a pipeline of other clients.

Take a Risk; Send a Surprise. Texting is tremendous. Email is efficient. A phone call can be fun. But if you really want to get the attention of a potential client or to thank a recent client, send a lumpy envelope in the mail. You will surprise them, and if your "prize" has been well chosen, you will delight them.

Market with Your Card. Your business card may be one of the least expensive and most valuable ways to get attention. There are so many unique shapes, designs, and alternatives. And I do not mean the kind you can print yourself. You could use special paper that is firm and has a different color on each side. Business cards can have rounded corners, be die-cut into shapes, include your picture, have raised lettering, be square, and have content on both sides. The card that I am using today is printed on clear plastic, shaped like a credit card, and yes, you can see through it!

The Cost of Doing Business | 6

Error is only the opportunity to begin again, more intelligently.

Henry Ford

Mateo was having a beer at his favorite microbrewery when his friend Josh pulled up a stool. "Man, what happened to you? You look like you were rode hard and put away wet!" said Josh. "You look like you lost your best friend. What's happenin'?"

"I feel like it. I just left my accountant and she is not happy with me."

"What did you do? Embezzle from your own company?"

"Very funny," Mateo replied. "Well, you know how those accounting bean-counter types can be. I guess I missed a few details and she is uber upset. She just went on and on! But, man, I've been so busy getting clients and then delivering on the proposals. I barely have time to think. Thanks for asking."

"What are friends for? Let me grab a brew and you can tell me all about it." Josh left and returned with a couple of beers for both of them and a platter of loaded chips to munch on and said, "Okay, so how did you irritate your bookkeeper?"

"I don't even know where to start," said Mateo. "I guess it all began when I walked in with a greasy McDonald's bag in which I had been keeping my parking receipts, airline tickets, and other stuff she told me to save. I started saving stuff about six months ago. You know, stuff that would be deductible. I guess she wanted me to put them into some kind of a filing system and she wasn't very happy when I couldn't tell her what each receipt was for that made it a business expense. I didn't have a mileage log either."

"Yeah, well, you probably should have at least found a bag that wasn't greasy," snorted Josh. "What else?"

"Well, I couldn't tell her if all my clients had paid their invoices—something about a paper trail," said Mateo. "I overdrew my account at the bank a couple of times because I was out of town. I guess the overdraft charge is almost as much as I make an hour. I hate reconciling my checkbook. She didn't like the late fees I'd been paying on insurance and some other bills, either. But what really got her fuming was that I forgot to pay my quarterlies!"

"Wow!" said Josh. "You've got a problem. What are you gonna do?"

"She wants me to do something called revenue projections and to track my cash flow. I feel like I am back in Accounting 101! I guess I'll hire someone to help me get organized. Do you know anybody?"

■ ■ ■

Oh, Mateo. You are in trouble. It's quite clear that Mateo has lost money and may never be able to identify how much. He's already lost money on unnecessary bank charges and late penalties. He may never recoup payments from clients if he doesn't have clear records. And he's about to lose more. Late invoices have set a tone of mediocrity for his start-up business. He'll pay higher taxes without good expense records and the IRS will most likely penalize him for late quarterly taxes. Even worse, messy books may limit his options for getting a loan if he needs one.

Mateo is not unlike many new business owners. He's busy with many tasks and clients who are clamoring for his attention. All the immediate needs make bookkeeping tasks one of the last things he thinks about.

Every new consultant needs to start with a process of tracking money that is coming in and going out. Without good records you have no data, and without the data you have no way of analyzing your success (or failure), forecasting the future, or even paying your bills—in short, your business suffers. Good bookkeeping may make the difference between a successful consulting practice and an unsuccessful one—especially if it becomes another casualty of a started, failed, and closed small business.

KEEPING RECORDS FOR YOUR CONSULTING BUSINESS

Even if your business is up and running quickly, you land a couple of big contracts, and you have satisfied customers, you must study the numbers to know whether you are financially successful. Study your numbers? Here's what you are looking for.

- *Cash flow.* Will you have enough money to pay your bills this month?
- *Expenses.* Where is all the money going? Which expenses are constant (those that do not change when business increases or decreases, such as rent, salaries, and insurance)? Which expenses vary depending on the level of business, such as travel, printing, and professional fees?
- *Overhead.* What does it take to keep your business open?
- *Profitability.* Which contracts are the most lucrative?
- *Capital.* What business expenses are good investments?
- *Invoices.* How readily are they being paid?

This chapter helps you examine various aspects of recording, tracking, and reading your numbers. It also provides suggestions to improve your financial picture. Forms are also provided that will save you weeks of work. The advice in this chapter can prevent dozens of mistakes.

Plan for the Worst

To keep myself out of financial trouble, I follow this advice: Plan for the worst-case scenario, but act as if you're living the best case. There are two messages inherent in this statement: First, *don't spend your money until it's in your hands.* One of your clients may not pay you on time; the loan you were counting on may not be approved; an unexpected expense may occur, such as replacing your computer.

Plan for the worst-case scenario, but act as if you're living the best case.

The first message is practical, but the second message is philosophical. "Act as if you're living the best case" refers to the message you are sending to yourself and others. As a strong believer in positive thinking, I am convinced that much of my company's success is due to the fact that I expect it. I believe I will succeed. You must also live the best case for your clients. Never hint to a client that business is less than great. Suggesting that your business is having finan-cial difficulty will make clients nervous about your stability and even wary about your ability to perform the job. I've noticed that even the smallest complaint, such as "Our paper wasn't delivered on time," can cause concern. So do not men-tion your problems to your clients. You want confidence, not sympathy.

---

*Do not mention your problems to
your clients.*

Whenever you play with your numbers, remind yourself to "plan for the worst-case scenario, but act as if you're living the best case." Most consultants do exactly the opposite. And by the way, if you should ever find yourself in the red, know that the IRS allows you to carry operating loss back two years and to use it to offset the income from those years. This may result in a refund. See? Taxes aren't all bad!

Plan for problems. Portray prosperity.

WATCH YOUR CASH FLOW

You can be very profitable and still go out of business. A surprising statement? Yes, but true. Your books can display a 20 percent profit on every project, but if cash flowing into your business does not exceed cash flowing out, you will find yourself in a very difficult situation. Cash-flow problems are the number-one reason that small businesses fail. You can control cash flow. Try some or all of these sugges-tions to prevent cash-flow problems.

---

*You can be very profitable and still
go out of business.*

Bill Immediately

Make billing for the work you have completed your number-two priority. (Meeting customers' needs should always be your first priority.) Complete and deliver your clients' invoices as soon as you finish the work. The same day is not too soon. Many organizations, including federal government agencies, have a 30-day time frame from the date they receive the invoice to the day they cut the check. If you wait a week or two to send the bill, it could be a full 60 days before you receive cash for the work you completed. Remember, they cannot pay you if you don't bill them!

They cannot pay you if you don't bill them!

Billing immediately is important for reasons beyond preventing cash-flow problems. The sooner you bill, the more pleased the client will be about paying immediately. Unfortunately, the value of your services diminishes with time. A client may begin to think that what you accomplished was actually a very small aspect of the total success of the project or even that the solution was his or her own, not yours! The lesson? Bill while the client is most satisfied with your work.

Use a Reliable Delivery System to Send Invoices

Ensure that your client receives your invoice. You might be emailing your invoice. In other instances, an organization may want a hard copy of the invoice. If so, send it in a Priority Mail packet. The cost will be a little over $6.00, as opposed to a first-class stamp, but the U.S. Postal Service will give Priority Mail better attention. Your invoice will have a better chance of reaching its destination in a shorter amount of time. We could give many examples of delayed or lost mail. In general, we have seen first-class mail between our offices in Virginia and Wisconsin take as long as 5 to 10 days. The Priority Mail packets usually arrive in fewer than 5 days—often in just 2 days. In addition, your client may give it special attention due to the packaging.

Tip: Get paid faster.

Take advantage of any electronic billing system your client offers—no matter how magical it may seem, it will most likely ensure a faster turnaround than the post office process. If your clients do not mention the process, ask. Your client may advise you to contact accounts payable. Do so. It is always good to have that department on your side.

Monitor Accounts Receivable Methodically

At the end of every week, the bookkeeper on staff provides me with a cash-flow report. It identifies the amount in our checking and savings accounts, overdue invoices, and those due this month and next. The report also highlights significant expenses, such as noting that payroll will be taken out the following week.

Know Your Clients' Reputation for Prompt Payment

The strategy you have chosen will often define how readily your clients pay you. Most clients I work with pay within our 30-day expectations. Some industries are notoriously late; some of your clients may be late on occasion.

For example, if you have decided that providing service to the federal government is your niche, learn more about what you are getting into. First, although there is a prompt payment law, some agencies have a difficult time paying within 30 days. This is not due to a lack of funds, but to a lack of efficient processes. In the past, it was not uncommon for a government agency to be two months behind in paying us due to some technicality or awaiting money from a specific source. We know we will always be paid, but we do not know when! This can be detrimental to your cash flow if you are not prepared for it. Second, government work is fickle. Here today, gone tomorrow. Even with a signed contract, the federal government has the right to cancel at any time. As a taxpayer, I am fine with that. I don't want my tax dollars used on a project someone deems unnecessary due to changes.

_____

Government work is fickle.

_____

The federal government also offers you the choice of accepting payment for your services in the form of a credit card. The advantage is that you can be paid immediately upon completing the work. The disadvantages are that you will take a discount of approximately 5 percent and pay a monthly fee to the credit card company to maintain the service.

Serving government agencies, especially our Department of Defense clients, has always been a rewarding part of our work, so we don't want to eliminate it. Our strategy is to have government contracts generate a maximum of 35 percent of our revenue. This strategy has helped us balance working with great clients and maintaining a healthy revenue stream for the business.

Include Project Initiation Fees in Your Proposals

You can prevent cash-flow concerns by requesting a sum in advance to initiate the contract. Put an amount in your proposal, normally a few thousand dollars, to cover initial out-of-pocket expenses such as travel. Your contract could read, "$10,000 is due to initiate this project and to cover initial out-of-pocket expenses." We prefer to avoid this technique, because we always want to project an image of success—including financial success. The technique, although perfectly legitimate and used by many successful firms to show commitment from the client, can suggest a shortage of cash. Your business philosophy will determine your decision on this business practice.

Offer a Prepayment Discount

Some consultants offer their clients a discount of 3 to 7 percent if they prepay. Others offer a 1 to 3 percent discount for early payment, say within five days of the invoice date. I have never done this, but those who use it like it. I admit that the reason I do not use this technique is that it feels amateurish. This is only my opinion. The decision is yours.

Refrain from Paying Client Expenses

Rather than paying for copying, research, or other direct client costs out of your pocket, send the invoices to the client. Paying for them yourself and then asking for reimbursement can tie up your cash for over 30 days.

Make Your Money Work for You

Cash-flow problems can be reduced if you ensure that the money you do have is working for you. Few people think of a business as having a savings account, but the interest you earn is as valuable as working a few extra hours! Talk to your accountant for other ideas.

Bank on Good Advice

Selecting a bank and banker is second only to selecting your accountant. It is important that you keep separate accounts for your business. Commingled business and personal funds may raise tax or liability issues. Your banking needs may not seem critical initially, but you will find that a good banker can become a close and valuable partner. How do you begin? Ask your accountant and your attorney for recommendations. You benefit when the members of your support team know each other and work together. Be sure that the bank is small-business friendly. What should you look for in a bank?

- Is the bank federally insured?
- Like your accountant, does the bank support accounting software integration?
- Does it offer the services you need: loans, checking accounts, money market accounts, advisory services, notary public, safe-deposit box, direct deposit, IRA or 401(k) services?

- How experienced is management?
- What experience have they had with consulting firms?
- Is the location convenient for your business? What are their hours of operation?
- If you plan to work internationally, can the bank handle foreign currency and offer wire transfers?
- Can the bank help you set up payroll deductions for IRAs?
- What kind of fees will you pay for your checking account? Is it free with a minimum balance?
- Will the bank place a holding period on your deposits?
- How soon will you need to order checks? How much will they cost?
- What business advice does the bank provide and in what format, such as brochures, phone, or through seminars?
- What networking capabilities does the bank have? Can it put you in touch with suppliers, potential clients, or other business owners?
- How well did you connect with the people you interviewed? How comfortable will you be discussing your financial needs with them in the future?

> **Tip: Bank efficiently.**
>
> Be sure to ask your bank whether you can bank electronically. Also be sure to order checks that can be used by your accounting system and printed using your computer.

Obtain a Line of Credit for Your Business

As quickly as you can, talk to your banker about a line of credit. A good banker will understand the need and its connection to cash flow. During your start-up phase, you could use your home as collateral if your banker doesn't find equity in your company's reputation, accounts receivable, or contracts alone. A line of credit is invaluable during a tight spot. Generally a phone call to your bank will deposit the amount you request into your account the same day. You can pay back the loan on your terms, sometimes paying only the interest each month.

Use a Business Credit Card Wisely

A business credit card can delay a payment for up to 45 days. For example, let's say your credit card billing period runs from the first of the month to the end of the month. You purchase office supplies during the first week. The credit card company doesn't send your bill until the thirtieth of the month, and you have two weeks before it is due, on the fifteenth of the month. You have delayed payment for 45 days from the date you purchased the supplies. This period can be longer if your credit card company gives you longer to pay or shorter if you make your purchase later in the month. No matter what the dates, a credit card can help cash flow. One word of caution: The best way to use a credit card is to pay the balance every month to avoid the huge interest rates of 14 percent, 22 percent, or even higher. Don't run a credit bill up so high that you are stuck paying these high interest rates.

Compare Leasing and Purchase Rates Carefully

I have always been a "buy it with cash" kind of person to avoid interest rates. In fact, I was in business for 10 years before I even considered leasing equipment. One year we needed a new copier and we were short of cash. I studied the leasing agreement. It compared favorably to a cash purchase when I considered the maintenance agreement and the outright purchase option at the end of the leasing period. Since that experience, I always compare before I buy.

Play Up Your Small-Business Status

If you are a small business, you can type "Small business. Please expedite payment" at the bottom of your invoices. We've never used this technique, but have been told that it works with empathetic accounts payable departments.

Act on Late Payments Immediately

Even when you stay on top of invoices and send them out in a timely way, late payments will create a cash-flow issue. First, determine why the payment is late. It can be any of the following reasons:

- The client did not receive the invoice.
- One or more of the organization's processes caused a delay.
- The client may be deliberately paying late to manage their cash flow or for other reasons.

How do you deal with late payments? First, call the organization's accounts payable department to learn whether the invoice was received. If the organization is notoriously late, you may wish to call soon after you submit it to ensure that it is in their hands.

Act on late payments immediately.

Next, call the client for whom you completed the work and ask if your work was satisfactory. Assuming that the answer is yes, say that the reason you were asking is that the payment is past due and you were wondering if it was being held up for anything for which you were responsible. This will usually result in your client taking some action to help expedite your payment.

Last, submit a second bill that includes a new date, a statement that this is a "second bill," and a late-payment charge identified on the bill. Often consultants want to give the client another chance and not add the late-payment charge. You may if there was an unusual processing problem. You should if the bill never arrived. However, if the payment is more than a week late without good reason, submit a second invoice with the additional late fee added.

What amount should be charged for the late payment? Charge 1 to 2 percent per month. The very last line on our invoices reads, "A late payment charge of 1.5 percent will be assessed for all bills over 30 days." Some consultants use a 10- or 15-day payment schedule. If you choose something other than the conventional 30 days, it should be spelled out in the agreement or contract you have with the client.

How can you mitigate late payments? If you have had experience with a late payer, you may wish to request staggered payments including a start-up fee, a mid-project fee, and a completion fee. You could also try billing more frequently, on the fifteenth and thirtieth of the month as opposed to a once-monthly billing cycle. You may wish to offer a prepayment discount, as suggested earlier in this chapter. And, as Laurie Lewis (2000) in *What to Charge* states, "Do not accept more work from a client who owes you a bundle!" Make it your company policy that you do not accept new work from clients who are late in paying.

Pay Bills When They Are Due, Not Before

Have you ever received a bill to renew a magazine when the subscription still had four months left? This is a common practice. Watch the due dates on bills for professional organizations, magazines, clubs, and others whose process is to bill you three or four months before the due date. You can file the bill you receive for later payment or even toss it! One of my professional organizations bills me four times before they really expect payment.

Compare Actual Expenses to the Budget Monthly

Use a form similar to the one in Exhibit 6.1 to keep you informed about the status of your expenses: What's been paid, what's due this month, and which categories are ahead or behind budget? The amounts may be a real guessing game your first year, but it is a learning tool. The amounts for the second year will be more accurate if based on your first year's final totals.

Exhibit 6.1. Monthly Expense Worksheet and Record

Account	Budget	Jan.	Feb.	Mar.	April	May	June	July	Aug.	Sept.	Oct.	Nov.	Dec.	Total
Accounting, banking, legal fees														
Advertising and marketing														
Automobile expenses														
Books and resources														
Clerical support														
Copying and printing														
Donations														
Dues and subscriptions														
Entertainment														
Equipment leases														
Insurance														
Interest and loans														
Licenses														
Meals														
Office supplies														
Pension plan														
Postage														
Professional development														
Professional fees														
Rent														
Repairs and maintenance														
Salaries														
Seminar expenses														
Taxes														
Telephone														
Travel														
Utilities														
Total														

> **Tip: Accounting software.**
>
> If you have not selected your accounting software, speak with your accountant first. Life will be easier if your software is compatible with your accountant's software and if your accountant is familiar with the package you choose. Commonly used accounting software used by small businesses includes QuickBooks Pro, Freshbooks, FreeAgent, or Zoho Books. These packages are reasonably priced. If you are not familiar with accounting software, have your accountant help you select and set it up so that you will be able to manipulate the data to produce the most useful reports for you.

By the way, the accounting software you choose should produce most of the forms I've shared with you in this book. My examples are simply samples of the kind of information you will want to use to keep you informed about your business.

TRACK YOUR EXPENSES

Where is all the money going? If you are not good at handling the details of book-keeping, find someone else to do it for you. Although you are a consultant, you must also consider yourself a business owner. Tracking every expense is imperative. You may be lax about requesting and saving all those $4 parking receipts when you visit the library each week. Indeed, $4 does not seem like much. However, if you visit that library once or twice a week for resources, your parking receipts could easily add up to $200 worth of expenses. If your total state and federal tax bracket is 40 percent, you've just thrown away $80!

Now think about how many other things you might "forget" to record, such as tolls, business-related books or magazines, client gifts, mileage, seminar supplies you purchase on-site, office supplies you pick up on the weekend, light bulbs, cleaning supplies, or paper products you bring into the office from home.

What's the solution? Develop an easy way to gather and track expenses. For example, our consultants use envelopes for tracking expenses and for filing receipts. The 9×12-inch envelopes identify the consultant, the client, the date, and a list of the expenses. We had a printer print several thousand for a very reasonable cost. They serve several purposes: They provide a place to put the receipts while we are collecting them; they provide a method for tracking expenses by client, even if we are in the same city for two separate clients; and they are neatly stored by project for easy retrieval at a later date if necessary. Even if you use a mobile app such as Expensify to snap an image and upload it to your accounting system, the envelope is convenient to store the receipts in until you have a chance to file them electronically. In addition, I use the same envelope system to store office supply or repair receipts for the month.

In Chapter Four I listed items that might be in your monthly budget. These same budget line items are your expenses. You will want to track them for two reasons.

First, you will want to study them. Your expense record will provide the most information about your financial situation. It will tell you where you might cut back if you need to save, what you can expect in upcoming cash flow, and what you could prepay if you show too large a profit at the end of the year. (Perhaps the last item is surprising after the discussion about tight cash flow. You should assume that you will be so successful that you will face that problem in a year or two!)

Second you will want to track your expenses to ensure that you can easily compile your records prior to filing your taxes. You will want to claim as many legitimate deductions as possible because it reduces your tax bill. Poor record keeping takes cash out of your pocket.

---

*Poor record keeping takes cash
out of your pocket.*

The monthly expense record in Exhibit 6.1 will be valuable for tracking your monthly expenses. The following categories identify where your money will go.

Accounting, Legal, and Banking Fees. Find an accountant as one of your first tasks. Good accountants will save you five times what they cost. There is no way (unless you are an accounting consultant) that you can keep up with all the tax law changes. For example, whenever new retirement plans are offered or changed, my accountant informs me and helps me decide whether I should maintain the plan I have for me and my employees or switch to a new one. You will have few legal fees beyond your initial incorporation, but you will likely have some minor monthly banking charges.

Advertising and Marketing. Initially, you will have the expense of creating a website and printing a brochure or introductory piece to let people know who you are and what your capabilities are. I started out with a simple one-page introduction printed on good-quality stationery. I never have completed a mailing of our corporate brochure, but it is useful as an introduction piece or as something to leave when I visit a potential client. Expenses here may include a special announcement mailing, books or articles you purchase to send to clients or potential clients, or marketing firm expenses you may incur.

Automobile Expenses. Establish a good tracking system for your automobile expenses. If you use the same vehicle for personal and business use, you will most likely track mileage only. Review the apps that are available to determine how easy they are to use, their accuracy, and their cost. You probably wouldn't think about a bookkeeping system tracking your mileage, but it can! QuickBooks Self-Employed will track and categorize each trip as business or personal. Since we use Quick-Books, this is our choice, and it's quite comprehensive. At the end of the year it will also automatically compare your business miles with other actual automobile expenses and recommend which deduction is greater. It does have a cost—$10 per month. If you want a free app that tracks mileage and logs your expense receipts, try MileIQ or Hurdlr. Compare them and check into the details for reports you can export or share, how the trips can be categorized, and tax summaries. Both have a premium version that does much more for a small subscription fee.

If your time is limited and you need a fast tracking system now, download Exhibit 6.2, where you can track date, destination, purpose, beginning and ending odometer readings, and total mileage. Remember, you cannot deduct mileage going to and from your office. Your accountant will assist you with the nuances of mileage.

Books and Resources. Keep up on the latest books in your field. A good library is a real time saver when it comes to developing new materials or writing proposals.

Copying and Printing. If you do not purchase or lease your own copy machine, build a good relationship with the employees of your local copy center. There will be days when you will need a rush job!

Donations. Your business may make monetary or equipment donations to local charities. We donated a lettering machine to our local Head Start and old computers and software to the Salvation Army and a nursery school. Both were in good condition, but we had outgrown their use.

| **Tip: Purge first.**
| Be sure to purge any confidential or sensitive information from your computers before donating them to charity or giving them to anyone.

Dues and Subscriptions. Dues to professional organizations and subscriptions to professional journals and newspapers, online or physical, are tax deductible.

Entertainment. Although you can only deduct 50 percent of the expense incurred when you take a client to dinner, you must still track it and maintain receipts. Track the full amount. Your accountant will take care of the reduction.

Exhibit 6.2. Mileage Log

Name: _____   From: _____   To: _____

| Date | Destination | Odometer | | Business Purpose | Number of Miles |
		Begin	End		
				Total Miles This Sheet	

Equipment and Furniture Purchases. You may think these are only one-time purchases, but you may upgrade computers or need a new desk sooner than you think. Depending on the amount you purchase or on your financial situation at the end of the year, your accountant may suggest that you depreciate larger purchases over several years to capture the greatest tax advantage.

Equipment and Furniture Leases. Be sure to check the advantages of leasing against purchasing. Sometimes it's just a matter of preference, but there also may be savings with one or the other.

Insurance. This is a broad category and may include fleet insurance if you own a company vehicle, fire and theft if you rent or own an office, group health if you have employees, business liability insurance, disability insurance, and a number of others. See the sidebar for more information. Again, your accountant is the best source for determining which would be better as business expenses and which would be better as personal expenses. For example, my company has group health insurance for all employees. If you are self-employed in the United States, you are (this year) eligible to deduct these premiums and qualifying long-term-care insurance coverage.

Insurance and the Rational

From day one, a consultant is exposed to risks, and in most countries you cannot operate a business without certain kinds of insurance protection. You need to be prepared for problems that you do not want to happen—but if they do, you'll have a backup. That's why it's important to make time to plan for your insurance needs. Your accountant can probably help you with the basics, but you may also want to consult an insurance broker with more detailed questions. You might consider these types of insurance:

- *Professional liability.* Also known as errors and omissions (E&O) insurance, this covers a business against negligence claims from mistakes or failure to perform.
- *Owner's disability.* You are the primary force of your business, as well as the bankroll. Disability is coverage when you get sidelined due to an accident or a medical problem such as heart disease, back problems, or cancer.

- *Commercial property.* Covering equipment, inventory, and furniture in leased or owned office space is protection in the event of a fire, storm, or theft. Note that mass-destruction events like floods and earthquakes are generally not covered under a standard policy.
- *Workers' compensation.* Once you hire your first employee, you must purchase workers' compensation insurance. It covers medical treatment, disability, and death benefits if an employee is injured or dies as a result of work. Workers' comp is very inexpensive for consultants.
- *Home-based businesses.* Your homeowner's policy may not provide coverage the way commercial property insurance does. You may be able to ask for additional coverage.
- *Commercial auto insurance.* If company vehicles will be used, they should be fully insured to protect your business against liability if an accident should occur. Even if you use your own vehicle, many of your clients will require you to have a floor limit of at least $1 million per occurrence.
- *Business interruption.* More critical for businesses that require a physical location to do business, such as a retail store, it compensates a business for its loss of income during disasters or catastrophic events.

Having the right insurance in place prevents financial loss due to a lawsuit or catastrophic event. In the end, it is much better to be safe than sorry.

Interest and Loans. You may have taken out a loan to start your business. The interest is tax deductible. Although the principle is not deductible, it will still appear as an expense, affecting your cash flow. By the way, even if you loaned yourself the money to start your business, you should track it and pay it back.

Licenses. Check into state or city licenses that are required to do business in your city. There is usually a small annual fee.

Meals. Local meals are tax deductible when they are business-related only. In addition, keep all receipts for food when you travel. Again, as with the entertainment category, only 50 percent of the actual cost is tax deductible. Your accountant will assist you with this process at tax time. Keep your receipts.

Office Supplies. This category includes things such as paper supplies, ink cartridges for your printer, rubber bands, pens, paper towels, glass cleaner (to clean your copier's glass), floor mats, light bulbs, and anything else that it takes to keep an office operating. Track these carefully.

Pension Plan. Excellent plans exist for small businesses. Check into them soon, even if you don't think you can afford it. Your accountant may demonstrate to you that you can't afford *not* to invest in a plan.

Plan for Retirement

I am a big proponent of aggressively using tax-advantaged retirement plans such as a 401(k) or SEP IRA. The SEP IRA may be one of the best options for consultants and other freelancers who want to save for retirement. The SEP IRA is a plan that receives special tax treatment from the U.S. government. At this writing, the biggest advantage is that the limit you can save is set higher than most plans—the lesser of 25 percent of your compensation or $53,000. This is about 10 times the amount in a traditional IRA or Roth IRA. This is particularly good for consultants, whose income may sway radically from one year to the next. In addition, these plans are available to almost anyone making money at a side hustle.

Count on your accountant to guide you to the right plan.

Postage. This is, of course, the cost of sending proposals, marketing materials, books, and other correspondence using the postal service or private carriers.

Professional Development. Stay current with the changes in your field. This category includes the costs for conferences, training, or local professional meetings you may attend.

Professional Fees. This category is for subcontractors you may hire to assist you with larger projects. You might hire a consultant or a freelance designer to support you.

Rent. Track your office rent expense in this category.

Repairs and Maintenance. Often these expenses are included in an office lease. However, you may need to hire your own cleaning firm. In addition, if you own your computers, copier, and other equipment, their repairs will be tracked in this category. If you drive over your iPhone, you'd record the cost to repair it here.

Salaries. Pay yourself first. You've heard that advice before. This category also includes anyone else you have hired, such as your secretary, receptionist, assistant, or professionals who are on your payroll.

Seminar Expense. You may need to purchase a video to use during a training session. You may require some materials that you use in your sessions. For example, I use crayons, Play-Doh®, clay, jump ropes, and other toys in my creativity sessions. Sometimes it is easier to purchase these on-site than to ship them. I also purchase in bulk to save money.

Taxes. This category may include local business taxes, personal property taxes, unemployment taxes, self-employment taxes, FICA, and other payroll taxes. You may have several subcategories here.

Tax Talk

You will select your own fiscal year. To make it easy, I selected the calendar year. If you have specific reasons to choose differently, just let your accountant know.

Most consultants will pay quarterly taxes based on their estimated amount. Your accountant will determine the amount based on your previous year's income. You generally have to make the payment if you expect to owe taxes of $1,000 or more.

The Internal Revenue Service has established four due dates for paying estimated taxes. Typically, the due date is the fifteenth of the month in which they are due. If the fifteenth falls on a weekend or a federal holiday, the due date is moved to the following business day. A payment not postmarked on or before the due date will be considered late. You will likely be penalized.

Estimated tax due for income received:

• January 1 through March 30	is due April 15.
• April 1 through June 30	is due July 15.
• July 1 through September 30	is due October 15.
• October 1 through December 31	is due January 15.

Telephone/Internet. Telephone calls, fax transmissions, and your email expenses are listed here.

Travel. Travel expenses include taxi fares, Ubers, airfares, hotel rooms, shuttle buses, parking, tips, and other costs incurred as a result of getting to and staying at a site to conduct business. The expense report in Exhibit 6.3 will help you to track travel and other out-of-pocket expenses you incur throughout the month. When you or an employee turns the report in at the end of the month, it can also be used to compile all that is due for the month.

Utilities. Electricity, water, heat, or air conditioning may be included in your office rent. If you are working out of your home, your accountant will assist you to determine what percentage of the total you can consider a business expense.

Breaking expenses into categories like this creates a system that makes it easy for you to track expenses, manage cash flow, and predict revenue needed for next month as well as next year. In addition, the structure will pay dividends in time saved when preparing your tax statement.

Savings and Your Business

Although a business savings account is not an expense, you should plan to sock away 30 percent of your revenue in a business savings account. A portion of that will pay for your taxes and the rest for the proverbial rainy day. What could go wrong? A client could cancel a big project a month before it is to start, which is probably too late to land a new project. You may need to replace computers or your copier during a month that is already soft. You may have a delayed payment from a client. Or perhaps several of these things happen at the same time. Yes, hopefully you requested a line of credit, but don't dip into it unless you really must.

In the end, it is not what you make, but what you keep. Watch your expenses!

SET ASIDE PETTY CASH

If you find yourself digging into your own pocket to pay for postage or other small purchases during the month, you may wish to create a petty cash fund. Having cash on hand eliminates the need for you to record every little expense for reimbursement. To establish the fund, write a check out to petty cash. Keep the money in a safe place separate from your personal money. The form in Exhibit 6.4 provides an easy way to track these expenditures.

Exhibit 6.3. Time Sheet and Expense Report

Name: _____ Work Period: _____

Date	Activity	Mileage			Other Travel Expenses*			Employee Tax Record
		Specify	Miles	@.55	Travel	Lodging	Meals	Gross =
								– State Tax
								– Federal Tax
								– SS Tax
								+ Expenses
								– Deductions
								Net =

Miscellaneous*

Specify	Amount

Totals

Signature: _____ Date: _____ *Attach Receipts in Expense Envelope Expense Total: _____

Exhibit 6.4. Petty Cash Record

PETTY CASH   From: _____ To: _____

Date	Paid to Whom	Expense Account Debited	Deposit	Amount of Expense	Balance
	Balance Forward ———————————————————————→				

CHARGE YOUR CLIENT

In general, consultants are not very confident about what we charge our clients. Perhaps this is due to the many jokes and cartoons referencing consultants and their fees. I remember how difficult it was to state my fee when I first raised it to $1,000. "I charge one th-th-th-thousand dollars a day," I would stutter. Certainly the exercise in Chapter Three showing how easily a $2,000 daily charge can accumulate should allow you to feel more confident. Although it is important that *we* know that our prices are fair and value-filled, it is even more important that *our clients* be satisfied that they receive value for their investment.

If consultants have difficulty in stating fees, we have even more difficulty in ensuring that our clients know what we did for them. Granted, much of our work can be elusive, intangible, and invisible, but that does not mean that it is not valuable. Keep your work in front of your clients—not bragging, but informing. Try these suggestions:

- Itemize your invoice to include specific results and accomplishments.
- Itemize things you did without charge and specify the amount as $0.00. We often list books we have provided at no extra charge or an unscheduled, impromptu meeting.
- Submit your invoice in person, discussing what it covers.
- When on-site, save the end of your day to update your client about recent activities and their results.
- Submit a brief ongoing status report if visits are not practical.
- When your client requests something special, follow up personally with the results.
- Keep the client informed of what is happening behind the scenes. What should the client expect to see or hear?
- Make a phone call during extended time periods when you are not on-site to stay in the loop and to show that you care.
- Send books or articles. We all read something and think that it is perfect reading for a particular client. Make it possible by sending it!

The Cost of Doing Business

Each of these ideas ensures that you keep your client informed of the value you are adding to the organization.

Keep your client informed of the value
you are adding to the organization.

Invoices

As mentioned previously in this chapter, issuing invoices should be one of your top priorities. They should be submitted as soon as the project has ended. If the project's duration is greater than 30 days, bill monthly or every two weeks for deliverables you have completed, plus the expenses incurred. This is best for you and for your client. You prevent cash-flow problems, and your client will find it easier to pay several small invoices than one large one after four months. The invoicing summary in Exhibit 6.5 provides an easy method to track the date you invoiced the client, what services you invoiced for, and the date the client's payment was received.

Your invoice should provide all the information necessary for a client to quickly approve payment. Include these items:

- Your corporate name, address, and telephone number. (During start-up, use your stationery rather than have actual invoices printed.)
- A numbering system for tracking invoices.
- The billing date.
- The address and the name of the person to whom the invoice is sent.
- An itemized list of the tasks completed, dates, and hours, if appropriate.
- The name of the person completing the tasks.
- An itemized list of the expenses incurred.
- Total of the entire invoice.
- Terms of the invoice, such as due date and consequences of late payments.
- Your Federal ID number
- The name of the person to whom questions may be addressed (optional).

Tip: Customize your invoice.

Your accounting software should have an invoice format; however, I recommend that you adjust it to meet your needs and to have a more professional look. Check to see whether you can add your logo. Once you have an invoice format that meets your needs, save the template on your computer to make it easier to invoice each time.

Exhibit 6.5. Invoice Summary

Work Date	Organization	Consultant	Invoice Number	Billed	Paid	Facilitator Fee	Materials Fee	Expenses	Total Due
Total									

In addition to the invoice, attach copies of receipts incurred as expenses—for example, a hotel bill, meal receipt, or copy-center invoice. Although your client may not require these receipts, I believe it builds trust and is a good practice. Exhibit 6.6 is a simple yet complete invoice format.

Exhibit 6.6. Invoice

INVOICE
100-000111-2025

TO: Mr. Dale Woodward
Gilbert Manufacturing
333 Ridge Road
Anywhere, NY 10000

Invoice Date: January 24, 20XX

For: "Talent Management Applied: Learning from Our Experience" for Gilbert Manufacturing on January 23, 20XX.
Elizabeth Drake, Facilitator
    Facilitator Fee ....$ 4,000.00

EXPENSES: Mileage Round Trip to Airport:
      80 miles @$.50 per mile $40.00
Airfare $710.00
Airport parking $30.00
Lodging................................... $190.00
Books $0.00
    Expense Total $970.00

Amount Due: $4,970.00

Terms: Due upon receipt

Payable to: ebb associates inc
Box 8249
Norfolk, VA 23503
Federal ID# 33-5333XXX

1.5 percent late fee charged per month for accounts due over 30 days

---

The Clients' Expenses

For what expenses can you expect the client to be responsible? In almost all cases, the client will reimburse all travel expenses incurred when you are away from home: airfare, taxis, mileage to and from the airport, parking, reasonable lodging, meals, and tips. If you have agreed to it, a client may also cover material costs, audiovisual equipment and supplies (for example, LCD or video rental), seminar supplies, room rental, or refreshments. Depending on the industry you serve and your pricing structure, your client may also reimburse you for telephone expenses, overnight mail, computer time, or computer program development. We consider telephone calls and express shipping a cost of doing business and include them as a part of our overhead.

Do not expect a client to cover laundry, dry cleaning, liquor, upgraded hotel rooms, entertainment, or unrelated phone calls when you travel. Local travel and meals are not reimbursable. Postage is not generally reimbursed, unless you have a large mailing to send as a part of the contract.

In any event, all reimbursables should be clearly spelled out at the beginning of any contract.

PROJECT REVENUES

Equally as important as tracking expenses is projecting revenue. We project revenue by the month. This works for us because we have been able to adjust our accounting processes so that we pay bills only once each month. You may wish to track revenue weekly, especially if cash flow is a concern. The revenue projection form in Exhibit 6.7 can be transferred to a spreadsheet so that you can keep a running total by month as well as by organization.

DEAL WITH BAD DEBTS

Bad debts occur when your clients do not pay you for the services provided. They occur infrequently in the consulting business, but when they do, they can be devastating to a small business. Although we have never experienced a bad debt, professional firms may experience bad debt rates from 5 to 30 percent.

If this should occur, you may use a collection agency to assist you. In some cases, you may choose to take the matter to your local small claims court. They are generally well informed and very helpful.

Exhibit 6.7. Revenue Projections

Organization and Project	Jan.	Feb.	March	April	May	June	July	Aug.	Sept.	Oct.	Nov.	Dec.	Total
Total Revenue													

KEEP AN EYE ON YOUR NUMBERS

Although you are a consultant, you should never forget that you are running a business. Businesses exist to make a profit. The numbers will spell profit or loss for your business. You must establish processes for gathering the numbers and then keep an eye on them. As a good business owner, you will want to know where you stand financially at any given time, which means that you must read the numbers, compare them, and play with them. Read them and know what they mean. Increases? Decreases? Compare them to the last project, last month, last year. Are they better? Worse? And finally, play with them. What if you invested in a new computer system? Prepaid bills before the end of the year?

Never forget that you are running a business.

What specifically can you look for when you are studying your numbers?

Expenses

Certainly you should compare your actual expenditures with your budget. Are you over? Under? Both are worthy of investigation. If the actual is over the budget, look at the detailed report. What pushed you over the limit? Is it likely to occur again? Should you adjust your budget to account for the difference? What about being under budget? That's good, so don't worry—right? Wrong! If you have budgeted for something and the money wasn't spent, you need to examine this as well. Perhaps a marketing mailing you budgeted for was not done. This may affect income several months down the road.

Businesses exist to make a profit.

It could be worse. Once I discovered an extra $600 in the budget. First I felt smug; then I became curious. When I finally discovered what had caused the difference, I panicked. The fire insurance on our new office building had not been paid! Remember, being under budget can be as bad as being over budget.

Value

Compare some of your expenses to the time invested to determine whether the value warrants the expense. For example, you have hired two associates to help you deliver services. Your receptionist is stretched, but you cannot justify hiring a bookkeeper. So now you find yourself doing the payroll every other week. Check into the payroll services that abound. They do it all: figure salaries, compute the taxes, write the checks, deposit the taxes, and provide monthly as well as year-end reports and W-2s. And they do it for a reasonable fee. Consider the time you are investing in payroll or any other administrative task. Is it the best use of your time? Is this where you should invest your value?

Growth

You will certainly be comparing income to expenses, but you should also watch the overall growth trend. Is the number of projects increasing? Is your gross income growing proportionately? Are expenses growing at the same, greater, or lesser rate? You might think that growth is always desired. That isn't so. It is not desired if you have overscheduled yourself. It is not desired if you have decided not to hire employees. It is not desired if the projects are less profitable. And it certainly is not desired if you are working harder and enjoying it less.

Seven years into my business I wrote a letter to Peter Block, the guru of all consultants. He had published *Flawless Consulting* a few years before that. This is what I wrote:

> Dear Peter,
>
> For the past year I have been working harder but making less money. I have searched the library for a book, an article—anything that will provide me with a benchmark against which to compare my business. I want to know what the average consulting firm spends on marketing. How can I determine how much my employees should be billing? What is considered a good profit margin in "the business of consulting"? I will call you next week to find out whether you can recommend a book.
>
> Thank you.
>
> Elaine

Peter Block read my note. When I called him, he said, "I'm going to do much more than recommend a book. I want you to pull all your records together, such as your expenses for this year, your taxes from last year, your income summaries for the past three years, and your projected cash flow and income for the next year. After you have everything together, call me back. Plan to talk to me for two hours! And by the way, there isn't a book to read about this stuff!"

I couldn't believe my ears! Peter Block was going to consult with me on my consulting business! We had a great conversation. He provided me with sound business advice—you might say it was "flawless consulting"!

Peter's advice encouraged me to examine marketing dollars wisely, study business numbers and data carefully, and explore the advantages and disadvantages of hiring employees and forming partnerships. And the fact that there wasn't a book—well, that was a downright shame! It was also what prompted me to write the first edition of *The Business of Consulting* in 1999.

All of the topics in this book—especially this chapter—are written in the same spirit—sound advice and practical suggestions for *your* business of consulting. My phone call with Peter resulted in developing several forms to monitor my business.

Exhibit 6.8 is a form for you to track the time and materials used on individual projects. If you want to record and compare the profitability of various projects, you will find Exhibit 6.9 at www.wiley.com/go/newconsultingbiech, entitled Program Development Cost versus Revenue. It can assist you in determining which projects are the most profitable and can help you with bidding on new projects. It may also signal that it is time to fire a low-profit-margin client!

Certainly, growth can be exactly what you desire and what you have planned for. Given that, there is still one more thing to watch for. Fast growth can lead to cash-flow issues. You may need to invest in new projects up front that are not in your budget. Check the cash-flow suggestions earlier in this chapter and keep an eye on the numbers.

Consider Capital Investments

You are running a business. That means that you have capital investments, and with that goes responsibility. If you own equipment, put each item on a preventive maintenance schedule. Clean phones, computers, copiers, printers, and other equipment regularly. You will benefit in the long run. Equipment will last longer and it will not break down just when you need it to complete the last-minute details of a program you will conduct the next day!

Your library is a capital investment that can easily walk out the door without your vigilance. We have a complete library that can easily compete with any area library in the training, business, consulting, leadership, talent management, creativity, and communication categories. Many of our local clients and other consultants, as well as employees, borrow volumes from it. Although we want to share the resources, a Library Sign-Out Sheet allows us to do so without worrying about unreturned books. Exhibit 6.10, which you can find at www.wiley.com/go/newconsultingbiech, is a copy of that form.

This chapter should have driven home the importance of tracking and monitoring your income and expenses. You could be the best consultant in the world, but if you do not make money, you will not remain in business, and the world will never know about your consulting expertise.

Exhibit 6.8. Project Time and Expense Record

Date	Team Member	Task Performed or Materials Used	Hours or Expense	Salary or Cost

For the Consummate Consultant

Yes, there is a cost to doing business, and it requires your eagle eye to ensure that the cost doesn't outpace the revenue. Never fear, with the right tools in your toolbox you will build a solid foundation and use them to track your success.

Don't Mingle Your Money. Commingling personal and business accounts can cause problems downstream. Don't even think about it! Creating the right accounts and structure for your business from the outset can help prevent future financial missteps and headaches.

Repeat Business Is Good. Aim to bill 50 to 75 percent of your annual revenue from the previous year's clients. Experts estimate it takes 7 to 10 times the investment to sell to new clients. You don't want to be dependent on one or two large clients, but you still want to balance enough repeat business so that you are not constantly on a client hustle.

Study Your Numbers—Religiously. Other than billing your clients as early as possible, tracking your numbers every week at a specific time is the best activity to keep you in business. Know your numbers to:

- Predict cash flow concerns well in advance.
- Stay on top of your marketing plan to keep your pipeline full.
- Forecast big-ticket purchases.
- Prevent excess spending.
- Know what you need to earn each month and how much money you owe now.
- Track when money is due to you.
- Discern which projects have been the most profitable and why.

Your numbers will predict much of what you need to know—including whether you are fizzling out on the job.

7

Building a Client Relationship

Hold yourself responsible for a higher standard than anybody expects of you. Never excuse yourself.

Henry Ward Beecher

Eliana could feel the perspiration trickle down her back. Wow, this was one long sales call! She'd been meeting with the CEO, Nicholas Marino, and his senior level staff for almost 90 minutes now. She had been fielding questions for the last hour. She wasn't sure whether she should be feeling good about the questions or not. This was a big project: It would last about nine months. She was excited, because she was certain she knew how to take the company from where it was to where it needed to be.

She had a fleeting thought about all the preparation she'd done for this meeting. Did she do enough? She reviewed her mental checklist: confirmed she understood the RFP, met with the COO to identify his thoughts about measurable outcomes, spoke with the talent development director to review the engagement study results, and analyzed the evaluations of the project she'd completed with the company the previous year. Had she missed something?

Maybe they didn't like how strongly she declared the commitment that would be necessary? Maybe she shouldn't have been so adamant that their culture would not support the intensity the plan required? Maybe she should have used their names more often? Maybe she had scoped the effort wrong? Ah! She could reframe the plan with less emphasis on operations. "So what you'd like me to do, Mr. Marino, is to . . ." Eliana started.

"Nick, Eliana, please call me Nick," he interrupted. "We've been working together for almost two years. This project is important to the company, right, everyone?" He looked around as all the team members smiled and nodded their heads. "Our competition is snapping at our heels and we need to increase our agility—our ability to get in step with our customers' needs faster—much faster."

He went on, "I think your response to the RFP and your clarifications today about our concerns have been spot on. You know us well and you should be challenging us the way you have. We need to support this effort and we need someone like you to hold our feet to the fire!"

"Thank you for that. I do know a great deal about your company and its personalities!" She smiled as everyone around the table chuckled. "So as I surmise from your questions, you would like me to . . ."

"Stop right there, Eliana. I like your plan. I think we all like what you proposed. The concern that I have is that you haven't priced this properly," he stated. Eliana started to sputter, saying that she thought she'd given them a great deal.

"Now, wait a minute, Eliana, let me finish. I wanted to say that I think that you have underpriced this project. We will gain great value when this project is completed. I think I speak for the team when I say that your projections are achievable and they will make a difference—a huge difference. But to do that, I'd like to increase the number of interviews you've suggested; we need to tap into your expertise more, and everyone in the company should have more access to you throughout the process. What you are offering ensures that we will maintain our competitive edge and will grow our customer base. We're all in and you're the right person to take on this challenge. So if you are all in, too, I'd suggest that you increase your fee. The value to us far outweighs the price tag you've offered. Are you with me?"

All Eliana could do was grin and nod.

■ ■ ■

You started your business to serve clients. Serve them well! This can only happen if you are continually aware of building the relationship you have with each of your clients. That's apparently what happened to Eliana. She had been successful with her past projects. She had built a relationship with her client. And she had delivered value above and beyond what was expected. Before you think that this is just a fairy tale, I need to tell you that something very similar to this happened to me.

You started your business to serve clients.

Your initial contact with a new client is more important than you can imagine. Your comfort with one another and your ability to communicate clearly and candidly are critical to start on the right foot.

RELATIONSHIPS: IT'S WHY YOU'RE IN BUSINESS

The success of your interactions and the results of your project will establish and build your relationship and help you to maintain a client for a long time. There is an interesting phenomenon that the longer you have clients, the longer they will continue to be clients. Now mind you, this is not about building a client's reliance on you. It is about a client who thinks of you whenever a new project comes up. With the frequent changes that businesses go through today, that can be often.

In these relationships, you become too valuable to lose. Your reputation for getting results, your knowledge of the organization, your rapport with key managers, and your experience with the political and operational factors of the organization cannot be replaced—at any cost.

Why would you want to encourage repeat business? Here are a few good reasons:

1. Repeat business means you will not need to expend time marketing your services. The client knows you—knows your capabilities and how you might help. Also, because you know the client, there will be less lag time between the time the client hires you and the time you begin the project.
2. The client will call you regularly to assist in many different situations. Each will build on past projects, and you will continue to increase in value. We are frequently referred from department to department or from division to division.

3. You will have a leg up against your competition. You have already built a relationship with the client. The trust you have built will count heavily on your side when the need for a competitive process arises.

4. You will not lose clients during difficult economic times. In fact, your expertise may be readily called on to help them through.

5. You will develop a valuable marketing vehicle. A client's referral is the most potent marketing tool you can have. If your project is successful and you have built solid relationships, your clients will refer you to others. Our clients market us to other organizations. This happens because we pay attention both to doing the job with quality results and to building the relationship. I am firmly convinced that without the effort we put into building the relationship, this marketing by our clients would not occur.

Are there times when repeat business is not valuable? Sure. Check the sidebar for reasons.

Reasons to Reject Repeat Work

Repeat business has so many advantages. Are there ever times that repeat business could be detrimental to your consulting business? Yes. Repeat business can be a disadvantage if:

- The work produces no profit and the client doesn't have the ability to increase payments from your current fees.
- You can't price the engagement in a way that makes money.
- The client hasn't implemented your previous recommendations and you believe that the requested work is dependent on them.
- You don't like the type of work you receive from the client.
- The client is in an industry that is outside the niche you have defined for your consulting work.
- You are trying to diversify your client base and believe that is more important than repeat business.
- The location is inconvenient.
- Something has changed; perhaps the client's reputation has been tarnished and you no longer want to be associated with the brand.
- You have changed your consulting focus and need to spend your time learning new content, processes, or techniques.

So how can you get to a point at which your clients market you? First, you must identify the project and how you can add value; your first meeting will most likely determine that. Next, you must build the relationship. Every interaction, every product, and every result will make a difference. Finally, you must maintain the relationship. The project ends, not the relationship. Your sincere follow-up will maintain the relationship.

The project ends,
not the relationship.

THE FIRST MEETING

Your initial meeting is critical. It sets a tone for the rest of the relationship, which is why it is important to be yourself in this meeting. Many consultants come prepared for their initial introduction with a "dog and pony show"—a slick PowerPoint® presentation, materials in a bound folder, and a precisely worded presentation. If that's your style and it works for you, continue doing it. We try to create a conversation with the client; that's our style. It's natural, and it sets the tone for the rest of the relationship. How do we fare? We are regularly pitted against the top consulting firms in the United States—many of those listed in Chapter One. We are awarded the work a much higher percent of the time than not. Be yourself. If you land the project, it will be difficult to continue the charade you used to get it.

The skills you need for this first meeting read like an Interpersonal Skills 101 class:

- Read the client to determine whether to make small talk first or to get right down to business. Conversation based on the client's communication style will lay a foundation for the rest of the discussion. Consider each person in the meeting. An analytical style will want data and proof. A creative style will want to hear all your ideas. A controlling style will expect a fast-paced, logical approach. And a collaborative style will expect to hear how the collective team will fit in.
- Listen for understanding, especially to determine the critical points. Sometimes clients will not be clear about what they want. Read between the lines and interpret meaning or structure the content to make sense of

the situation. Remember that every statement has at least two messages: the content and the intent.

- Ask pertinent and thought-provoking questions. Before you attend the meeting, develop three to 10 questions based on what you know about the situation. Three well-thought-out questions will usually start a discussion. You will probably not have time to ask 10 questions, and if you have more than 10, it will be difficult to prioritize while you're trying to focus.
- Put others at ease by remembering and using their names, by showing interest in their needs, and by balancing the discussion appropriately in a group. Ask for a list of attendees and their positions before your first meeting. Study the names before the meeting. After you are introduced, subtly make a seating chart as a reference. Then use people's names throughout the meeting.
- Exude self-confidence without arrogance. You will display your self-confidence with your body language as much as anything, so use good eye contact, a pleasant demeanor, and confident posture. The client will want to know about your past experience. Providing examples or relating similar situations should be a natural part of the discussion. Take care to avoid bragging, giving too much detail, or sounding as if you have rehearsed a rote speech.
- Project a professional image. First impressions count. A firm handshake, appropriate attire, and genuine interest in the client and the organization you are visiting will help you make a great first impression.

Your personality, not your expertise, will land most contracts. That may disappoint you, but it is the truth. Sure, you must have the basic skills in place, but that's a given. Your wit, charm, sincerity, professionalism, and interpersonal skills will be the deciding factor at this stage.

Your personality, not your expertise,
will land most contracts.

A quick measure of how you're doing can be determined by how much you are talking. If the clients are doing the majority of the talking, it's a sign that they feel comfortable with you and that you are asking appropriate questions. If you are doing more talking, more selling than listening, your chances of successfully landing this contract are decreasing.

The Importance of Listening: An Exaggerated Case

I'd flown from Wisconsin to Virginia to meet a potential client. I'd just started my consulting business and didn't even think to ask for reimbursement for travel. This client had the name recognition that I needed and a project that was a piece of cake for me. I knew I could do this.

I met Bill in his office. He had scheduled a one-hour meeting with me. As I sat down I sensed that he wanted to get to know me better, so we started off with some small talk. The more questions I asked, the more he talked. I tried to guide the discussion to the project and why I was there, but Bill continued to talk about his situation. I heard about his kids. I learned that he really wanted to be a college professor. And I heard about his back problems.

The hour passed quickly. As he looked at his watch he said, "Oops! I'm late for a meeting. Gotta go." I dropped the proposal and a brochure on his desk, shook hands, and said it was great to meet him.

All the way back on the flight home I berated myself. I was never really very good at closing a sale. And now I couldn't even open this one! What a waste of time and money.

A week passed and I was still upset with myself. Then I received a phone call from someone I knew inside the corporation who asked me, "What did you do to Bill?"

"Why?" I asked warily.

My friend said, "Bill says you are going to design a corporate communications class for us, teach our sales force some new tactics, and coach our senior executives. I've never seen him this excited about a consultant! Congratulations!" I hung up the phone in such shock that I don't remember thanking him for the information.

Was this a fluke? I think it was. Do I recommend that you conduct your sales calls like this? Absolutely not! This experience, however, does demonstrate the value of listening. If you are doing more than 50 percent of the talking, you have probably already lost the sale.

FOUR PHASES OF BUILDING A CLIENT-CONSULTANT PARTNERSHIP

The relationship you begin to establish during the first meeting lays the groundwork for a solid client-consultant partnership—in which both the client and the consultant are equal, contributing counterparts in an effort to accomplish a mutual goal.

Building a partnership with your client may be similar to building a friendship or a team. Let's explore building a client-consultant partnership in four phases: (1) finding the right match, (2) getting to know one another, (3) being productive, and (4) creating independence.

Phase I focuses on finding the right match and deciding whether you and the client can work together. When you are introduced to someone, you make decisions about whether you want to pursue a relationship. Even though you and your client may already be discussing the project, a final decision about how to move forward has not been made. I have been in this phase for as little as 10 minutes and as long as a couple of months.

Phase II focuses on getting to know one another. At this point a commitment exists to move the project to the next level. The relationship is moving forward as well. Both parties are learning everything they can about each other and how to work together effectively.

Phase III occurs when you and your client are productive. The project is in full swing. If you and your client have worked on the relationship, your partnership is in full swing as well.

Phase IV focuses on helping the client become independent. The project is coming to a close. By focusing on the client's independence, you ensure that the organization continues to be successful. Equally as important, you ensure that your relationship continues to be healthy.

Phase I: Finding the Right Match

During this phase, you will focus on two areas: obtaining information and setting expectations. Both lead to a final decision about whether to move forward with the project.

Getting Information. Prior to meeting someone of interest, you may ask questions and try to gather information about them. Prior to meeting a client, you may choose to obtain the best information available about the organization on the Internet. How? Ask people. Go to the client's website, visit the library. Check the industry journals. Obtain a copy of the client company's most recent annual report.

If you are meeting someone from an industry that is new to you, become familiar with the general industry jargon. Reading several industry journals will help.

This is also the time to define the scope of the effort. Your client may not be able to answer all questions at this time, but it is important that you clarify the scope as much as possible. You may find that the project is larger than you want to take on.

We've found it valuable to discuss past projects for which the client used consultants. Answers to simple questions such as, "What went well?" and "What would you do differently?" provide information about how the client likes to work.

Your client will be obtaining information from you, too. Be prepared to provide references, and encourage the client to call them. Speaking with your former clients gives a potential client confidence in your abilities. Last, discuss your consulting fee and how you invoice.

Setting Expectations. Establishing expectations between you and your client lays a solid foundation for the relationship. The process is often referred to as "contracting."

Contracting is the process by which you and your client identify, clarify, and agree on both of your needs, wants, and expectations. Contracting is critical in the first phase, because it is here that you and your client will begin to build your partnership, begin to clarify the project, and begin to understand and appreciate one another's principles, styles, and values.

In his best-selling classic *Flawless Consulting*, Peter Block (2011) explains contracting as the process to reach "an explicit agreement of what the consultant and client expect from each other and how they are going to work together." Your contracting discussion should explore and come to agreement on the following:

- Your role, the client's role, and how they are related.
- The project's time frame.
- The expected outcome of the project.
- The support, resources, and information you will need from the client.
- How this project fits into the larger organizational picture and the organization's vision.

As a result of this discussion, you should have a better idea of the client's ability to support the effort, some of the values that you share and where you differ, the client's vision for the project, the organization's support for the project, and your desire to complete the project.

In addition, you should have determined who your primary client is. The primary client is most often the individual who hired you for the project, but on a

Building a Client Relationship   **195**

few rare occasions it may be another department; human resources, for example, may actually bring you in and provide the budget for work you conduct in another department.

You will also have secondary clients and stakeholders. They are the individuals who are affected by your work, but are not directing it.

Exhibit 7.1 identifies a list of questions you can ask yourself. Use it in two ways: it was designed for you to evaluate your behavior after the contracting meeting and to use it before the meeting as a reminder of all the things you must remember during the meeting.

Exhibit 7.1. Contracting Checklist

Evaluate the contracting meeting with your client.

Did I:

		Yes	No
1.	Do my homework before the meeting?	☐	☐
2.	Determine the primary client?	☐	☐
3.	Determine the secondary clients and stakeholders?	☐	☐
4.	Define the scope of the effort?	☐	☐
5.	Elicit the clients' specific needs and expectations?	☐	☐
6.	Identify shared values and differences?	☐	☐
7.	Evaluate the clients' expertise and ability to support the effort?	☐	☐
8.	Discuss my rates and consulting approach?	☐	☐
9.	Clearly state my needs and expectations?	☐	☐
10.	Obtain a sense of client commitment to the effort?	☐	☐
11.	Provide references?	☐	☐

Asking Questions. Questions represent the means by which the client and consultant determine whether they have found the right match. Either you or the client may find the following questions helpful:

- What are your mission, vision, and guiding principles?
- How would you define your organization's culture and values?
- What values are most important to your organization?
- What value will this effort bring? By what percent do you expect (sales to increase, profits to increase, turnover to decrease, productivity to increase, or others)?
- How frequently will we measure progress? How will we do that?
- What questions do you have about how we conduct a front-end analysis?
- What logistics do we need to clarify (shared copyright, scheduling, reporting)?
- Has money been earmarked for this engagement?
- What would happen if we did nothing?
- Why now? What is unique about this timing?
- Who will make final decisions?

Additional questions you might ask to learn more about the organization include these:

- How do employees feel about my being brought into the organization?
- What's it like to work here?
- How will this organization be different as a result of this intervention?
- How will resources be made available (time, people, space)?

Phase II: Getting to Know One Another

When you build relationships with individuals, you spend time getting to know them. You can do the same thing with your clients. This phase is typically considered the data-collection step in consulting. It is natural that, as you build the relationship, you learn everything you can about the client. You learned things about the client in Phase I, but now you are on-site, asking questions, touring plants, observing meetings, interviewing employees, or eating in the corporate dining room.

As with a personal relationship, the more you know about the organization, the better you will understand its people, its problems, and its culture. Every time you interview key employees of the organization, you influence the relationship. You will be gaining information about the organization's attitudes, skills, and climate.

During this phase you have the opportunity to invest in the relationship by modeling appropriate skills. Every interaction is an opportunity to model good communication, teamwork, and high-quality work. The relationship benefits in two ways: you gain respect from the client and the client has an opportunity to observe your professional skills.

Tip: Create your gig onboarding.

As a consultant, you need a good onboarding. Although many companies are taking advantage of gig workers, they have not updated their onboarding processes. You can be a hero by outlining your ideal gig onboarding plan. Then share it with your client to be used with other gig workers.

Initial planning takes place during Phase II. You will provide an analysis of the situation, recommendations, and a plan for proceeding. You will reach consensus around the plan as well as on how to keep the client informed. Provide ample opportunity for milestone meetings, progress reports, and other communication that will keep the client informed of progress. Maintaining an open line of communication will continue to build the relationship. If you spend the time getting to know the people and the organization, you will begin to build a trusting relationship.

Phase III: Being Productive

Several books have been written about how to manage an external consultant. Chances are good that your client has not read any of these books and will be expecting you to manage the project and the relationship. During this implementation stage, you have the opportunity to continue to build the relationship through what you deliver and how you deliver your services.

What You Deliver. All clients I have worked with believe that they are special and that their business is unique. Perhaps that's human nature. Although you will find plenty of similarities from client to client, you must still study the situation with an open mind. Look for the differences. Those allow you to create customized solutions for the client more easily.

You will probably need to conduct one-on-one coaching sessions. Be honest and helpful. Building the relationship does not mean that you will agree with everything the individual does or says. In fact, once individuals reach a certain level, they rarely receive candid feedback from anyone within the organization. How many employees give feedback to the president?

Become an active member of the client's team. You can do more as a part of the team than by maintaining your separateness. Become involved. Be aware of the "magic wand" syndrome. Some clients may believe that you have arrived to "fix things." Permanent fixes only occur if you and the client work together in a partnership.

Things Will Go Wrong. You will uncover things you wish you had not. The unexpected will occur. In every instance, be honest, candid, and timely about issues, problems, and concerns. Don't be afraid to say, "It's not working." Keep the right person informed. Your honesty and candor will be respected by everyone.

While you're in the thick of implementation, it may be difficult to focus on the day when you will no longer be involved in the project. However, this is the ideal time to plan for the skills your client will need to ensure continued success. Your client will brag about you if you make this happen. That means you must attend to it now through coaching, mentoring, and development. Continually create ways that lead to the client's independence.

Communicate, Communicate, Communicate! Keep everyone informed. You will not be able to communicate too much. Guaranteed! Find many ways to keep employees informed, such as memos, email, posters, telephone trees, town hall meetings, presentations, Q&A sessions, and paycheck stuffers. Help your client develop a communication plan.

How You Deliver Services. As in any business, how you deliver your services is as important as the service you provide. Build your relationship with your client by providing superb service. As with any business, the eight commonly accepted elements of service that follow apply to your consulting practice:

1. *Time.* How much time are you spending on the project? Too little and your clients will wonder what they are paying for; too much and your clients will wonder if you have moved in! In addition, plan time to build the client relationship. It's a key element in delivering high-quality service.
2. *Timeliness.* Do you do what you say you are going to do when you say you will? Do you return their phone calls promptly?
3. *Completeness.* Do you do everything you say you will? Do you do everything you should do? Always?

4. *Courtesy.* Do you treat everyone in your client's firm respectfully, politely, and cheerfully? Do you greet the receptionist with the same positive attention with which you greet the CEO?

5. *Consistency.* Do you provide the same high-quality services to all clients and to every department and to everyone within each organization?

6. *Convenience.* Are you easy to reach? Are you able to turn on a dime to meet special needs that may come up?

7. *Accuracy.* Is your service provided right the first time? Do you aim for "flawless consulting"? Do the results demonstrate the accuracy that was agreed on initially?

8. *Responsiveness.* How quickly do you respond if something goes awry? Do you accept the responsibility for problems?

Tip: Time to assess.

Use the eight service expectations to conduct a self-assessment of your most recent client gig. How'd you rate yourself? Would your client rate you the same way?

Phase IV: Creating Independence

As the excitement of the project winds down and you complete your final tasks with the client, you may not feel as enthusiastic about the project as you did when you started. This is natural, something like the post-holiday letdown that sometimes occurs. Some consultants avoid this unpleasant feeling by focusing on their next clients. They just drift away. This is unfair to your client. Finish the project completely. Maintain your standards of quality.

You still have work to do. Although you should have been building your client's independence throughout the project, this is the time to confirm that the client has the tools and skills to continue without you. You may want to ensure that trainers are certified to teach ongoing classes, that supervisors are comfortable using the new computer program, that the project manager knows where to obtain additional information and support, or that the internal coaches know how to use the resources you designed for them.

You will want to ensure that the client knows to contact you with questions or concerns after the project has ended. We tell our clients that they can't get rid of us! What we mean by that is that our initial consulting fee grants them the privilege to call us at any time with questions, when they need ideas, if they need advice, or if they just need to vent.

There is a fine line between making the client dependent on you and providing help when it is really needed. After you have worked with clients and know them well, it's easy to provide additional ideas and support.

During this phase you will want to discuss continued communication. Identify who will be the best point of contact for future communication or follow-up. Let your client know that you will continue to maintain contact by sending articles, books, or notes and with periodic phone calls. Find out what the client's needs are as well.

Celebrate the project's success with your client. Celebrations are a great way to establish closure to the project. You could take the client to lunch or give a small gift that represents the partnership you have developed.

When you return to your office, don't forget to send a follow-up note thanking your client for the business and the opportunity to provide service.

Exhibits 7.2 and 7.3 provide two Client-Consultant Partnership Checklists—one for you and one for your client. These can serve as reminders for what you can do during each phase to build the relationship or can serve as discussion starters for you and your client during the early part of your relationship.

Exhibit 7.2. Client-Consultant Partnership: Consultant Checklist

Phase I: Finding the Right Match

- ❑ Obtain the best information available about the organization and the industry.
- ❑ Learn general industry jargon.
- ❑ Define the scope of the effort.
- ❑ Require that the client specifically define expectations and who does what.
- ❑ Evaluate the client's ability to support the effort.
- ❑ Identify shared values/differences.
- ❑ Identify the client's vision for the project.
- ❑ Provide rates and anticipated invoicing plan.
- ❑ Obtain feeling for the organization's support.
- ❑ Provide references.
- ❑ Discuss previous consultant efforts and biases.

Exhibit 7.2. Client-Consultant Partnership:
Consultant Checklist cont'd.

Phase II: Getting to Know One Another

- ❑ Learn everything possible about the client.
- ❑ Get inside the organization to understand its culture.
- ❑ Interview key people.
- ❑ Develop baseline information about attitudes, skills, climate.
- ❑ Model skills at every opportunity.
- ❑ Provide an initial plan.
- ❑ Build consensus around the plan.
- ❑ Plan for milestones, progress reports, communication.

Phase III: Being Productive

- ❑ Study the situation with an open mind.
- ❑ Create customized solutions.
- ❑ Conduct one-on-one coaching sessions.
- ❑ Become an active member of the client's team.
- ❑ Determine client self-sufficiency needs for the future.
- ❑ Be aware of the "magic wand" syndrome.
- ❑ Be honest, candid, and timely with issues and concerns.
- ❑ Continually create ways that lead to the client's independence.
- ❑ Communicate, communicate, communicate!

Phase IV: Creating Independence

- ❑ Validate self-sufficiency.
- ❑ Develop a system of continued communication.
- ❑ Determine best point of contact for future communication or follow-up.
- ❑ Continue to maintain contact with articles, books, notes, and periodic contact.
- ❑ Celebrate success with the client.

Exhibit 7.3. Client-Consultant Partnership: Client Checklist

Phase I: Finding the Right Match

- ❑ Meet with lead consultants.
- ❑ Request a proposal to ensure that the consultant understands the situation.
- ❑ Learn about the consultant's company.
- ❑ Contact references and past clients.
- ❑ Obtain information: length of time in business, consultant's background, type of clients served, repeat business, general reputation.
- ❑ Observe consultant in action, if possible.
- ❑ Check consultant's experience in your industry.
- ❑ Identify shared values and differences.
- ❑ Determine capabilities versus needs.
- ❑ Determine flexibility and availability of consultant.
- ❑ Clarify specific expectations and who does what.
- ❑ Identify desired time frame.
- ❑ Discuss limitations (money, time).
- ❑ Discuss known/suspected roadblocks.
- ❑ Think in terms of a long-term relationship: Is rapport evident? Is there a personal fit?

Phase II: Getting to Know One Another

- ❑ Choose one person as a point of contact.
- ❑ Include the consultant on the team.
- ❑ Ask the consultant to help identify the problem as well as the solution.
- ❑ Provide telephone directory, rosters, email addresses, and other contact information.
- ❑ Add consultants to in-house mailing list for newsletters and updates.
- ❑ Add to distribution list for pertinent teams.

**Exhibit 7.3.   Client-Consultant Partnership:
Client Checklist cont'd.**

❑   Provide feedback on employees' initial reactions to the project.

❑   Discuss risk factors.

Phase III: Being Productive

❑   Establish regular feedback sessions.

❑   Develop a tracking system for continuity.

❑   Be honest and candid with information and concerns.

❑   Communicate, communicate, communicate!

Phase IV: Creating Independence

❑   Validate self-sufficiency.

❑   Ensure that a system of continued communication is in place.

❑   Ensure that management is aware of next steps.

❑   Continue to provide news, success stories, and other insightful updates.

❑   Keep the consultant on the mailing list.

❑   Request advice if issues arise.

❑   Plan a success celebration.

ADDING MORE VALUE

Consulting is about creating value for your clients. Read that statement again. Sometimes we as consultants know that to be true, but we sell our activities and think the decision will be made on price instead. News flash: Your clients probably do not care about what you do and how you do it. They have problems to solve and are only interested in whether you can solve their problems. They want results. That's how they measure value.

A successful client-consultant relationship provides more value for the client than the client expected. Think about how delighted you are when you receive more than what you expected: fresh flowers in your hotel room, a complimentary mug with your breakfast buffet, or a free car wash with your oil change. However, none of these will ensure that you are a satisfied customer unless your original problem was solved. Was your hotel room clean, comfortable, and peaceful? Was the breakfast hot, tasty, and nutritious? Was your oil changed quickly and professionally? If yes, that's when the extra value kicks in.

A solid client-consultant relationship with high-impact results is built when two things happen.

1. First, the job is completed on time, within budget, with the highest quality possible, and meets or exceeds the client's expected return on investment.
2. Second, both the client and the consultant would be pleased to work on another project together.

You need a value and a relationship focus. Value happens when you solve the problem. A relationship focus occurs when you add extras to the project that have value to the client.

Selling: Helping Clients See the Value

Next to "How much should I charge?" the second-most-asked question by consultants is "How do I get more clients?" What they are really asking about is selling. We discussed marketing in Chapter Five, where I introduced you to the foolproof warm sales call. It is the best way that I know to get in front of your targeted clients.

But once you are in front of clients, you need to sell to them. Lots of consultants—me included—do not like what we perceive as "selling." Think about it differently. Do you like to help your clients solve problems? Of course you do. How can you help solve their problems if you don't work with them? You can't. So some transaction needs to occur that allows you to help them. If it is helpful, stop thinking about it as selling your services. Stop thinking about it as clients buying your services.

Instead, help your potential clients see the value in what you offer by asking a few questions. Your questions should lead your potential clients to tell you the value of solving their problems.

In addition, create a conversation that gives them value immediately. These conversations can be so positive to the client that they will look forward to speaking with you again. You can do this by asking a few powerful questions. Remember earlier I said that if you are speaking 50 percent of the time you've lost the sale? Well, this is what you do instead. You ask questions that get them to do most of the talking. People like to talk about themselves. To help your clients understand how you can help them, ask four kinds of questions. I call them the 4Rs, and I plan one or two in each category before meeting with potential clients.

Relation Questions. Start by building and strengthening the relationship with questions such as, "What's happening in your organization these days?" or "I read about the big award your company received. Congratulations! Tell me about it." Or "What's changed since the last time we talked?" You could move into questions related to the problem, such as, "What experience have you had with . . .?" This gives you a chance to test the water, but should not be leading in any way.

Requirement Questions. This is where you can address the value of solving the problem. You probably know what the problem is they are trying to solve, but now you can gather more information about it. For example, you might ask, "How important is . . .?" or "By what percent could sales increase?" or "How would this affect profit margins?" or "If you don't solve this, what will happen . . .?" Or even gather more data if you know what the problem is, such as how many people they lose each year; how it is affecting revenues; or by how much accidents have increased.

Relatable Questions. To get your potential client to relate to your solution, ask questions that draw comparisons or create a contrast between now and the future. It might sound like, "How does your current situation compare to what you want in the future?" or "Several of our clients are reporting the same issue . . . Do you find that too?" Another is, "If we could show you that . . . would that solve it for you?"

Rationale Questions. These questions will inform you about the decision-making process. For example, you might ask, "What criteria will be important to make this decision?" or "How will the decision be made?" or, my favorite, "If there were no constraints, what would you change and why?"

Finally, demonstrate how you can add more value to the discussion. Can you share your unique perspective or insight? Can you use an example about how you can help them avoid making bad decisions? Can you share pros and cons or a process to help them make the right decisions? Can you share testimonials? What data or information can you share to help them justify the purchase to someone higher? Can you discuss return on investment, or how the value will benefit the organization?

As a result of not selling, but instead asking questions that help to target the value the potential client is searching for, you will be able to help them justify a decision to buy from you. Help potential clients get clear on the value, rather than just seeing it as a cost. A good result for you is that by not "selling" you have convinced them that you can solve their problem and provide value.

Sales Objections

Sometimes the reason consultants won't go on a sales call is that they fear objections. Often the objection starts out that it costs too much, but that is rarely the real reason. It is more likely that the consultant didn't ask enough questions to help the potential client see the value, the potential ROI, or the cost of inaction. Here are a few others I hear often, with a suggested response.

- "I'm not interested." Ask, "In what?"; then focus on the problem they want solved and how you've helped others solve the same problem.
- "It's not my decision." Say that you understand and ask what their decision process is. Then ask how you can help justify the solution to those who will make the decision.
- "It's not in the budget." If they really care about the problem, help them find a way to move budget from a lower-priority item.
- "Send me some information." This is a soft objection. Say, "Sure. Happy to. Let's make sure it is relevant to you."

Sometimes providing options for a project gives you the edge over your competitors and provides a sense of control. Usually you will position the option that you think will best serve the client in the middle. See the example.

Option 1	Option 2	Option 3
	Everything in option 1 plus	**Everything in option 2 plus**
Team interviews	Industry focus groups	Three months of director coaching
Competitive analysis	Presentation at the offsite	Three months of executive coaching
Recommendations	One month of director coaching	Three monthly strategy sessions
	Weekly implementation support	
$11,000	$21,900	$42,500

Once the project starts, consultants can add value for clients in numerous ways. Sometimes you will be able to include these examples in your initial discussion to demonstrate how you add more value than was originally expected. Adding value is the mark of an excellent consultant. What do we mean by adding value during the project? We already mentioned adding a guarantee to your work. Here are three additional examples that can be differentiators to transform your work from good to great.

1. **You customize the solution for the client.** No stale answers, no been-there-done-that solutions, no Band-Aid approaches. You add value when you search for an original answer that addresses the client's unique needs. Although there is a place for best practices, a great consultant provides fresh advice and distinctive solutions that build on best practices.

2. **You challenge the client.** We consultants are paid well because our work is not easy. We push back; we force clients to crawl out of their boxes and push them out of their comfort zones so that they can see themselves—both personally and organizationally—as they really are. We do this to help clients see that it is not usually the defined situation that is the problem, but that in many cases the individuals or the organizations may be the roadblocks to success. Once clients see themselves as they are, there is a better chance for them to envision how they could be. A great consultant builds a trusting relationship as a foundation on which to provide constructive, candid, and, at times difficult, advice.

3. **You create the client's independence**. You are not there to make the client dependent upon you, but to ensure that clients receive the maximum return on their investment. A lasting impact only occurs if you ensure that the client has the competency required to sustain lasting impact. Before walking out the door, the great consultant ensures that the client owns the solutions. A great consultant inherently knows that this is the best way to be invited back.

Building the client-consultant relationship is a process that takes time and energy. Building the relationship is equally as important as your expertise. Do it because you care. Caring—truly caring—is a powerful business advantage.

---

*Caring—truly caring—is a
powerful business advantage.*

Attracting High-Value Clients

A hot topic in the consulting world is high-value clients. Who are they? How do you attract them? Why does it matter?

High-value clients are those who hire you as a consultant because they know that they need you. They value your insight, experience, and expertise. The assumption is that they also pay well because they are looking for someone who can solve their problems. They realize that there is a better way to evaluate consulting services than the lowest bid.

Generally, high-value clients recognize that they have a problem to solve. They don't look at it as a project to complete, such as designing and delivering a training program. Now, there is nothing wrong with that, but if you are seeking high-value clients, you need to focus differently.

How do you attract them? The key is to ensure that they know you are available. If you are producing value for others, you need to let the world know. How many times have you ended a conversation with an open-ended invitation, such as: "If you ever have anything we can work together on, let me know." Or "Here's my card. If you need my support, call me." When you are asked what you're doing and you say, "I'm working with a client," can you say something instead that would get them excited? Attract them to you? Perhaps "You have a crazy situation there and I can help you work through it." Or "I can call you tomorrow morning and lay out a plan for you." Or "I'm working with Brand Name Client to double their profits."

How else can you attract them? Well, of course, blogging about your expertise (without bragging, I might add), speaking at high-profile conferences, featuring testimonials from quality clients on your website, featuring case studies on your business pages, and other things you've already read about in this book. The key is not "what" you do, but "how" you do it. For example, if you use networking to find new clients, make it purposeful. While networking, listen for substantive business problems. You are there to learn, not sell. Listen more than you talk and you will likely leave with a handful of business cards and opportunities to follow up. Then, before they forget your conversation, follow up with them the very next morning.

Why does it matter? Well it's really up to you. It's not a requirement to work with high-value clients, but if you feel like you are working with clients who don't appreciate the value you can add, if you want to increase your profits, or if you simply want a different kind of work, then consider following what is in this book. Again, it is not a requirement to be a good consultant. It is your decision.

What can you do? To begin working with high-value clients, return to some of the things we've covered in this book: identifying your ideal client, knowing what is valued by your ideal client, understanding your value proposition, positioning you as the solution to their problem, following the warm-call process in Chapter Five, building relationships, and staying in touch beyond the project. It's all your decision.

Seven Selling Mistakes Consultants Make

Yes, few of us like to sell. And when you're a consultant, you are selling yourself. Ick! What are the biggest mistakes consultants make when trying to land a new client? There are dozens, but these are the ones I see most often.

Talking Too Much. The biggest one is doing too much talking. I've said it before: If you are talking more than 50 percent of the time, you may as well go and have a Starbucks specialty, because you've already lost the sale.

Not Selling the Solution. You already know that people buy to solve a problem. Otherwise why would they part with their money? Focus on how you will help your client solve the problem.

Asking the Wrong Questions. Questions need to build rapport and then get to the problem. Why is it a problem? What will be better once it is solved? What will happen if it isn't solved?

Missing Clues. I've attended meetings with consultants and watched $50,000 worth of work fly right over their heads. Consultants may be so intent on selling what they originally scheduled the meeting for that they can't hear these other opportunities. They become too dependent on their sales presentation.

Waiting Too Long for a Call to Action. Again, it's a matter of not attending to the client and presenting long after the client had tuned them out. A simple change To asking "Have you seen enough to make a decision?" will help.

Bragging. Really? Consultants are there to learn about the potential clients and how they can help them. If you must share some important data, do it in more subtle ways through examples and the questions you ask.

Believing Price Is the Answer. Except for the federal government, few clients buy on price. Often a client may seem obsessed with price, but in the end it's usually an excuse for something else. Clients want a problem solved. If you demonstrate that you can solve it, they'll find the money.

HOW MANY CLIENTS DO YOU NEED?

Just how many of these client relationships does an independent consultant need? It depends on a lot of things: how long your typical engagement lasts, what percent of face time or billable time you have with the client during the engagement, how many days per month you intend to work, and how much you are charging. All of these create a formula for the number of clients one has. Perhaps another way to look at it is that about half of your work should come from dependable, regular clients. The other half should come from those unique or unusual new efforts, one-and-done clients who hire you for a quick project. This offers you a good balance of stability and creativity. It also ensures that you receive a paycheck while you are marketing to new clients.

I currently have 11 clients. This could change tomorrow, since I am waiting for a call from a potential new client. I work with one of my clients every other week on-site. I work with three once every month. I coach one twice a month by phone. Two are periodic, but I do intense work with them for at least five days every other month. The other four are at different levels at different times. These clients will change throughout the year. One or two projects will end and then a new client will come onboard, or a client from five years ago will call with a project. Eleven is actually more than I'd like. I'm busy.

Take care that you do not end up in a position with only one or two clients. A change in the economic climate or the industry or even a change in leadership could end a project abruptly. The average (if there is such a thing) consultant will work with five to 10 clients at a time. This allows for the gentle shifting of the client tide as one moves out and another moves in.

Keep in mind that this also means that while you are serving your five to 10 clients, you are also marketing so that you have clients ready to move into the empty spots when you complete one of your projects.

HOW TO IMPROVE THE RELATIONSHIP CONTINUOUSLY

A sale is not something you close; it closes itself while you are busy serving your customer. Having a positive relationship with your client makes it easier to close your next sale, due to referrals. Do such a good job of completing the project and building the relationship that your client brags about you.

*A sale is not something you close; it closes itself
while you are busy serving your customer.*

What can you do so that your client will brag about you? The following ideas will help you start. Then think of 20 more that are unique to you.

- Deliver more than you promise.
- Demonstrate the return on investment as value to the client.
- Make opportunities to meet as many employees as possible.
- Request copies of the organization's newsletter and employee directory.
- Learn something personal about your most frequent contacts.
- Keep everyone informed; publicize project status as appropriate.
- Keep both company and individual information confidential.
- When you are on-site, arrive early, stay late.
- Adapt your work style to that of the organization.
- Meet—or beat—all deadlines.
- Deepen your relationship with a key buyer.
- Keep them informed of the next burning platform.
- Find ways to build trust.
- If you cannot meet a deadline, inform your clients as soon as you know and tell them why.
- Invite the client to shadow you when appropriate.
- Make the client feel like the only client.
- Send articles and share books that would be helpful to individuals.
- Be tough on the problem, but supportive of the person.
- Openly offer information about yourself.
- Explore a non-business-related topic you both enjoy discussing.

Tip: Picture this.
Use your cell phone or digital camera to take pictures at your off-sites of the participants and their work. Email the photos back to the clients after the session.

- Discover common acquaintances.
- Discover locations where you have both lived or visited.
- Discover common experiences you have had.
- Write thank-you notes and how-are-you-doing notes.

- Call frequently when not on-site.
- Be available when not on-site.
- Follow through on special requests from individuals.
- Provide treats for special meetings or when they're not in the client's budget.
- Offer and provide resources.
- Assist with developing outlines for future needs that support the effort.
- Send surprises, such as puzzles, posters, cartoons, or tools to make the job easier and more fun.
- Be prepared to help your client deal with the stress of change.
- Support your clients. Find positive aspects in situations that they may not see.
- Avoid internal politics.
- Discuss the organization's successes, but also discuss your objective thoughts about what could be done better.
- Discuss small problems before they become big problems.
- Be prepared to deal with unplanned delays—cheerfully.
- Openly discuss delays caused by the client that may prevent you from meeting deadlines; resolve them with the client.
- Plan and work as partners.
- Give the client credit for success.
- Attend the organization's social functions.
- Coach individuals.
- Teach by example.
- Ask for feedback.
- Apologize.
- Smile.

Tip: A photo op.

My husband is a pilot. Recently we took the plane up to take pictures of our house. One of my clients recently built a new complex and so we also took pictures of his buildings. The pictures turned out so well with the digital camera that we emailed the photos to the company president. We also enlarged three of the best and had them matted and framed. Too farfetched for you? Remember, you are looking for ways to get your clients to brag about you. What do you do or have access to that is unique?

Decisions

Building a solid client relationship may create situations that require you to make decisions. For example, it is possible to become too friendly with your client. This prevents you from maintaining your objectivity. When that happens, ethically you will need to sever the professional relationship. This is definitely a drawback to building a solid client-consultant relationship and has happened to me several times. I've always decided that the long-term friendship was worth more than the business I lost.

Another decision you may need to make is of a more positive nature. You may receive job offers. If you are good at what you do, it's going to happen. A client respects your professional approach, admires your results, and enjoys working with you. These are the ingredients that lead to a job offer. This is the kind of validation that consultants appreciate. Do you want a job, or do you want to continue as a consultant? The decision is yours.

Communication

Even if you are being paid to give advice, listening is the most critical communication skill, both for completing the project and for building the relationship. Learn and use good questioning techniques so that you are asking the right questions in the right way. Neither a wimp nor an interrogator be! Learn and use paraphrasing, summarizing, and clarifying techniques.

Remember the critical role that nonverbals play in the communication process. You may wish to pair up with someone periodically who can give you feedback about the nonverbal messages you may be sending.

IT'S THE PEOPLE

Perhaps the most important aspect to remember about building a strong client-consultant relationship is that it's all about people. You are not really building a relationship with the client organization. You are building a relationship with the individuals within the organization.

You may be working on a project *for* ABC, Inc., but you are working *with* individuals like Jack and Ilona. ABC, Inc. may pay your consulting fee, but president Francis and receptionist Lee will determine whether you earned it by adding value. You may receive a referral from ABC, Inc., but Jose will write it.

Build a relationship with everyone in the organization. They are all important to the company. Building a relationship with all employees is equally as important as building a relationship with the president. Kowtowing to the president will be observed by the employees—and by the president. Don't do it.

For me, building a relationship with my client is equally important to completing the project and exceeding the results my client expects. It is part of my philosophy of doing business. If building relationships is not a part of your business philosophy, you may want to review the beginning of this chapter. Reconsider the business value of building relationships.

MAINTAIN THE RELATIONSHIP AFTER THE PROJECT

It would be foolish of you to ignore a relationship you have spent months to build. Many of the ideas in this chapter can be used to maintain a relationship after the project ends. Continue to stay in touch with your clients. You will find ways to maintain the relationship. Let me share some of the ways I do this.

- I purchase article reprints and books that will be interesting to my clients and send them on a regular basis. A former client called recently to say that he wanted to move from his government job to a COO position in private industry. He wanted advice about how to prepare. I bought him the most recent copies of *Harvard Business Review*, *Fortune*, and the *Wall Street Journal* and dropped them off at his office the last time I drove past.

- I stay in touch. I continue to send notes and cards. Usually I've learned a great deal about a client's likes, dislikes, pet peeves, hobbies, and interests. I may find items or reading materials about any of these. I find reasons to call the client.

- If I find that I will be near a previous client's location, I will call the client and plan to have breakfast, lunch, dinner, or just a visit. I drop in and visit clients' business locations when I can.

- I encourage my clients to call at any time. I enjoy helping them find resources or materials. I enjoy helping them track down a bit of information or someone who could help them. As I write this book, I received an email from Melanie, who was tasked with building a team and was wondering whether I could provide several team-building activities. We sent her an entire book of them. Clients call to ask if I know of available jobs or people to fill job openings that they have. They call for recommendations about conferences or books. It is a sign of a solid partnership to have requests coming my way regularly.

Tip: Tap into your network.

Use your network to conduct mini-research for your clients. Several months ago a client contacted me asking who was using gamification to develop their people. I emailed eight people and seven responded. They provided company names, individual contacts, and contact information. I passed the information to my colleague. The whole process took a week to get the answer.

- I sell my clients to others regularly. I find new customers for them. I recommend them to serve on boards. I sell their products. For example, Land O'Lakes is one of my clients. If a restaurant uses Land O'Lakes butter, I never hesitate to compliment them on using the best butter in the world.
- I also call clients if I need help. I call them if I know of available jobs. I may call them to serve as a resource for someone else or to ask if I can use their names as references. Always ask permission before you use a client as a reference for another project. Even this continues to maintain the relationship.

Maintaining the relationship can be whatever you decide it should be. We have lots of repeat work. I believe that is primarily due to providing high-quality, results-oriented consulting. However, I believe that a solid relationship makes it easier to remember us when new projects evolve.

We have other clients whom we simply enjoy staying in touch with. There is little chance that additional work will ensue. That isn't our primary reason for maintaining the relationship. We do it because we like to.

ENSURE SUCCESS

If you see yourself as a business owner first—not simply a consultant—you are on the road to success. You own a business and you must act like a business owner, or you will be out of business—no matter how good a consultant you are. Observe the following to be a successful business owner.

Commit to consulting. Do what you love. Owning your own business isn't a hobby. It's a lifestyle. Starting your own business is risky; running it is challenging. If you really love it, it is worth it. If you don't, you will most likely fail. It takes commitment.

Understand the value of your services and price accordingly. The biggest mistake new consultants make is to underprice their services. Price your services high enough to stay in business. Have confidence in your ability to deliver value. Don't be shy about charging for that value.

Strengths—know what yours are and build on them. Hire someone to support things that aren't your specialty. This frees up your time for the things you excel at and love doing. Isn't that why you went into business for yourself in the first place?

Team—build a strong one. Build a team of smart professionals who know more than you do about their areas of expertise: an attorney, accountant, banker, and insurance broker. Choose wisely and trust the advice they give you. Hire the best people you can afford.

Observe others to perfect your people skills. Your potential customers want to do business with someone they like. Your success is directly related to your ability to build and maintain relationships. Clients hire personality over expertise every day.

Measure and monitor every aspect of your business with a one-page "snapshot." You can include sales, receivables, payables, trends, profit averages on one page. Monitor against your business plan to know when things need tweaking. Know your numbers.

Expect to succeed. Why just hope your business will succeed? Decide that it will. When things are going wrong, it takes drive from within to push forward, no matter the consequence. You know you can do it—and that is the difference.

Recognize the importance of your clients. Cater to your customers. Your services improve people's lives. Put yourself in your clients' shoes. The ability to empathize with your customer helps you understand the real value in what you do.

The list spells CUSTOMER—the center of every successful business. Without customers you will quickly be out of business. Taking care of your customers and adhering to each of these principles will ensure your success. You will find a longer, printable version with more content at www.wiley.com/go/newconsultingbiech.

For the Consummate Consultant

You need your customers. But they need you, too. They have problems and need you to solve them. Remember that there are two ways to evaluate your work with clients. Did you resolve their problem and leave them with a solution that added value? And did you build a relationship with the client so that they would be delighted to work with you again?

Stack the Odds. Competing on price alone will get you nowhere fast. Be unique. Stack the odds in your favor by determining what your clients value. You could be the only consultant that guarantees results. Perhaps you have the ability to really get to the root cause. Perhaps you have a testimonial from a respected organization in your industry to share. Remember, if you've got it, flaunt it.

Don't Be a Secret. What's your expertise? Make sure the world knows. You can't make an impact with clients and potential clients if they don't know about you. Are you published? Do you blog? Do you present at conferences? Be sure to send a message of confidence and expertise in all that you do.

Question Queen (or King). Create a list of questions that work for you. You can find them everywhere. This task is so important to me that I have a running list of questions on a document on my desktop, filed in a drawer, and in my briefcase. It changes as I discover new and better questions to ask. My all-time favorite is how I end almost every interview: "What question should I have asked you but didn't?" It often leads to another five minutes of information.

Growing Pains

8

A goal is a dream with its feet on the ground.

Anonymous

Kyle sat on the park bench, looking out at the lake. How had things gone so wrong? He had been excited about starting his business five years ago. Corte Consulting grew quickly—well, at least according to his standards—$2.4 million and seven employees. It had started with a $20,000 savings withdrawal and a six-month contract with the new glass manufacturer in town. Things had been humming along and growing in spurts. He had a client list from coast to coast that would make many consulting firms jealous. The travel was a bear, but every job had its drawbacks.

Growth had been stagnant for more than a year. Kyle was the sole marketer for the company. He knew he had no one to blame but himself: he was a big part of the problem. Now he had to make a decision. To grow or not to grow—that was the question. Did he want to grow a business with real equity value so that he could sell it at some future date? Or did he want to remain the small company that "worked harder"? He knew this tagline would have to go, no matter what.

219

Everyone at Corte Consulting was working long hours. And while Kyle claimed to like it, he had to admit that working weekends was getting old.

Did he want to grow his business? It would require huge changes to crack through the $2.5 million glass ceiling he was bumping up against. According to Pat, from Equiteq—an M&A advisory firm—Kyle would need to maximize his firm's growth and scale the business. He'd have to transition from doing the work to increased delegation. He wasn't sure about that, since he loved working with clients to solve their problems. Yes, he had to admit that there was very little planning in the company's growth to date. It was profitable—usually—and he paid his employee consultants well. But he also had huge turnover. His employees joined the company, learned the tricks of the trade, and left to start their own competing consulting companies.

His other option was to settle for a lifestyle business and not grow. This felt better to him today—but then it just could be exhaustion from the latest round of proposal writing. He'd continue to be the sole rainmaker and continue to work directly with clients. He'd probably need to scale back on employees, too; he was more profitable when he had four consultants. Perhaps he could use a couple of subcontractors. The big question was whether his ego could handle it. A company that didn't grow? Who'd respect that? On the other hand, a different lifestyle was the reason he'd left his 8-to-5 (which was more like 7-to-7) position with the big New York firm.

Decision time. It was easy when he turned in his laptop and decided to start Corte Consulting. He left and never looked back. But that was different. It felt like he was going forward. Now one of his options felt like he'd be going backward. He was never very good at decisions, and this one felt overwhelming. What to do? Well, he knew exactly what he'd do. He had all the advice from the experts. He had the data. It was time to talk to his long-time confidant, Lisa, who was at home preparing his favorite, chicken cacciatore.

■ ■ ■

All business owners reach a point at which they begin asking themselves questions about growth. In this chapter we explore a few of the many opportunities for growth.

What does growth mean? We can probably assume that it at least means more income. Does growth also mean more people in your organization? In what capacity? Do you want someone who replicates your skills? Complements them? Do you want a staff?

Growth may mean many more questions than answers. Are there ways to increase income other than increasing the number of bodies? Do you need to figure out how to level the peaks and valleys of your business cycle? Do you have products that you could market? Could you offer other services? For example, if you are a training consultant, do you also want to offer to be a keynoter at conferences? Perhaps you want to design an online training course. Or perhaps it is simply time to increase the fee you charge.

Think long and hard about this step. Once you change the makeup of your business, it will never be the same. You have dozens of options and combinations of options to consider. For example, when I decided that I wanted a "partner" in my business, we sat down and came up with the following list of possibilities for the business configuration:

- I own; you're employed.
- You own (buy me out); I'm employed.
- Equal partnership.
- Unequal partnership.
- I own the primary business; you own a subsidiary.
- We both own the primary business (equally or unequally); I own a related subsidiary.
- We create a franchise arrangement.
- You start your own business; we share overhead.

We were creative and tried to identify all the possibilities. You will want to do the same. Think hard and long, do all your homework, and talk to others who have done what you are thinking about doing before you make the move to grow. If growth is on your mind, this chapter presents several options for you to consider.

ADDING PEOPLE

Because increasing the number of people is usually the first thing people think about when the issue of growth comes up, let's begin there.

Should You Hire Staff?

Beth was the first person I hired. I hired her to work part-time, to be in my office when I wasn't in to answer the telephone. This was in the early years of answering machines and voice mail. An answering machine was a dead giveaway that you were new to the business and probably working off your kitchen table. In the early 1980s, working from your home was not regarded as professional. Wow—has that changed! Now being a freelancer, solopreneur, gig worker, and, of course, a consultant, is viewed as having flexibility and control of what you want to do.

After I hired Beth, things started to snowball. I hired Beth for her telephone voice. I knew she would be great with clients. In addition to having a great voice, Beth also loved computers. She immediately started to do some of my word processing. That freed me up for more billable days. I took on more clients with more sophisticated needs. Therefore, we needed a better computer and a copying machine.

To pay for the new equipment, I started to take on larger projects. I was unable to provide the highest-quality services by myself, so I started to hire other consultants. Beth could no longer keep up with the demands of additional clients, so we hired additional administrative staff for support. Of course that meant we needed more computers and a larger office. To pay for the additional equipment and . . . well, you get the idea.

Before you begin to hire staff, have a clear plan in place for exactly how much growth you desire and how you will fund this growth. Study the various glass ceilings that consulting firms hit, typically at $2.5 million, $5 million, $10 million, and $15 million, and what needs to occur to break through. To push forward, owners need to make different things happen at each point. The pain points can also be predicted by the number of employees. I have experienced the diminishing returns, and I can tell you that they are real.

Hey, wait! You're just starting out. Let's not talk millions yet. As a solopreneur you will experience similar roadblocks, although not so well defined or researched. See the sidebar for what you might expect.

Stages of Growth

As a solopreneur, your business will move through several stages. Here's what I can tell you about each stage. In this outline you will see gaps between amounts because once you solve the issue in each category you will tend to move quickly to the next stage.

$25 to $75k. You will be in the largest business classification in the United States, with around 22 million other business owners. It is likely to be stressful and you will have feelings of doubt. Most of your business has come from friends and other contacts. You may have started out accepting all work. Actions that are required are constant marketing, but you need to improve the consistency of your marketing. This may be difficult because you may not be 100 percent sure of what you are marketing. You will not be likely to move forward until you figure this out. You need to clarify your niche.

$100 to $200k. You now have consistent marketing in place but realize you can't do it all on your own. This is the point at which you are likely to hire someone to support you. You may hesitate because you aren't certain that you can afford it. You may have a confidence crisis to get through. You'll need to scale your marketing plan, since much of your work is coming from referrals, which is good; it's just not completely sustainable.

$300 to $600k. At this stage you'll likely experience capacity constraints and may not be able to fulfill all the marketing requirements. You may have been reluctant to hire the caliber of people you need, but it's time to let go. The only thing that will allow you to break into seven figures is to hire the kind of people you need to support you and the business. Now listen up—that does not necessarily mean you need to hire staff. You might, but there are other options. Review your business plan and develop procedures for each function so that you can increase your efficiency and everyone knows what's expected.

$800k to $1.5m. At this stage you are in constant demand. This is flattering, but exhausting. This is the point where you have one to three employees and need to decide whether you are going to grow, stay the same size, or create another growth strategy. You are still expected to make every decision. If your goal is to grow a business with employees, it's time to step back to determine whether your employees are too reliant on you. You probably feel as if people are not pulling their own weight. It is likely that you are putting out fires instead of making decisions. In order to grow you need to make time for planning. Also, this is the point at which you need to be sure that you have a diversified client base—that you are not too reliant on one or two clients or too many clients in the same industry. Be sure you have someone to talk to about your business. You need a good listening ear—a mentor.

If you have decided to hire additional consultants, hire those who are passionate and love what they do. Experience is important, but passion is more important. You will also want to hire employees who are willing to take a few risks. If you want your business to grow, risks are required. In addition, be sure that your new hires are reliable, confident, and detail-oriented, but see the big picture and have a high level of emotional intelligence.

Advantages. The greatest advantage to hiring staff members is that they will be a part of your organization. Clients will see that you are growing. Some clients will be impressed with the number of employees that you have. In my early years of consulting I was often asked, "How many employees do you have?" I noticed that clients' interest levels rose in direct proportion to the number of employees we had. That has changed. The gig economy has influenced how we think about self-employed individuals. Hiring a subcontractor or a part-time employee is more accepted, so there are fewer questions.

A larger staff affords you the luxury of pursuing larger, more complex projects, and it is usually easier to manage several large projects than many small projects.

As staff members become a permanent part of your organization, you will become familiar with their talents and limitations. That means you will be able to more knowledgeably match them to the project, the client, or the industry.

Disadvantages. The greatest disadvantage of hiring staff is the ongoing payroll commitment. When our company was at its peak, I worried about how many people, roofs, tires, braces, and dogs were dependent on the success of the company. You need to engage in more marketing activities to keep up with payroll and benefits demand.

It may be difficult to find productive work for employees. You've read that the true cost of employees is twice as much as their salary, and if you want to make a profit you may want to triple that. The question you will face is whether a client will pay that much for the employee. So you need to pay more to hire good people so that clients will be willing to pay what you need just to break even! Yes, one of those circular issues.

So how do you make that work? You need to scale. Having several employees gives you a bit more wiggle room. But that's not a simple solution either, because:

- You'll likely need larger office space.
- As Kyle experienced, you're likely to be in a near-constant hiring mode due to turnover.
- You'll need to keep more client engagements going to keep your consultants billable.

- Consultants will have downtime. If you have staff who have specialties, they may experience gaps in their billable time. For example, employees whose specialty is lean six sigma design may experience downtime between these large projects. Do you assign them to designing creativity training? Probably not if you want to do right by your clients.
- You'll need to invest time orienting, training, and developing new consultants.
- You will be busy with all these additional tasks on top of what you've already been doing.

More administrative tasks are required. As soon as you hire one person, you become an employer and the paperwork mounts: you need unemployment insurance, new federal and state tax configurations, an "office" where they can work, and a dozen other employee-related items. You'll also need more administrative staff to manage the increased workload.

One of the greatest disadvantages is one that you might think is an advantage: If there are other people in the organization, they can do more of the client face-to-face work and you can do more marketing. Wrong! It has been my experience that clients will want you to do the work. You have the reputation, and it's your name on the door. No matter what you do, clients will still want you. The only way to keep all the demands from falling on you is for the consultants in your organization to generate some of their own work. They need to make face-to-face contact with clients and also do their own marketing.

---

*No matter what you do,
clients will still want you.*

You might wonder, can't the consultant employees generate some of the work? Yes, they could, but I learned that few want to sell. If they did, they would probably have their own consulting firms.

So if having additional consultants on staff was your solution to freeing yourself up from the grind of billing, go back to the drawing board. Unfortunately, it isn't likely to happen.

Exhibit 8.1 explores additional advantages and disadvantages. If you are considering hiring employees, take time to add your own thoughts under each item. When you have finished, go back and look at what you have written. Which side appears to be the stronger for you?

Exhibit 8.1. Building a Firm

Advantages	Disadvantages
Increased ability to serve more clients	Increased time necessary to educate new employees
Increased availability and types of services	Increased time in managing others decreases time to serve clients
Increased earnings base	Increased overhead, responsibilities, and accountability
Security of backup in an emergency	May invest time in those who will leave and compete with me
Spread my philosophy and increase name recognition	May have different values from employees

The New Business of Consulting

Should You Recruit a Partner?

I had a partner for five years, and I would do it again if I could find another exactly like him. We were alike in some respects and very different in others. We communicated well, trusted one another completely, made decisions effectively, and complemented one another's skills. I've heard it said that taking on a partner is more like a marriage than marriage itself. So the choice of who to partner with is not a simple one.

---

*Taking on a partner is more like a
marriage than marriage itself.*

According to small business owners, the single biggest mistake entrepreneurs make is choosing a partner too casually. A trial relationship can be established to explore the likelihood of a successful permanent one. I highly recommend an arrangement that allows you and your potential partner to work together for six to 12 months before making the relationship permanent.

How to configure your partnership is a second concern. We decided that, although we were going to be partners, it made more sense for us to incorporate legally as a subchapter-S corporation. (Chapter Four described the advantages of this legal entity.) We also decided that because I had more equity and eight years in the company, I would maintain slightly more than half of the ownership. Although we didn't consider it at the time, my slight edge of more than half of the ownership meant that the company would be a woman-owned business. Some organizations use that designation to make final decisions for awarding contracts.

We agreed that we would draw the same salary after the partnership was formed. The split of dividends, of course, is governed by law. We would each receive an amount proportionate to the percentage of ownership.

Prior to becoming a partnership, my partner and I agreed that he would work for at least one year at a reduced salary. The salary not taken was his way of buying into the company. We established several other parameters. One was that, in addition to working for a year, he needed to show that he was generating an equal amount of work.

Tip: Plan ahead.

In the excitement of forming a partnership, you may forget that something could go wrong in the future. Put all agreements in writing and devise a plan for the details of a breakup, should one be necessary. Depending on your situation, you may want to tap your attorney to help make it official.

Often, dividing responsibilities and roles is the most difficult task. If you can be as lucky as I was, you can have roles and titles that clearly define the responsibilities. For example, a founding partner can focus on work with major clients and maintain the corporate vision, while a managing partner can manage the daily operation of the company, including taking over responsibility for sales and profitability. In our case, we were separated geographically: my office was in Wisconsin and his office was in Virginia. Each of the offices was responsible for different aspects of the business—for example, invoicing clients, bookkeeping, or producing client materials. Each of us had responsibility for an office.

Exhibit 8.2 is a discussion generator for checking partner compatibility. Each partner completes the questionnaire separately. At least half a day should be set aside to discuss both partners' responses. The discussion will uncover concerns and issues that could create problems within the partnership. Take care of them before a legal entity is formed.

Exhibit 8.2.   Partnerability

Each potential partner completes this questionnaire. Set aside at least one-half day to discuss your responses.

Rate each item on a scale from 1 to 7, with 1 being low and 7 being high.

		Low						High
1.	The importance of my title	1	2	3	4	5	6	7
	My ideal title would be . . .							
2.	The importance of salary	1	2	3	4	5	6	7
	My ideal salary would be . . .							
3.	The importance of responsibilities	1	2	3	4	5	6	7
	The responsibilities I want are . . .							
	The responsibilities I do not want are . . .							
4.	My commitment to this partnership	1	2	3	4	5	6	7
	Because . . .							

Exhibit 8.2.   Partnerability Cont'd.

5. My willingness to challenge you   1 2 3 4 5 6 7
    Because . . .

6. My level of trust with you   1 2 3 4 5 6 7
    Because . . .

7. My willingness to take risks   1 2 3 4 5 6 7
    Examples are . . .

8. The strengths I bring to this partnership are . . .

9. The liabilities I bring to this partnership are . . .

10. My five-year vision for this partnership is . . .

11. My "must haves" or things I will not budge on are . . .

12. My philosophy about travel expenses is . . .

13. My philosophy about quality of work is . . .

Advantages. Consulting is a lonely business. Often the thought of having a partner seems like the perfect answer. There would be someone to bounce ideas off of (consultants like to bounce ideas) and someone to cover for you if you became ill.

A partnership broadens your business capabilities, expertise, skills, and experience. This is one reason for partnering with someone who is unlike you—someone who complements what you bring to the business.

A partnership sends a message to the world that you believe the person you have elected to partner with is at least your equal. This is important if your present clients are to accept the person as a qualified substitute for you.

From a business perspective, there is someone to share the responsibilities or the cost of doing business—someone with whom to share the decision making.

Disadvantages. The greatest disadvantage to having a partner was already listed as an advantage: you must share the decision making with someone! Depending on your agreement, each of you will probably need to check with the other before making a change. If you like independence and not having to ask permission to do something, shared decision making could get in the way of your relationship. In addition, it may take more time to make decisions.

You will need to share resources. This can be a concern, especially if one of the partners is either generating or billing a greater proportion than the other.

Guidelines for Selecting a Partner

If you are considering bringing a partner into the business, use this quick checklist to help you make the decision. To make it more helpful, make notes for why you think each item is critical for you. Look for a partner who:

- Shares your values and vision
- Is a natural entrepreneur
- Is financially stable
- Brings credibility to the business
- Brings skills, experience, resources, and contacts to the business
- Is good in sales and marketing
- Is ethical and trustworthy
- You respect and genuinely like

Should You Consider a Practice?

Although you will find various definitions, I think of a *practice* as having one key person (you) with others on staff in assisting roles, and a *firm* as having numerous people who can do the same thing (many you's!), plus support staff (receptionists, administrative assistants, or researchers). A practice focuses on providing services and doesn't usually sell products.

Advantages. The greatest advantage of a practice is having dedicated support. Someone is there to help with the ordering, scheduling, typing, copying, cleaning, filing, billing, packing, and the dozens of other things that need to be done. Someone is available to pick up the slack and share the administrative stress. If you're on the road and need something, someone is available who can fax or mail it to you.

Disadvantages. The greatest disadvantage of a practice is having someone on payroll who is not billable and cannot generate income. This means that you are working to support two people. If you decide to hire someone, make sure that it is worth your while. Will the person free up enough of your time so that you can easily pay the individual's salary, benefits, and added overhead? If not, it is not a worthwhile pursuit.

As an author, I frequently receive requests for advice. The sidebar shares an actual example that occurred in August. Misha had a question that pulls together many of the concerns we've touched on.

A Question about the Business of Consulting

I frequently receive requests for help from consultants. This past August I received this interesting request.

Hi!

I've been reading and really enjoying your book *The Business of Consulting*. I read it because it was recommended by my friend and mentor Geoff Bellman (whom I think you know, too). I wonder if you might be able to answer a question about something you wrote in the book.

I work mostly as a trainer, teaching communication and collaboration skills. After years of working alone, in the past year, I've

---

started to work with a couple of part-time people—one who helps with sales and one with general admin work. I love it! It frees up a lot of my time, and also makes the work a lot more enjoyable.

Both of these folks want to increase their roles: They want to work more hours, and get paid more per hour. You wrote in your book, on the subject of hiring help, "Will this person free up enough of your time that you can easily pay the individual's salary, benefits, and overhead?" I'd love to know more about that. Do I need to consider the 3× Rule here, too? I'd be really grateful if you were able to shed any light on this.

Thanks!!!

Misha

I responded with this:

Hi Misha!

Let me begin with a general comment about what the 3× salary statement refers to. The 3× Rule applies when you are hiring another trainer/consultant. The consultant needs to sell (generate) and deliver (usually called billable time) at a rate that is at least three times his or her salary in order to be profitable for the organization. This is common practice in large consulting firms. Why? One-third is, of course, the individual's salary; the other two-thirds include benefits, equipment, supplies, office rent, company liability insurance, electric bills, moving costs, furniture, at least 10 percent profit to your business, your time to train, supervise, and mentor them, and on and on. *But* this is not the job role you are asking about.

In your case, you are asking for two very different kinds of support staff. It is wonderful that they both want more hours with you—you must be doing some very good things. And of course everyone wants a higher salary! Me, too! The fact that they want more hours and more money does not justify your rationale to schedule more hours or to pay them more money.

Let's look at each situation.

Assistant: I discuss hiring Beth, my first employee. I actually hired her over the phone, sight unseen, because I wanted someone with good telephone presence. Beth had it. She was with me for 20 years until I closed the office in Wisconsin and she had other plans in life. The key to hiring an assistant is to ensure that you find someone who has a passion for the work he or she has to complete. Too often I hear about people who hire assistants who want to be "trainers" instead. It sounds like a good idea at first, but the truth is you will have someone who is dissatisfied until he or she is a trainer. And then you will face the same issue you have today—needing to find an assistant.

How much more do you need to make? The person's salary, of course, + benefits + any additional office trappings you'll need to purchase (e.g., one-time costs such as a desk or new phone system) + equipment and software to make both of you more efficient. You'll also need to consider the cost of additional internal services. Will you now need an accountant to do payroll and your quarterly taxes (in the United States), and the additional bookkeeping that comes with staff? The advantage is that an assistant can free you up to do other things. And I always advocate for hiring an assistant if you can afford it. The drawback is that you are now responsible for keeping a roof over someone else's head. It's a big step.

Sales: One of the lessons I learned is that sales staff are paid differently and are motivated differently. I learned early in my business that the reason sales were stagnant in my company was that I was being too generous with the base salary. Salespeople are generally paid on a base salary plus commission—or a percentage of the dollar amount of what they sell. You may be working with your salesperson on a customized situation in which he or she also delivers, so your plan may be customized. I have learned that employees have no idea of the cost to run a business—some of which I noted in the book. They don't see that you pay liability insurance, that you do not get a "paid" vacation, that your website requires a monthly fee, or that you work on Sundays to get a proposal out. The key here is to be as transparent as possible.

So the bottom line is that you have two different kinds of people you are asking about. It sounds like everyone is happy working together—especially you. That's wonderful! Start any increases in pay slowly. It's always easier and more practical to give a bonus at the end of the year than to overpay during the year and come up short in the end. Make sure that all employees know exactly what they are expected to accomplish. What are they accountable for? And how will they be rewarded when they meet their goals? And what happens when they don't? Oh gosh, I don't mean to take the fun out of all of this for you. I just don't want you to trip up in the same places that I have been.

You had a question about the 3x Rule. You need to be making 3x YOUR salary plus the salary of the person plus the cost of having that person on staff, such as I listed above. I guess the real question here is if you pay these two individuals a higher rate for more hours, will YOU be able to sell and deliver enough business to pay for them? And also, can you see a direct correlation in the value you create to the time they save you? In other words, what is the dollar proportion of (billable to clients) to (cost of employees)? I don't like to be that crass nor do I think the only reason we are in business is to make money. *Not at all!!* I just don't want you to lose money.

Working as a freelance trainer/consultant can be a lonely job. There are other ways to build collegiality, alliances, friendships—and just to have someone to talk to—than to hire employees. You could create your own monthly network where everyone gets together for coffee and to chat or share ideas. You could (or maybe should) meet with your mentor regularly. You could just have another consultant you meet for coffee or drinks after work several times a month. Or maybe you do all of these. It is critical that you network with your colleagues to share ideas and let off steam.

Good luck to you! I hope I've helped you.

Say hello to Geoff for me!

Elaine

Do You Want to Hire Subcontractors?

The gig economy has seen subcontracting increase dramatically. Companies must be agile, and subcontracting is one way to ensure that can happen. It can be helpful to consultants, too. If you accept a project that is too big for you to handle alone, you may choose to hire subcontractors. It is an excellent idea from a tax perspective because you can add people on a temporary basis.

In addition to being helpful for large projects, the arrangement allows consultants to tap into one another's expertise. This allows you to seek projects for which you may not have all the qualifications.

Although I often work on a handshake, if you have a large project for which you will use multiple subcontractors, I recommend that you use a subcontractor agreement. The more people involved, the higher the chance for mistakes, misunderstandings, and disagreements. An example of a subcontractor agreement can be found in Exhibit 8.3; head to www.wiley.com/go/newconsultingbiech to check it out. In addition, the subcontractor expense record in Exhibit 8.4 can be adapted for your use. Using subcontractors is a great time to check in with your attorney. Consider using clear "paid-when-paid" terms and milestones in your agreements to avoid issues.

Advantages. Subcontractors can be hired on a per-project basis. That means that there will be no ongoing payroll expense. You will not be required to withhold income taxes or pay any share of their Social Security or Medicare taxes. Generally, you will hire people who are skilled and professional. Subcontractors increase your flexibility, as you are able to hire the talent you need on a project-by-project basis.

Because they are independent, they know how important it is to produce high-quality work. They will work hard to satisfy your needs because it could lead to repeat work for them. They also require less administrative overhead. Your only obligation in the United States is to send completed 1099 forms to them by the last day of January.

Disadvantages. The greatest disadvantage is actually only a potential one. The Internal Revenue Service has adopted common-law rules for differentiating between an independent contractor and an employee. The rules cover things such as whether you have the right to direct the person's work, whether you supply the person with tools and a place to work, whether you establish the hours of work, and whether you have a continuing relationship with the individual. Even if you have studied the guidelines and are complying with the law, the Internal Revenue Service could tie you up in an investigation for months. As an independent consultant, you can imagine what this might do to your business.

Tip: Tax tip.

Learn the language of the 1099. For additional information about the how the IRS differentiates between subcontractors and employees, contact your accountant or attorney, from whom you can obtain up-to-the-minute information and learn how the laws clarify the difference. For example, the IRS does not allow a subcontractor to work full-time for one company. No more than 80 percent of a subcontractor's income can come from one source.

Exhibit 8.4.   Subcontractor Expense Record

Contract _____   Invoice # _____
                              Invoice Date _____

Consultant Name_____
Session Number and Location _____ Dates _____
Team_____ Number of Team Members____ Billable Days _____

Travel Costs *To be completed by Facilitator. Attach receipts for all (*) items.*

Airfare*/Train*/other. . . . .$_____
Rental Car* $_____   Fuel*$_____ . . . . .Total $_____
_____Transportation* from_____airport to hotel . .$_____
_____Transportation* from session to_____ airport$_____
Meals* (itemize) . . . .$_____
Hotel*. . . . .$_____
Airport parking*. . . . .$_____
Local Privately Owned Vehicle # miles_____× $.58/mile or
   Other Transportation* from residence to airport . . . .$_____
Local Privately Owned Vehicle # miles_____× $.58/mile or
   Other Transportation* from airport to residence . . . .$_____
                                          Total Travel Costs $_____

Session Costs *This section to be completed by ebb associates inc*
Facilitation fee $_____
Other $_____
(explain)

                                          Total Session Costs $_____
                              Total (Travel and Session Costs) $_____

Subcontractors are not always available when you need them, and because they most likely substitute for other consultants, they will not know your projects well and may not understand your consulting preferences. This means that you may need to spend almost as much time bringing them up to speed for a project as if you did it yourself. You can only hope that the investment of time will have a payback in the future.

Subcontractors may also become your competitors. Ethically, subcontractors represent your company when they work for you. In addition, they are not supposed to discuss their own business nor are they to market themselves to your clients while on your project. Even if they do not, your client may discover the arrangement and may want to hire them directly to save money. This can be uncomfortable for everyone, especially you. By the way, check with your attorney; the last I knew is that you can't have a subcontractor sign a noncompete agreement because it reclassifies the sub as an employee. And that is probably not what you want.

Don't Assume Business Acumen

Subcontractors, are likely to have their own businesses. Unfortunately, that does not mean that they really understand how a business works. I remember one of my subcontractors bringing a "deal" to me. She was excited about working with this company in our city. I was, too. They had name recognition and the potential for repeat business. When I read the proposal she was about to send under our name, I quickly saw that she was going to make her normal daily subcontractor rate. Yet the client was going to pay a couple thousand dollars less. My company was going to lose money on this "deal"! What?

What was worse is that as I tried to get her to explain why I would want to lose money on an engagement, her only response was, "because they could be a good client." Yes, they could be a good client, but first, I was going to lose over $5,000 (by the way, she was unwilling to cut her daily rate). And second, when you set the price lower than we could afford, you have to explain why the next engagement would be priced higher. To this day, I am not sure she could understand why I turned the deal down, or if she was trying to pull the wool over my eyes.

Bottom line, don't assume that anyone with whom you work understands business basics. Kevin Cope (2018) is my go-to guy for learning more about business acumen.

Can You Use Graduate Students?

University graduate students may be hired as interns for project work under arrangements similar to those of subcontractors, but you must still follow all IRS guidelines. You could also hire them as part-time employees, in which case you put them on your payroll.

On occasion, you may be able to locate a student who will work for credit only. If you have a thriving practice that provides an opportunity for learning to occur, this may be an option you should check into. Call at least the business and communication departments of your local campus. There may be other specialty departments to call also.

Advantages. Graduate students usually are interested in the experience more than the salary. That means that you can find lots of talent at a very good price.

You can complete projects that you have been unable to tackle in the past due to a lack of time. For example, you may assign a student to one specific project, such as researching and developing a new seminar.

Disadvantages. The greatest disadvantage is that graduate students usually lack experience. They may have lots of knowledge, but not the practical hands-on experience that your clients expect. Even if they work as support staff, they may have little experience with running a copy machine, creating computer graphics, or answering client questions.

University students are generally short-term employees. That means that you will not often have them for more than a school year—and usually for just a semester.

Due to class schedules, they may not be available when you need them the most. Sure as heck, they will have a big exam scheduled when you have a major project due for your best client.

GROWING WITHOUT ADDING PEOPLE

As soon as you hire your first employee, you change the complexity of your business. You no longer have choices about where, when, and how much you will work. You now have a responsibility to another human being. Before you take that big step, consider growing without employees. How can you increase profits and yet maintain your practice as a sole employee? First, consider using your local temporary services to help you out on occasion. Second, try several configurations involving other consultants: subcontracting for or collaborating with another consultant; joining a joint venture; offering other related services; or selling products that are related to your consulting work.

As soon as you hire your first employee,
you change the complexity of your business.

These are all viable options. Consider the advantages and disadvantages of each.

Could a Temporary Service Meet Your Needs?

One of the fastest-growing industries in the nation is temporary services. Corporate America is outsourcing almost every kind of job. We use temporary services when we have repetitive tasks or simple processes to complete. Temporary services are useful when we have huge mailings (envelope stuffing, stamping, labeling) or for a large amount of computer input or copying.

We find temporary employees to be especially helpful when everyone in the company is busy with a huge project and we need someone to serve as a receptionist.

Advantages. Temporary services can provide the specific skills necessary for repeat work. It is a reasonable price for short-term prequalified support. If you are in a bind, temps can fill in at the last minute.

Disadvantages. The disadvantage of temporary employees is that the individuals have to be trained each time you are sent someone new. It is highly unlikely that you will be able to use the same person more than twice. If the person is good, he or she will be offered a permanent position.

Another disadvantage is that you will not always have the best person from the agency if there were many requests ahead of yours. Also, no matter how clearly you define the task, the person who shows up may not be able to live up to your standards of quality.

> **Tip: The temps have it.**
>
> More employees are turning to gig work either as a side hustle or as their primary career. There is a site to locate almost any kind of skill you need for your consulting practice. The freelance marketplace has created three levels. The most basic level includes sites like Fiverr.com (which claims to be the largest) and microWorkers.com. The second level is still aimed at low cost, but freelancers bid for jobs. It includes sites such as Freelancer.com and UpWork.com. Finally, the last level includes Toptal.com and ScalablePath.com to support the best freelance talent. Know what you are getting into before using any of these.

Do You Want to Subcontract?

You could become a subcontractor for another firm, offering your services directly or perhaps completing design and development behind the scenes. Remember that, as a subcontractor, you must be seen by the client as an employee of the firm for which you are doing the work. Many consultants' egos will not allow them to do that.

Advantages. As a subcontractor, you could continue to run your own business while subcontracting with others. This provides an opportunity for you to fill in the gaps when you don't have billable work. If you have been offered a long-term project, it could provide a steady income.

A big advantage is that you will be able to work for or with other professionals. This will certainly give you experience and knowledge that you might not acquire any other way.

Disadvantages. The greatest disadvantage to subcontracting is that you will most likely make one-third to one-half of your daily fee. It is possible that you may need to turn down a full-paying project to fulfill your subcontracting responsibility.

You may have a difficult time working under someone else's business name—especially if you have had your own consulting business for any length of time. As stated earlier, we consultants typically have healthy egos that may create dissonance within ourselves.

Have You Considered a Joint Venture?

Some use the term *virtual partners* to describe a temporary arrangement, usually aimed at completing one project at a time. The parties involved may be separated geographically, but that is not a requirement. The partners in the joint venture may work under a name that represents the group. That name may remain while partners may come and go, depending on the project.

Typically no legal agreements are made. However, you should not become involved in a joint venture without some written agreement among all parties. This will save you time and energy should something negative occur.

Advantages. A joint venture provides a temporary arrangement. This allows you to work with others on an experimental basis. It allows you time to determine whether you would like to create a more permanent arrangement with some or all of these individuals.

The individuals have a shared responsibility for the outcome of the project, for completing the work, and for the financial success of the project.

Disadvantages. Because the joint venture operates under a loosely drawn up agreement, it is likely that something will be forgotten. The temporary arrangement exacerbates the situation, as individuals in the venture may not be as dedicated to its success as if they were in for the long term.

One of the biggest disadvantages is that the decision-making process may become convoluted—especially if more than two people are involved.

Do You Want to Collaborate with Another Consultant?

A collaborative arrangement is a fashionable growth option. You may hear a number of terms, such as "alliance" or "coalition" or "consortium," to describe a loosely formed arrangement of shared resources, clients, and decisions.

Although a collaborative agreement is similar to a joint venture, there are some key differences. A joint venture is project-oriented; a collaboration is relationship-oriented. Membership in a joint venture is temporary and ends when the project ends; a collaboration is a continuing relationship and is maintained whether or not there is a project.

Collaborating is similar to a partnership but has fewer legal ramifications. Sometimes consultants collaborate with one another as a way to determine whether they would like to form a partnership or corporation. Although the consultants may have good intentions, using the arrangement for that purpose is rarely a good idea. The loose agreement between two collaborating consultants is not the same as truly working together under a legal description that encourages individuals to make the best of any situation.

Before becoming involved in a collaborative arrangement, scrutinize the other individuals and the arrangement. Does the person's image reflect favorably on you? His or her values, ethics, expertise, experience, and reputation should be similar to yours. In addition, you will want to ensure that there is value in the relationship.

Working in a collaborative effort will most likely result in a greater investment of time than you may have originally thought. It will take longer to make decisions. It will require long, time-consuming communications. Sorting out support mechanisms and staff issues will take time. Planning will take longer. There are some common elements that should be in place for a successful collaborative effort to flourish:

- *Trust.* The effort should be based on trust by both consultants.
- *Value.* Each party must recognize the value he or she brings as well as the value the other consultant brings. In addition, each must clearly articulate the added value that neither of you would create if working alone.
- *Risk.* Both consultants must recognize the risk and the pros and cons of that risk.
- *Alignment.* Both parties must determine the degree to which they are aligned in mission, goals, values, and priorities and to what extent the differences may prevent success.
- *Guidelines.* All must agree on the guidelines, which will include communication, responsiveness, the ability to withdraw financial support, and so on.

Advantages. Some of the greatest advantages are for your clients. Collaborating with someone allows you to add services to those you presently offer. The collaboration means instant growth in your customers' eyes. Another advantage to your clients is that you will have backup if something should occur that prevents you from being available on a scheduled date.

Another advantage is that the collaborating parties have more for less. The collaboration allows two consultants to pool resources for efficiencies in marketing, product development, and other high-ticket items. In addition, it allows them to share support staff.

A collaboration also increases opportunities for you to learn from another professional. I recently formed an alliance with Halelly Azulay to produce online training for new training consultants. We each bring a different expertise. She is knowledgeable about the online training phenomenon and I bring the resources that will form the content for the course. It's a win-win for both of us as well as for the clients we will serve.

Disadvantages. Time becomes one of the greatest problems in a collaborative effort. Joint activities usually take more preparation time than solo events because you must discuss and plan as a team. Sometimes the projects each party brings get in the way and limit the time for joint activities. It is difficult for the individuals to give up these projects, because they are loyal to their clients, and the projects most likely are their source of cash flow. In the end, it becomes difficult to find time to generate collaborative efforts.

Lack of a legal agreement causes continued separation, which can prevent the collaborating parties from learning to work together. The logistics may cause problems if the individuals live a distance apart. If they rarely see one another, they may not find the time to begin to meld their businesses together. If your values clash and you are not working together, the collaboration is doomed.

As with most things, money can create problems. Because the collaborative arrangement keeps the individuals separate, they may not make final decisions about how much to charge, how to share revenues, how to determine required investments, and a host of other issues.

If the two individuals are working in the same field, there may be crossover of clients. If this creates a competitive situation, the collaborative arrangement will end.

Do You Want to Offer Other Services?

If you are a trainer, you might consider offering keynote addresses for conferences. Keep in mind that the two require very different skill sets. You could offer other services. For example, a computer consultant could teach evening computer classes at the local college. Consultants can also write newspaper or journal columns, write and sell articles, tutor college students in their professions, or create and sell subscriptions to a for-profit newsletter.

You could monetize your most popular service into an online course. What is your most popular service? Does it lend itself to creating an online course product? It would teach others how to do what you do. You have to choose carefully, because many topics have been so commoditized that they sell for under $25. If you can make the numbers work, go for it, but with just a little personal attention you can raise the cost to $99 or $999. It really depends on the topic and the audience.

Tip: Join the online course sensation.

You may be inundated with many offers to teach you anything online. You can launch a product for almost anything. Before you do, note that several pioneers have perfected the process and are happy to sell it to you. If this interests you, I suggest that you check out Jeff Walker at www.productlaunchformula.com. He seems to have done the most research and claims to have done over $400 million in product launches. That seems like a record you can launch from!

Before you decide to take on a new service, decide what effect, if any, it will have on your business image. You may decide that it will have a positive effect and will enhance your consulting business. On the other hand, you may decide that it will engulf your consulting business or be detrimental to your image.

Advantages. The advantage of offering other services is that you broaden your skills and capabilities. There is always the possibility that you may discover another career that you like even more than consulting!

Disadvantages. The greatest disadvantage is that you may spread yourself too thin, taking on too many different things. You may not focus well. You may also become so tied up in a new venture that you will not be available for a consulting project when it comes up.

Tip: Try coaching.

Have you considered coaching? Much of the work can be conducted through email and telephone calls. The field of executive coaching has been in existence for several decades. Today, it's not just the executives who have coaches; people in other key positions also avail themselves of coaching. I have a friend who has had the same coach for over 10 years. When I met him he was a new director, and he is now a vice president of the same organization. That is one measure of success. He has never met his coach in person. All of his coaching is conducted using the phone and email.

Most other jobs, such as teaching at a college or writing a newspaper column, require you to meet a consistent schedule—for example, show up every Tuesday and Thursday to teach. This does not fit into the erratic schedule of a consultant. You will need to determine whether two different services can live together under the same hat.

Can You Expand into the Product Market?

If you have been in business for a number of years, you probably have enough potential products in your files to fill a small library: questionnaires, activity pages, surveys, survey results, reading lists, topic papers, quotes, checklists, tests, quizzes, summary sheets, games, puzzles—books' worth of things you have used once. Could they become products to sell to clients?

The members of the National Speakers Association (NSA) are truly experts at turning their content into products. They take the best quotes from their speeches and turn out planning guides, pins, T-shirts, plaques, posters, videos, workbooks, newsletters, and special reports! They may sell such products in the back of the room or to the client, who distributes them after the presentation.

> **Tip: Write a blog.**
>
> Making money from a blog is possible and isn't even difficult anymore. Make money by putting ads on your pages (check out BlogAds or Google's Adsense). Use affiliate marketing, whereby a company agrees to pay you a commission for helping to sell their products (Amazon, Linkshare). Get sponsored by a company; deals range from including obvious advertising to adding a company's name, logo, and brand to an existing blog. Or get hired by a company to keep their blogs going. And finally, sell your own and others' intellectual property through your blog.

As a consultant, you don't want to open a store, but surely there is one book among all your stacks and files. Turn your favorite workshop into a how-to book for managers. How about a collection of self-evaluations or 10 activities that will improve [you name it]? An interesting phenomenon occurs after you are a published author (even if you self-publish). You become an "expert." This automatically gives you the authority to increase your fees!

How about recording your next presentation and selling it? You could create both video and audio recordings. Many listen to audiorecorded books in their cars during a long commute to work each day. Perhaps the next book they listen to will be yours!

Tip: Record a podcast.

And as long as you are taping content, consider podcasts. Podcasts present a way to distribute an audio or video episode via the Internet for playback at any time. Podcasts allow development in the form of event capture, new product information, negotiating ideas, or even new employee orientation that can be delivered on demand to anyone, anywhere. Before you start recording your first podcast, consider these suggestions for success: keep them short. Depending on your topic, the podcast could be as short as 10 minutes or, for a more in-depth topic, 60 minutes long; plan a series released on a specific schedule; script them just as you would any show; incorporate music; focus on one succinct idea; maintain professionalism; and archive your old podcasts. Perhaps you are a sales training consultant. Wouldn't it be great if past training participants could download one hot tip every Monday morning to start their week? The cost could be included in your original fee as a featured benefit for choosing you over your competitor. Or it could be sold as an add-on component.

Before you jump up and grab your iPhone, think about distribution. Who will sell your products for you? You could approach some of the large training product catalogs or publishers. It takes specific knowledge and special skills. For minimal sales, you could advertise on your website.

Tip: Look like a pro.

If you decide that recording in any format is something you want to try, be sure to check with the experts about what to wear, how to format, and how often to change scenes. For me that would be Jonathan Halls. Check out his book, *Rapid Media Development for Trainers*.

Product possibilities are endless. Here's a list that may pique other ideas:

- Sell an e-book.
- Publish and sell a newsletter.
- Print and sell articles, checklists, templates, or other tools to clients.
- Publish and sell instruments or surveys.
- Sell articles to magazines and trade journals.
- Syndicate your articles electronically.
- Conduct research, compile the results, write a white paper, and sell it.

Advantages. The advantage of producing products is really twofold. First, you have ways to make money while you sleep; you could be selling an asynchronous webinar on the other side of the world at the same time that you are consulting for a client in your own city.

Products may help to even out the dips in the uncertainty of consulting. Products can provide not only an additional revenue source, but a *steady* revenue source.

Second, your products keep your name out there. Not only are you making money from them, but they will serve as marketing tools as well.

Disadvantages. Products take time and an investment of cash to produce. Then you must distribute them and let people know that you have them for sale. Although most print media can be done print-on-demand, if that's not an option, products won't do you much good sitting in your garage. You must put them into potential buyers' hands.

Again, this is something you should discuss with others who sell products to determine whether it is a viable option for you to consider.

> **Tip: Use your IP to build new revenue streams.**
>
> Examine all the things you do for your clients. What intellectual property is hidden among all the client folders you file? What stand-alone products, processes, tools, or methods exist that would be valuable to others?

EXPAND YOUR GEOGRAPHICAL MARKET

If your business has been located in the same geographical area and you want to expand your horizons, you may want to look across the country or even to another country.

Do You Want to Expand Domestically?

You might ask your current clients for references to other similar organizations. Sometimes clients have locations in other cities, but they assume that you do not wish to travel. Let them know that you do.

You could also select cities or other states to which you would like to travel and identify several organizations for which you would like to provide services. Contact these organizations using the same process described in Chapter Five. If you live in Boston, Dallas probably sounds like a great place to go in January. Remember, however, if you do acquire work, it is doubtful that it will be seasonal and you will need to travel to Dallas in the middle of July's heat as well as the middle of January's welcome relief from Boston's blizzards!

Do You Want to Expand Internationally?

Perhaps you are interested in building business in Europe or Asia. How can you do that? One of the best ways to begin is to attend international conferences, such as IFTDO (International Federation of Training Development Organizations) or IODA (International Organization Development Association). Consider networking with the international attendees at domestic conferences. Many will have an international room set up for guests; visit them and exchange business cards. Of course, submit a proposal to speak at these conferences as well. You may meet foreign nationals who need someone to distribute their material in your country. This may grow into a two-way partnering. Let your clients who have global sites know that you are interested in working in their offices in other countries. Offer to provide similar services in other regions of the world.

My consulting in foreign countries all came because someone heard me speak at conferences held here in the United States. They asked me to take my message and my skills to Columbia, Peru, China, Taiwan, Malaysia, and Singapore. A couple of contracts led to repeat trips and over $1 million in additional consulting fees.

> **Tip: International contacts.**
>
> Would you like more information about IFTDO and IODA, the two international associations previously listed? Check out their websites at www.iftdo.org and www.iodanet.org.

Obtaining work in other countries may be difficult without someone to introduce you—someone who knows the culture. Unless you are a well-known "guru," it might be wise for you to work with a local firm or your own client organizations located elsewhere in the world. Read all you can about the culture before you go, and talk to people who have lived and worked there. Plan your trip so that you will have time in advance to meet with your local "coach," who can give you some guidance on the culture and specific organizational issues. Ideally, that same person will be available when you are with your foreign clients and provide feedback to you at breaks.

If you want to work internationally, the most important thing of all is to think of yourself as being a learner. You will be of the greatest value to your clients if you are a student of each culture that you visit and remember that no matter how competent you may be in your own fields, you are a beginner at the art of working, living, and learning in that new place. The rewards of being "at home" in the world are great. It all starts with being a learner and developing relationships that will make you a welcome visitor wherever you go.

International work brings two distinct advantages. The first is greater credibility among peers and clients. The second is that you will most likely be able to charge more for your services when working in foreign countries. By the way, always request payment in U.S. dollars and ask to have the funds wired directly into your account. As an alternative, request U.S. funds drawn on a U.S. bank. Fees for collecting from a foreign bank can be 20 to 25 percent of the transaction.

> **Tip: Get comfortable with the customs.**
>
> Once you land a job in a foreign country, gather advice about appropriate business etiquette, customs, protocol, and behaviors. An excellent website to help you is www.cyborlink.com.

DOING EVERYTHING YOU CAN TO GROW YOUR CURRENT BUSINESS

Ask yourself whether you have done everything you can to grow the business you now have. Sometimes we are so busy we forget the basics of the business we are in.

Some Questions

The following questions will jog your thinking about what you may be able to do with what you have:

- Have you recently studied your numbers? Have you compared them with past data? Have you conducted a reality check with another consultant to determine if your expenses are in line? If your income is reasonable?
- How closely are you following your business plan? Is that good? Or not? Just because you have a business plan does not mean you should shut your eyes to anything but what you have in the plan. Stumbling onto success may be just as good as planning for you. However, you do need to assess and redirect.
- Have you become overly dependent on one industry? Is it time to expand or at least to explore other industries?
- Have you expanded the coverage of your market area? Can you serve clients in the next state? On the other coast?
- Have you selected clients who hire you for the kind of projects you prefer? Who can provide repeat work? Who can pay the rate you charge? Who appreciate the value you bring?

- Are you selling the unique value proposition you can deliver, how to solve your clients' problems? Or are you still selling your competencies, processes, and tools?
- Have you professionalized your selling skills? Buyers buy, but they aren't sold to.
- Have you evaluated your consulting rate? Is it time to increase it?
- Have you kept up with technological advances? Are you current with how they affect your work? Have you incorporated them into your projects appropriately?
- Have you built relationships with your clients? With other consultants?

Your answers to these questions may contain some interesting answers for growth.

Ideas Outside the Norm

And then consider these ideas that go outside your business.

- *Invest in your business and yourself.* We all get too busy to do what we should to stay up to speed. I always return from a conference with a notebook full of ideas. Implementing just a few of them saves me time, improves my lifestyle, and increases profits.
- *Join a mastermind group.* Being a consultant can be lonely. You need someone to share ideas and solve problems with, and confirm that you are not crazy! Mastermind groups are excellent for holding you accountable for your growth plans.
- *Join an association.* There is a little-known association for consulting organizations called ISA—The Association of Learning Providers. Its purpose is to help training, performance, and talent development firms build, enhance, and share their success. Member companies range in size from $1 to $200 million. C-Level Forums, similar to mastermind groups, are held quarterly and included in your membership fee. More information at www.isaconnection.org.
- *Try a consulting matchup.* Check out PwC's Talent Exchange, where they connect independent consultants with PwC opportunities. I reviewed the roles available as I am writing this and found a finance transformation consultant on the West Coast; a benefits design lead in Irving, Texas; and a change

management lead in St. Louis, Missouri. MBO Connect is a similar sight. They are located at TalentExchange.Pwc.com and MBOpartners.com.

- *Identify the next big thing.* This takes a little research on your part. Try to predict the next urgent issue one of your clients will face. What's the next major challenge? Are they prepared for AI in their organization? Have they embraced agility? What's hot in their industry? Predict it and present it. Then offer to solve it.

Your Options

As a consultant you have many options. And because you are your own boss, you can decide which option to choose. Want to grow your business? First, define what you mean by "grow your business." Is it more income? More profits? More locations? More employees?

Next, review your strategic plan: Think about the kind of consulting you conduct, how your clients define your brand, and what makes your products and services unique. Also identify your ideal client. Third, determine the options for growth and the pros and cons for each and narrow your choices down to three or four. Then speak with consultants who have grown their businesses using these methods. Decide on the marketing techniques that will match your growth option.

Last, consider the implications for the bottom line, your time, and the added responsibility. Is it worth it? That's what Kyle was struggling with at the beginning of this chapter. His first three years in business were fun, but lately he's not feeling the same. Are there reasons to not grow your business? You bet. You could glean them out of some of the disadvantages listed in the early choices. We've summarized some of the key reasons in the side bar.

One of the advantages of being a consultant is that there are so many other avenues open to you. As you consider all your options, take care that you do not trap yourself into a financial commitment that you cannot support. If you decide to add individuals to your present business entity, consider the responsibility you have added and how it will affect you and your present business. Don't talk yourself into a situation that will negatively impact your lifestyle.

In the end it is all up to you. To grow or not to grow—that is the question.

Reasons to Stay Small

Growing a large consulting company is one route. But you may also want to remain small. Here are a few reasons to stay small.

- To maintain control.
- For a more balanced lifestyle.
- To have lower margins and higher profits.
- To gain agility for a faster response to market changes.
- For the ability to explore different specialties.
- To be able to choose your risk.
- It's less stressful.
- It doesn't require an office outside your home.
- It is easier to maintain quality.
- To limit your workload.
- To avoid regulation.
- To customize a personal retirement plan.
- For potential niche domination.
- To ensure customer reliance.
- Fewer distractions make it is easier to focus.
- It is easier to build and maintain a stellar reputation.
- To manage and supervise less.
- Your schedule is your own—mostly.

For the Consummate Consultant

Like most consultants, growing your business is always foremost in your mind. Be smart in how you approach this challenge. Growing your business does not always mean hiring more consultants. There may be more savvy ways to grow the bottom line without a huge office filled with consultants.

Trade a Name. Review your network of consultants to identify someone whose work you respect. Is there a way that you could each introduce the other to a current client? After the introduction make a warm call to expand your client base and land a new client.

Replicate Success. Review some of the engagements you've completed this past year. Which have delivered a substantial return on investment—200 percent or more? If they were implemented in only one department or at one site, can you replicate that success to the rest of the organization?

Grow or Go. Getting bigger is a choice, but getting better is essential. Don't follow the growth mantra without first examining what you really want out of your own gig.

The Ethics of the Business

9

It takes 20 years to build a reputation and five minutes to ruin it. If you think about that, you'll do things differently.

Warren Buffett

Asha was almost through her presentation. She was so excited she could hardly focus on what was happening. She was in the middle of her first sales call with a big client. She'd been a consultant for three years and was just not getting the traction she wanted—breaking through to a guaranteed six-figure income. Last year, she hired a consulting coach to help her determine what she needed to do. The experience was enlightening. Coach Carl helped her identify her target audience, develop her niche, create a marketing plan, and figure out how to set her rates. It was the rate issue that had been giving her the most heartburn.

Last month, Asha's coach insisted that she role play several sales calls. She hated role plays, but as she sat here in the hot seat with a potential client she realized how important it was to be ready to field questions and sales objections. Asha's coach recommended that she maintain control of the cost of the project until the end, and she'd done just what he suggested: She determined the value she anticipated the client would achieve from the project and then created three options at three price points, with the most logical option in the middle. Carl had suggested that she print the options out on heavy-duty classy paper and put the printout in one of her presentation folders along with her business brochure (something else Carl insisted she create).

"And so, as you see, I've addressed all your requirements and suggested a couple of additional components that weren't called out in the RFP, but that I think might . . ." Asha was saying when the client interrupted her.

"Yes, I am thrilled with how you interpreted what we need. And I am especially pleased with your insight and the additional ideas you've suggested. I am excited about sharing your plans with my boss this afternoon. But I am concerned. We've only budgeted $100,000 for this project. Will your additions add a great deal more to the cost?" the client asked.

Asha took a big gulp as she reached for the burgundy folder that held her pricing options. $100,000! Would it cover it? She thought, Well, there was no question that it would cover it! The client's budget was larger than her most expensive option! What should she do? She could give the client her investment proposal and leave $30,000 on the table—even if they selected her most expensive option. Or she could say something about providing the estimate this afternoon—now that she was clear about all the expectations. Yikes! What should she do?

■ ■ ■

Even though consulting is a high-paying, high-profile profession and 50 percent of people in MBA programs flirt with the idea of becoming a management consultant, jokes abound about consultants. Did you hear the one about the consultant who is asked the time by a client? The consultant asks for the client's watch and then says, "Before I give you my opinion, perhaps you could tell me what time you think it is." One of the best ways to ensure that consulting is not a joking matter is always to provide services in the most ethical manner, to build relationships with the highest level of integrity, and to run a business with the highest principles.

Perhaps I am just more sensitive to the negative jokes about consultants (Do you read "Dilbert"?), so I was surprised to learn that one of the motivations employees give for why they leave the corporate world to start their own businesses is ethical misconduct. Misusing company time, abusive behavior, lying to employees, employee theft, and violating company Internet policies are cited most often. Whether it is signing off on an exaggerated expense report or lying to a manager, employees no longer want to tolerate misconduct. The new independent workers want to set their own standards and live for a higher purpose.

Thomas Jefferson said, "In matters of principle, stand like a rock! In matters of taste, swim with the current!" As a consultant, your principles are always on the line, and your principles contribute to the ethics of the profession. Perhaps Thomas Jefferson could easily tell the difference between a principle and a taste, but it's a bit more complicated in the consulting profession.

One consultant will say it is appropriate to charge the full per diem for expenses, even if the full amount was not used, because the organization budgeted for that amount. A second consultant will say it is inappropriate to charge for what was not spent.

One consultant will justify varying what a client is charged if a client cannot pay the full amount. A second consultant will say that is absolutely wrong because it appears that the consultant is overcharging one client. Anything can be justified and argued for with facts.

Your reputation as a consultant will be created by thousands of actions, but may be lost by only one. It is imperative that you always model your high standards with clients, other consultants, and the general public.

Your reputation as a consultant
will be created by thousands of actions,
but may be lost by only one.

This chapter focuses on ethics in the consulting field. It will address the ethics issue from three relationship perspectives: consultant to client, consultant to consultant, and client to consultant.

I take a fairly hard stand with regard to ethics, for two reasons. First, I believe that the consulting profession's reputation has been tarnished by past practices and that taking a tightly focused approach may help to polish it to a reputable shine. Second, and more important, is that the practices I espouse here are those that my company follows and strongly believes are right.

If you intend to join the consulting ranks, support the profession by maintaining high ethical standards. You will benefit everyone associated with the profession.

CONSULTANT TO CLIENT

Let's first focus on the consultant's relationship with the client, because that's the one that probably concerns you the most at this time. We will discuss consultant to client ethics in two categories—delivery of services and business aspects.

Delivery of Services

Some pointers for delivery are given in the following paragraphs.

Deliver Only the Highest-Quality Products and Services. You have been paid to produce the highest-quality products and services, at a reasonable price, on time, every time. Provide quality first, last, and everything between. You will find that your clients will appreciate attention to details and services and products of the highest standards. One of the fastest ways to go out of business is by offering shoddy workmanship.

Accept Only Projects for Which You Are Qualified. Ethically, you must be willing to turn down a job that is beyond your competence. This does not mean that you should not accept projects that are a stretch or during which you can learn something. However, you should be able to contribute significantly to the client's needs. If you find yourself in this situation, share the name of a colleague who is qualified. Both the potential client and your colleagues will appreciate it. It will work in your favor.

Learn on Your Own Time. You will always need to learn something about the project or a new client, and there is often a hazy distinction about who is responsible for the investment. Our rule of thumb is that we will invest 5 percent of our time learning about our clients. That is, if we have a contract that is about 20 days in duration, we will spend at least one day learning about the client without charge. A more complex effort is usually a higher-ticket engagement, too, and the time will be incorporated. This is not something your clients will actually consider. It's just a guideline.

Turn Down Projects That Are Inappropriate. If you are asked to do something that is inappropriate from any standpoint, say no. Examples could include something that borders on discrimination, dishonesty, prejudice, unfairness, or is a conflict of interest to you or your beliefs. For example, a number of years ago, I was hired to conduct a team-building session. In the middle of the data-gathering step, I learned that the manager who had hired me actually wanted me to collect data that would support firing a specific individual. I wasn't as seasoned then as I am now, so I didn't end the relationship immediately; however, the next day, when I returned, instead of conducting the rest of the interviews, I turned in a resignation. This was one of the first times I saw a client sputter!

Cease Work If the Client Is Not Benefiting. Do not continue to work under a contract if you do not believe the client continues to gain from your involvement. You may have ended earlier than anticipated or circumstances may have changed that prevent the client from gaining any further benefits.

Place the Client's Interest Ahead of Your Own. This means that you will not take advantage of your client in any way—large or small. At the large end of the continuum, if you overbid the project, do not charge the full amount. At the small end of the continuum, it means not taking a limo when an Uber will do. You are charged with monitoring your own performance, as these are usually things that may never be uncovered.

Be Willing to Say "I Don't Know." Consultants must feel comfortable responding honestly, even when the answer is "I don't know." Some consultants think that they look weak if they do not have all the answers. Being honest with a client will gain more respect than will "faking it." As Mark Twain said, "If you tell the truth, you don't have to remember anything." Besides that, the truth may astonish some people. Almost everyone will react positively when you say, "I don't know, but I will find out and have an answer to you by tomorrow morning."

Accept Only Work That You Can Manage with High Quality. Consulting is notorious for having peaks and valleys. Therefore, consultants become nervous in the valleys and take on more work than they can manage later. They may fall behind on deadlines or cut corners to meet everyone's needs. How can you avoid overload without losing a client? I am honest up front and say something like, "We are looking forward to working with you, and right now we are swamped. I am sure you are disappointed; however, if we can put off the start date for three or four weeks, I can give your project the full attention it is due. Can we look at calendars now and determine when that might be?"

Accept Work Only from Organizations You Respect. When you work for organizations that you do not respect or whose business purpose may undermine your own values, you are hurting your own reputation. Watch for clients who may not appreciate your high standards of consulting or who try to reduce your quality. An advantage of being a consultant is the ability to choose your work.

Hold All Confidential Information Close. Never divulge any proprietary information or information about your contract. Although it might not be obvious why, it could give some other company a competitive advantage. You may also want to determine if you really need that confidential information to do your job. If you don't, you may not want to accept it; then you don't need to be concerned about keeping a close hold on it.

Avoid All Conflict of Interest. If you have the potential to benefit personally from any information you gain, you should not accept the project. For example, if you know that you will be in competition with the client in the future, do not accept the project. Some might think you are looking a gift horse in the mouth, but your conscience will know. This happened to us early in my career. Because I was on the board of directors, I knew that a competitive RFP would be released in a few short months by our association. At about the same time, another company asked me to work as a subcontractor to address a similar topic. I turned the project down and I also told them why. By the way, neither of us won the bid!

Accept Your Social Responsibility. Accept responsibility for and act with care and sensitivity to the fact that your work may alter the lives and well-being of people within your client organization.

Create Your Clients' Independence. The goal of every consultant should be to go into organizations, complete the work, and leave the clients better able to take care of themselves. An ad for a seminar entitled "How to Build and Maintain Your Consulting Practice" appeared in several newspapers. I was appalled to see that it touted

"How to build your client's dependency!" A few more ads like that and most consultants will not need to worry about their reputations!

Repay Any Loss You Cause the Client. Inform the client immediately when problems arise or errors occur. No matter what the error, if you are responsible, own up to it and take care of it. This is not only an ethical issue; you may be held legally liable if anyone is hurt or if the business is damaged in any way as a result of your error. This is, of course, why you need errors and omissions (E&O) insurance. *But* that does not mean you should think of insurance first. Think of doing the right thing first. Inform your client and fix the problem.

Complete All Work Yourself. If you find yourself in a bind and unable to complete an assignment, go to the client before you turn the project or even part of the project over to someone else. There could be another solution. Perhaps the client can take on more responsibility or was hoping to delay the project but did not want to change the agreement. You will never know unless you ask. Be up front.

Avoid Working with Competing Clients at the Same Time. Due to the sensitivity of information to which you may be exposed, it is likely that sharing such information with the competition, even inadvertently, could have negative consequences. We take this one step further. Due to the size and nature of many of our contracts, we will not work with clients' direct competition for a full two years after our last contact with them. In one instance, we designed a cultural shift for a client that would eventually be implemented by almost every large company in the country. Our client had the foresight to be on the cutting edge and start first. We agreed not to work with their competition for two years following the final payment of the project. What we didn't expect is that they would contract with us for a small project every year for several years to keep that agreement in place! I thought the client was very astute and creative—if not tricky!—with their solution.

Conduct Regular Self-Examination of Your Practice. During and after consulting engagements, assess your progress and results. Learn from the experience. The most valuable assessments occur when you can invite your clients to participate. We usually complete an after-action review (a term we picked up from our Navy clients) to uncover what went well and what didn't, as well as what we'll do differently the next time. We keep a lessons-learned book, too. It's amazing how short memories can be.

Continue to Provide Excellent Services That the Client May Never Comprehend. Someone will notice. Even if no one does, you know you did what was right. We conducted the same workshop for a large manufacturer for 18 months. Near the end of the contract, a participant said she signed up specifically to meet us. She was from accounts payable and said she wanted to see the only trainers who were not gouging the company on expenses! That was a true statement. The company was located 1,500 miles away from our offices and we were on-site about two weeks each month. Of course, that meant lots of travel. We are firm believers in keeping expenses down. If no one in the client/consultant partnership benefits, then the money does not need to be spent. This belief ensures that we work to get lower-price travel fares, stay in moderate hotels, and eat meals that are reasonably priced. In this case, someone noticed—the client.

Always Give Credit Where Credit Is Due. Never pass off someone else's work as your own. Obtaining permission to use someone else's work is easier than you can imagine. Tom Wood, owner of Watershed Associates, one of the best negotiating consulting firms in the world, shares his frustration with other consultants who make excuses for why they did not get permission to use someone's material: "It's not a big deal—I'm only going to use two minutes," or "I'm promoting the movie by showing the clip!" Tom uses several movie clips in his seminars and is proud to have obtained permission to use all of them. He says it feels good to be "squeaky clean"!

> **Tip: Get permission.**
> Yes, you need permission, and it's not that difficult to obtain. Use the Copyright Clearance Center at www.copyright.com to get permission for almost anything. Tom Wood gets permission for his movies from Motion Picture Licensing Corporation at www.mplc.com. Not sure? When in doubt, ask.

Copyright knowledge is so basic and copyright infringement is so detrimental, I would think that everyone would know the consequences by this time. Apparently not. I spoke at an association conference last week. The woman who followed me had a ton of technology to hook up. There were wires everywhere! Needless to say, she was anxious to get me off the stage. While I was packing up and answering a few questions from my audience, we were nearly blown out of the room with some loud top-hit music blaring from her iPhone. I am almost certain she did not have permission from all the bands she was featuring to use their music. But I also knew that to ask her whether she knew the consequences of playing copyrighted music without permission would upset her before her session. I let it go. Perhaps she'll read this book. Copyright is serious business. If you are not sure, ask.

Business Aspects

Can you be more businesslike while practicing integrity and being ethical? Here are a few things for you to consider.

Adhere to a Consistent Pricing Structure. If you followed our advice in Chapter Three to establish a fee structure and to stick with it, you have already created an ethical foundation for your business. We said there that you should identify a clear and consistent pricing structure for all of your clients. Your structure should clearly spell out any differences among clients, such as nonprofit groups or government agencies, different kinds of work, or where the work is completed. Be consistent. I know that pricing based on the value may be touted as the best approach, and many times it may be. Unfortunately, many clients are not in a position to look at your pricing structure that way. I also find that establishing a variable rate only works when you can clearly differentiate where the variation exists. Asha in this chapter's opening was using a variable rate structure.

I once hired a subcontractor with whom I needed to establish a daily rate. We would have more than 20 subcontractors on this job and the client wanted to pay each of them a daily rate, but was willing to pay different amounts within reason. When I asked the potential subcontractor what his daily rate was, his first response was $1,200 to $1,600. When I asked what constituted the difference, he could not give me a specific or measurable definition. Two weeks later, he came to me and proposed that I take 15 percent and he take 85 percent of some arbitrary daily fee. I responded that we all needed to try to give clients as much for their money as we could and that this client had specific requirements. He finally agreed to accept a fee of $850 for writing, data gathering, and phone interviews, and $1,100 for on-site strategy development. The client was able to accomplish about 30 percent more for the same amount of money. The real loser here was the subcontractor. Although he was good at his craft, his approach to business needed some work.

Charge for the Work That Needs to Be Done. It may be tempting to charge more just because you know the client has more in the budget. Don't do it. You will never feel good about it. Also, don't add on services that the client really does not need. Can you feel the struggle that Asha was experiencing at the beginning of this chapter?

What if you have quoted an amount and the project actually takes less time and effort? It's your call. You can justify charging the full price or you can buy surprised respect from your client by charging for only what was required. When I was first starting my consulting business, we returned excess money to a large firm—or, I should say, we *tried* to return the money we'd been paid. The company called us to say that there was no process for putting the returned fee back into the system! I have often wondered if that was actually true or if it was just a line to get us to keep the money. They contracted with us for more than a dozen years.

Charge Only for Reasonable Expenses Actually Incurred. Expenses are petty little things that can easily lead to a distrustful relationship. The easiest way to deal with them is to build things such as telephone calls and express mail into your project fee, so that you neither need to track them nor present them to your client for payment.

Expenses are petty little things that can easily lead to a distrustful relationship.

Travel expenses should always be charged at cost and verified with receipts. Do not exaggerate mileage and do not exceed reasonable expenses. The question you should ask yourself is "Would I spend this if I were at home?" For example, "Would I eat this $78 lobster dinner if I were at home tonight?" If the answer is no, it is probably not a legitimate expense.

Double dipping, or charging two clients for the same trip, is one of the worst ways a consultant violates the trust between consultant and client.

Bottom Line

Your fee structure, your expense report, and how you deliver your product are all important aspects of building an ethically strong relationship with your client. The bottom line, however, is that the ethical overtones will be dependent on the personal and professional relationship between individuals.

How can you determine whether you are doing everything possible to build this relationship? Ask your client. Discuss it. Your client may not be aware of your standards or what you do to maintain them. This kind of discussion will build respect for you and your consulting firm.

CONSULTANT TO CONSULTANT

A consultant's relationships with other consultants are critical. You will want to maintain your reputation among your peers. Let's discuss this first from a subcontracting relationship and then look at other situations that you may experience.

Subcontracting

Subcontracting is a special relationship. Some guidelines for subcontracting are given in the following paragraphs.

Subcontractors Shall Represent Themselves as a Part of the Primary Consultant's Organization. Most clients feel nervous when they believe a group of independents, a hodgepodge of consultants, will come in to work on their delicate problems. Thus, it is important to present a united front. As a subcontractor, you give up the right to represent your firm or to discuss it. You give up that right in exchange for steady work.

Subcontractors Shall Not Market to the Client. Even if the client approaches you, the client belongs to the primary consultant, who has invested in marketing to this particular client. Report any offers you receive to the primary consultant. Perhaps the two of you can work something out, such as one or the other of you providing the service and the other receiving a percentage of the fee. Some firms have their subcontractors sign noncompete agreements. We do not usually do that. We state what we believe is right and then trust the subcontractor to do the right thing. We believe that a client is not fair game for a subcontractor until at least two years past the final contract date. Noncompete agreements rarely stand up in court because of questions about whether the relationship has employee or 1099 status.

Subcontractors Shall Not Speak for or Represent the Client. Subcontractors should not speak for the client in contractual matters, changes in the delivery, or anything else. The primary consultant must take care of all issues and questions. The subcontractor should never discuss money with the client.

Subcontractors Shall Be Positive and Supportive. Subcontractors must support in word and deed the delivery of services—and that means no eye-rolling, either! The subcontractor's responsibility is to enhance the primary's performance. This is sometimes difficult. Egos get in the way. One tries to outguess the other.

Primary Consultants Shall Clearly Identify All Issues of Pay, Time, and Expectations Up Front. Be completely honest and candid. State doubts you may have about any aspect of the project, even if it has not been stated by the client and is only your gut feeling. If the primary consultant builds in a "paid-when-paid" provision in the contract, it should be clearly discussed before any work commences. As an act of good faith, the primary can include a net five days for payment to the subcontractor, once the client pays the primary.

Primary Consultants Shall Keep Subcontractors Informed. Subcontractors are very similar to employees, and you have the same ethical responsibilities to let them know if you have any concerns about the original plan. For example, let subcontractors know if a project will be extended or shortened. Keep them informed about any doubts the client may have. Build a team spirit.

Other Consultant-to-Consultant Experiences

You will find yourself in other situations that test your ethical stamina. Here are several.

Give to Your Colleagues More Than You Get. I believe there is very little new under the sun. I will always give credit to anyone from whom I get a new idea, but never think that my ideas are so unique that they cannot be shared. Therefore, anytime I can help someone, I do. I will send a book upon request or give advice or recommend another consultant. If someone asks permission to use my materials I always grant it—but I do expect someone to ask. I am not alone. There are many others who believe that collaboration sustains the consulting profession.

Julie O'Mara, for example is a world-renowned diversity consultant. Some years ago I sent her this email:

> I am working with a client who has had a couple of attempts at diversity efforts and they always fizzle out. They mean to do well, but just don't "take the time" to get the support from the senior leaders. In the past they have

had five years of external consultants who spent four to five days per week at the organization, and they have had a diversity council, but just don't seem to make any headway. Consultants have been gone now for three years. The organization has a new diversity coordinator, but she doesn't know where to start. Can you provide me with a bit of direction? Is there a book or plan or something that I can hand them—or work with them to create—that will get them started? If the answer is too long, or if what they really need is *you*—just say so. I am not looking for free consulting. Hope this explains it. I am sure it is a story you've heard before.

Julie, the quintessence of professionalism and a diversity expert, responded immediately, saying, "Not a simple answer. I have some thoughts. I have an hour-long drive to a client. I can call you from the car and would be glad to share some ideas. I'll be in the car from about noon until 1:15 PDT. Will that time work and what number can I call? I have other times to talk, but that would be the easiest. Attached are two documents that I'll refer to."

Julie spent an hour with me on the phone laying out the entire plan, what I needed to do, how the client needed to be involved, how to design the intervention, and what to do next. I followed up with a handwritten note and a thank-you puzzle. The client was finally successful.

Contrast this with another professional, who asked me to share an hour's worth of content, which I did willingly at 9 p.m. However, nine months later when I asked for similar support, he stated that his content was proprietary and he could not discuss it with me. I went to his website and printed off what I needed.

Here's another example of one of our stellar professionals. I received a message through LinkedIn from someone who had a dire problem. She'd read one of my books and didn't understand some aspect of it and needed to talk to me about it. Could I talk that night? I responded that I could and spent about an hour on the phone giving advice. The conversation was pleasant and I promised to send her a couple of my books. I ended up being generous and sending her about $200 worth of my books (and yes, authors do pay for their own books). A month passed and although she lived in another country with much higher postage, I never heard from her. I decided to send a message asking if the package had arrived. Her answer was, "Oh, yes. It arrived weeks ago." There was no thank you.

Asking for Help Is Okay, but Don't Expect Others to Do Your Work. As I said earlier, I will always assist where I can, but I can't do your job for you. This situation happened more than 10 years ago, but it is one I still think about on occasion. A man whom I had met briefly on one occasion emailed me in desperation asking me to help him with a consulting project: "I am enclosing the five PowerPoint slides and hope that you can suggest activities from the *Pfeiffer Annuals* or develop activities that I could use with my client—at least one for each of the five slides." He was in effect, asking me to design his training session.

I wrote back,

> I am sorry that I cannot help you. Coaching is not my area of expertise. It may seem like a simple request, but I do not select activities as you presented. It would seem to me that you need to design a full-day coaching course. If the slides you presented me are all the materials you have, you will probably need at least four days' worth of design. Then you will design the activities as a part of the holistic design. I rarely use the activities from the *Annuals* exactly the way they are, but, rather, I customize them for every situation and every client. So you see I do not have enough information to make a decision. Good luck to you!

He emailed again, "I thought I had the course designed, but the clients changed their minds. I have to redesign the material to fit the audience as much as possible. Is it possible to send me the list of activities for the 2002, 2003, 2004, 2005, 2006, and 2007 *Pfeiffer Annuals* (for both the Training and Consulting)? Then I could decide what might fit."

I wrote back, "I am on the road for the next week. I am with a client from morning until about 9:00 p.m. each night. I do not have access to email once I go into their secured office space and my office manager, Lorraine, is out until next Tuesday. So I am afraid we are no help to you. Check for the Table of Contents to the 12 Annuals on the Jossey-Bass website. You know, sometimes you just say no to the client too . . ."

He emailed *again*, "Thanks for telling me where to look, actually I still have a week if you could tell Lorraine to contact me in addition. The last time I checked, they did not list the table of contents." There were several more emails back and forth, plus a fax to him of about 40 pages.

In the end we never heard how his problem ended. He never acknowledged our support or thanked us.

Thank Your Colleagues. You knew that was coming! While it may not be an ethical issue, do not forget to thank your colleagues. At the least, take a couple of minutes to send an email. Even better, buy a cool thank-you card (you can find ones that sing!) and write a couple of personal words inside. Thank those who help your success. If you don't, they may feel used.

Do Your Part. Consultants are like mailmen: "through rain or sleet or falling snow...." No matter what, you do not let your colleagues down by being a no-show when you have agreed to support them. There is always a way. Find it.

Be Positive. When you discuss other consultants, it is unprofessional to criticize them. Take care with your nonverbals as well. Subtle signals may be observed by those around you. If you do have serious reservations about the competence or behavior of another consultant, you are ethically responsible for confronting that individual. As professionals, we must regulate ourselves to ensure high standards and ethical behavior.

CLIENT TO CONSULTANT

Although you have no control over your clients' behavior, you should be aware of some of the things clients may do that can undermine your relationship with them. I'd like to believe that some clients simply do not know better. In that case, it is our responsibility to educate them. If we all inform them of the effect any of their behaviors have on us, we will improve relationships for all consultants and clients.

In other cases, the client may have an agenda that does not meet your standards. Typically you would learn about this during the early stages of the relationship. Turn the project down and find something else.

Sometimes the client's agenda is not apparent until later in the project. You may see warning signs along the way. The client may have unrealistic expectations of you or may begin to withdraw commitment from parts of the project. Be honest and candid with the client to resolve your concerns. If the client will not move back on track, you can either work within the boundaries you have been given or quit. What unethical actions might you encounter? A few are listed in the sidebar.

Client Cues of Deception

You may encounter times when a potential client isn't in synch with you or is using you in some way. Watch for these signs.

Prior to contracting with you, the client:

- Wants to "pick your brain."
- Offers you lower pay than you quoted in your proposal.
- Has asked for your proposal in order to have the minimum number of quotes, without any intention of giving you the job. (Many clients have no idea that it takes four to 20 hours to write a good proposal.)
- Requests samples of product from several consultants, then puts them together and develops a program based on information that came from the consultants.
- Already has decided what the answer is to the problem.

During the project, the client:

- Fails to provide data and information as promised.
- Is slow to approve work.
- Is slow to approve invoices.
- Shifts gears in the middle of the project.
- Refuses to remove barriers for you, such as difficult staff.
- Ignores your recommendations.
- Asks you to do something that was not in the contract.
- Presents your ideas to management without sharing the credit.
- Requests that you omit information from a report.

PARTING ETHICS SHOTS

I hope you will not face too many ethical decisions as you start your consulting firm. Do recognize the importance of your decisions. Let's consider codes of ethics and how you might approach the ethics of international work.

Codes of Ethics

A code of ethics details the core guidelines of a profession. It highlights what is expected of a professional in the field. Most cover things such as conflict of interest, representing good faith, and the perception of the public. They usually cover broad topics of honesty, integrity, transparency, respect, fairness, and moral principles. A professional association or society expects its members to adhere to these ethics at the minimum.

Professional associations that represent consultants, such as the Institute of Management Consultants (IMC), the International Association of Registered Financial Consultants (IARFC), and the Professional and Technical Consultants Association (PATCA), have codes of ethics. If you do not know what your association's ethics code is, call the customer service line and ask that it be sent to you.

Tip: See their ethics.

To view IMC's code of ethics, check the website at www.imcusa.org.

As an independent consultant, you will establish your own code of ethics. You will develop a set of ethical standards that you choose to abide by as you do business. That is both a privilege and a responsibility. It is a privilege that you have been given. As a consultant, you do not need to live by others' ethics. It is a responsibility that you must accept. As a consultant, you have the ability to increase the public's respect and trust for the consulting profession.

Tip: Subscribe to an online ethics newsletter.

Ethics Today Online is a forum for exploring a broad range of organizational ethics and character development issues. It is published monthly and available at www.ethics.org. The Society for Business Ethics is an international organization engaged in the study of business ethics; its newsletter is available at www.societyforbusinessethics.org. Both newsletters are free.

International Ethics

Like everything in the world, ethics may not be black and white when it comes to international work. Business practices that are illegal, or at least frowned upon, in one country are allowed, or at least tolerated, in another. For example, in some Latin American countries, bribery and kickbacks are a part of doing business. In some Asian nations, insider trading is not a crime. I've conducted a great deal of work in China and wrestled with some things I've come up against.

A Chinese friend characterized some of the concerns I was having as, "In China, a handshake is only meant to be good until a better deal comes along." So I challenge you to wrap your head around that. I certainly didn't have to like or adopt this ethical philosophy, but it helped me to understand what was inside others' psychs. I think about that explanation often. Who's to say it isn't right?

If you have the courage to face the truth and do what is right, you will always feel good about the services you provide and you will do what is best for the profession. Place a high value on your talents and your high-quality service. Think highly of yourself. Do not sell out on your integrity; do not negotiate your reputation away. As a consultant, your principles are always in jeopardy. When your name is on the project, your reputation is on the line.

> *When your name is on the project,*
> *your reputation is on the line.*

For the Consummate Consultant

Your work and your company's future depend on clients. Without clients, there are no engagements. There is no future. Clients want to work with an ethical consultant to whom they can entrust their most pressing problems. Be that consultant. Build a trusting relationship, one that is built on solid integrity and ethical actions.

It's Not the Price. Avoid competing on price alone. Propose value for the client. Express and believe in your proposition's benefit to your client. Competing on price can just spell trouble. Either you won't have enough money to complete the engagement with the quality your client deserves or you will lose and damage your reputation in the process.

Don't Gloat. There are plenty of braggarts in this business. Do not be one of them. Modestly, and with all the dignity you can muster, give all credit to your client. They hired you because they knew you would be able to help them. Remember, it's a partnership. Make your client the hero!

Offer More. As the owner of your consulting firm, plan time to connect with the senior-level clients. You may have subcontractors or employees who are doing the work, but they still want to see you. And they want to know that you care. Are you meeting their needs? How could you exceed their needs? Demonstrate that you want to be the solution.

Exude Professionalism

10

If we did all the things we are capable of, we would literally astound ourselves.

Thomas Edison

Sarah stared at the raindrops trickling down her windshield, not trusting herself to drive yet. Wow, she hadn't seen this one coming. Her job had been eliminated. Eliminated! As if the work was going to go away. The merger had occurred almost a year ago, and many employees were let go soon after. She thought her job was safe. Then again, if she was absolutely honest, there were little signs: her move to a different office, being removed from the Thursday morning planning meeting, changed assignments. Yeah, there were signs, and she had a gut feeling for a while.

She was 54 and had planned to stay with this company until she retired. She'd dedicated her life to it. Now what? Well, there was her severance pay. That would get her through a few months. Wait! What's that blue envelope on the dash? That's right, Derrick, her friend from HR, had been waiting at her cubicle and helped her pack up her things. Of course, there wasn't much to pack, since the company

273

had gone to the open seating arrangement. He must have known this was going to happen. Well, of course he did; he's in HR.

Sarah opened the envelope and saw a quickly scribbled note saying, "I'll miss bumping into you in the breakroom. I have an idea. Call me at home tonight." Behind the card were pages he'd copied out of a book, "Competencies to Boost Your Consulting Success" from *The New Business of Consulting*. Hmm, he thinks I should be a consultant, Sarah thought. I wonder what he's plotting.

She scanned the list of eight competencies and the self-assessment: professional standards and awareness, business development, mindset. Yes, this could be interesting, she thought. There would be so much to learn. How would I find clients? Who would pay me? Can I do this? Can I reach professional consulting status? She put the article back in the envelope.

Ah, the sun is peeking out. Oh, and there is a tiny rainbow. That's a good sign. I think it's safe to drive now. I'll stop at Starbucks for a chai latte on my way home and complete this self-assessment. At least I have something to think about and a conversation with Derrick to look forward to tonight.

■ ■ ■

What does it take to be a true model of success and professionalism in the consulting world? Most likely the same things required to be a professional in any vocation, whether it's ballet, football, chemistry, landscaping, teaching, or writing. I once read that most people achieve only a third of their potential. Successful professionals in any position achieve much more than a third of their potential because they work at it.

Most people achieve only a third of their potential.

What It Means to Be a Professional

Professionals often have a reputation to grow into and live up to. Can you think of examples when you did each of these?

- Professionals assess where they are compared with where they want to be or where their customers expect them to be.
- Professionals continue to learn. They realize the value of expanding their knowledge and skills to develop and evolve the expertise expected of them.

- Professionals improve their processes continuously. They deliver services and products to their customers that are always on the cutting edge of industry trends.
- Professionals balance their lives and their businesses. They know the value of rejuvenation and renewal. They make conscious choices about how to spend their lives.
- Professionals manage their time. They are busy people who have learned ways to invest their time in the things that count.
- Professionals motivate and inspire others. Their authenticity paired with their enthusiasm sparks excitement and encourages others to aspire to a higher level of expertise.
- Professionals give back. No one "makes it" without the help and support of many others. True professionals give back to the profession, the community, their families, and their colleagues.

COMPETENCIES TO BOOST YOUR CONSULTING SUCCESS

Successful professionals step back and take stock of where they are and where they want to be. They determine some measure of success, drive a stake in the ground, and head for it. But what skills will be required? I often see articles such as "25 Qualities of a Rock Star Consultant," "Seven Essential Entrepreneurial Skills," or "A Dozen Attributes of a Successful Consultant." I started to collate several of the lists and found that almost none had the same skills. This told me that a successful consultant needs to be everything! Well, that's not helpful! Instead, I'll present the competencies that I share with those who are exploring or expanding their consulting roles.

The next few paragraphs will help you assess where you are as a consultant. Many ways exist for you to measure how well you are doing. I've coached a couple hundred consultants in getting started—some formally, other informally. The consultant competencies we are about to discuss are the things that most new consultants frequently skim over when they start. They are often in such a hurry to get a client, to sign a deal, or to determine how much they will charge that they skip some of the basics.

Who can blame them? Consulting is an exciting profession and a quick start will get them to results faster. There is another side, however, and that is laying the groundwork for a solid foundation. If these competencies are given little attention at the start, they may come back to bite you down the road. The sooner you start thinking about what you stand for as a consultant, where you are, and where you want to be, the more solid your foundation. Think about these eight competencies. Consider them guides to reaching much more than a third of your potential.

Competency 1: Professional Standards

Establish standards for yourself that are high enough to keep you on your consulting toes; position a bar that encourages continual reaching.

Establish standards for yourself that are high enough to keep you on your consulting toes.

Guarantee that your services will be the highest quality your clients have ever experienced. If you have employees, help them understand how important quality is to your business reputation. Put quality and your clients ahead of everything else—including profitability. What kind of a remark is that? Especially from someone who has just written a book telling you how to run a financially sound business!

It may very well be one of the best pieces of business advice in this book. The project will end; your relationship will not. You will learn from pricing mistakes and you will not make them again. Poor-quality service mistakes will follow you and your reputation for life. A project that goes in the red is a small price to pay for a lifetime reputation. You are only as good as your last client says you are. Set your standards high and never compromise them. Our standard is "Quality: first, last, and everything in between."

During your start-up:

- *Create your company's guiding principles.* What do you want your company to be known for?
- *Think of a company that you respect and interact with.* What does it do that keeps you coming back? How can you build those standards into your business?

Competency 2: Professional Awareness

Stay on top of the profession by having a clear understanding of consulting, its practices, and where it's going. This includes knowledge of state-of-the-art practices as well as the fads of the day; knowledge of the industry and consulting gurus as well as their philosophies; and knowledge of the professional organizations, journals, and newsletters that can help you stay abreast of the field.

One of the best ways to stay in touch with the field is to be an active member of your professional association. I often hear consultants say they "can't afford the dues." They have it all wrong. They "can't afford *not* to pay the dues"! Your ability to keep up with the profession is dependent on staying in touch. It is an investment in *you*. If you won't invest in you, who will?

It is an investment in you.
If you won't invest in you, who will?

Whether you have chosen the Institute of Management Consultants, the Association of Talent Development, or the ISA—The Association of Learning Providers, do more than just write the check for your annual dues. At a minimum, attend the organization's annual conference. Volunteering for a committee is also a great way to stay in touch with the profession. You will be involved in the work of the profession, communicating with other professionals, and working with colleagues in your profession. It's an enjoyable way to stay up to speed!

During your start-up:

- *Meet with two consultants you admire and respect.* Ask them how they stay up to speed with the changes within the profession and what they see on the horizon. Ask them what they are reading and who they follow on TED Talks or LinkedIn.
- *Identify several blogs written by other consultants you can follow.* Select a couple that seem to keep you abreast of topics that resonate with you and changes in the industry that are important to you and follow them. To start, I'd recommend Andrew Sobel.

Competency 3: Consulting Skills

Your ability to do the work is a basic requirement. A professional consultant knows the basics of the consulting process: defining a business need, clarifying expectations and reaching agreement (contracting), gathering data, recommending options, and implementing change. Continue to learn techniques and strategies that move you from being an apprentice toward being a master consultant.

In addition to becoming an expert at the consulting process, you will need other skills such as problem solving, managing meetings, designing surveys and materials, team building, and facilitating.

Certification or accreditation is available in many fields as a way of learning and achieving a professional standing in your profession. The accreditation could be related to your profession, such as a Certified Public Accountant (CPA) or a Certified Electrical Engineer (CEE). It could also relate to your specific consulting area, such as a Certified Professional in Learning and Performance (CPLP), a Certified Speaking Professional (CSP), International Coach Federation (ICF) Credential, a Certified Professional Facilitator (CPF), a Registered Organizational Development Consultant (RODC), or a Certified Management Consultant (CMC).

During your start-up:

- *Volunteer to help another consultant—without pay, if you need to.* This will give you an opportunity to view an expert in action. It also gives you a chance to build a relationship with someone to share ideas with in the future.
- *Learn the right questions to ask.* Sobel and Panas's *Power Questions: Build Relationships, Win New Business, and Influence Others* is high on my list of resources.

Competency 4: Communication Skills

The skill that goes awry the most often in any situation is communication. Therefore, you are probably not surprised to see communication skills listed as a critical competency. Your abilities to listen, observe, identify, summarize, and report objective information are important for a productive working relationship with your client. Equally important are your abilities to persuade, offer empathy, solve problems, and coach others.

Authentic communication, or stating what you are experiencing in the moment, is, in Peter Block's (2011) words, "the most powerful thing you can do to have the leverage you are looking for and to build client commitment." This statement indicates how important authenticity is to the client relationship. Authenticity means that you are able to express who you are and what you are feeling clearly without being inappropriately influenced by those around you. It is honesty, candor, and clarity, combined with sensitivity to others.

During your start-up:

- *Tap into your knowledge of communication styles.* If you have never completed an assessment to determine yours, do it today. The DiSC® is a good place to start. But don't just learn about your style; learn how to approach and sell to other styles as well, because it is unlikely that you will sell only to clients with a style similar to yours. You need to internalize the content existing in communication styles.
- *Review your last 360-degree assessment.* Look for clues that will help you be a better communicator in your new role as a consultant.

Competency 5: Mindset Success

Carol Dweck (2016) has given credence to the concept of mindset. Her research provides proof that what we think becomes reality—especially about our talents and abilities. How does this affect a professional consultant? Dweck's research wasn't available when I started consulting. The best that I had was the value of positive thinking—and I practiced it religiously.

When making the decision to leave my comfortable job and become an independent consultant, I remember thinking, "I can't not succeed!" I realize there's a double negative in that statement but it demonstrates where I started—not succeeding—so the words are meaningful to me. I was in my car driving from Madison, Wisconsin, on I90–94 when it all came together. Soon after, I discovered that a number of books had been written about positive thinking and I read all I could.

Your mindset and attitude are elusive. They cannot be measured or clearly defined, but we all know they are there. A professional maintains a positive attitude under all circumstances, asking, "What's good about it?" when something goes wrong. As a consultant, you'll need to be self-confident, cope with rejection, be open-minded and flexible, and believe in people. Professionals take responsibility for their actions and are accountable to their clients.

Your mindset about consulting will permeate everything you do. If you love the work, enjoy helping your clients, get a high from the challenge of difficult projects, and find consulting to be a rewarding outlet for you as a person, you have probably found your purpose in life. In *The Consultant's Calling*, Geoffrey M. Bellman (2002) suggests that you "Pursue this work as a personal calling, bringing who you are to what you do." Appreciate the value and benefits you bring to your clients and you will experience an increase in your confidence to win new client work.

Love what you do. I am delighted that I stumbled into the consulting field almost 40 years ago. I love the work and it shows. Don't get up and go to work every morning; get up and go to play. I am fortunate because I am allowed to play every day—and in the process make a good living. Consulting offers a good income, but if you are only in it for the money, you may not succeed.

Don't get up and go to work every morning; get up and go to play.

During your start-up:

- *Check your mindset.* What kind of self-talk are you practicing? A proper mindset allows you to address unplanned setbacks as learning opportunities. Although sometimes I do wonder how many more "learning opportunities" I can handle. You need to believe in your business and that you will be successful. Certainly, working on your business is important, too. Chapter Three opens with the quote "The harder I work, the luckier I get." The combination of a positive mindset and doing what you need to do will lead to success.

- *Find your positive corps.* No, that's not a typo for core. I do mean corps—the group of people you will hang around with who help you maintain your positivity. Meet with them when you are unsure. Celebrate with them when you are successful. And between times, enjoy their presence.

Competency 6: Business Development

Generating work provides the steady flow of projects essential to stay in business. You must know enough about sales and marketing to be able to analyze your present situation, clarify a marketing strategy, set measurable goals, and select marketing tactics to accomplish those goals.

You'll need to know how to develop an annual marketing planning calendar and how to monitor your results. You will want to determine how to even out your workload and income. Your ability to sell yourself and your services is the competency that keeps you in business. Return to Chapters Five and Seven for reminders. One last thing that we sometimes forget: Be sure clients are aware of your talents and expertise.

During your start-up:

- *Take advantage of your time.* You will never have the luxury of so much time for developing business as you do when you start your business. Use that time wisely. Identify the client problems you will solve, ask friends and colleagues for referrals, send personalized letters and emails to potential clients, add testimonials to your website, determine the best way to get your name out there, and finally, revisit (or create) your annual marketing plan and calendar from Chapter Five. Now is the best time to warm up your cold calls, following the process in Chapter Five. Again, use your time wisely.
- *Meet with someone who is a friend—but could be a potential client.* Review your business development plans with this person and ask for honest, candid feedback. Take good notes. Do not make excuses. And say "thank you very much" at the end.

Competency 7: Business Management

Staying in business is less dependent on how good a consultant you are than on how well you run your business. To stay focused, refer to your business plan on a regular basis.

Take care of the details of managing your business. Selecting a team of professionals to assist you (banker, accountant, attorney); tracking expenses and projecting income; invoicing in a timely manner; studying your data to learn how well you are doing; developing contracts and proposals; understanding office technology, systems, and equipment; dealing with suppliers; managing your money; scheduling, informing, and tracking clients and projects; and a myriad of other details are required to run a business. You will need to attend to these details to stay in business.

During your start-up:

- *Focus on your less-than-stellar skills.* Yes, you are brilliant at what you do—but can you run a business? Return to the entrepreneur assessment in Chapter Two to determine what you can improve.

- *Get your numbers in order.* Review the accounting/bookkeeping process you have chosen. Even if you don't have a dime to post, be ready when your first $10k contract arrives. If you are just starting up, you'll want to focus on how to bring money in and how to prevent it from going out. How can you conserve cash?

Competency 8: Building Relationships

Whether you are with clients, other consultants, or your employees, your success as a consultant is directly related to your ability to build and maintain relationships.

As a consultant, you do not have a tangible product that delights your customer. You have a service—one that may at times be difficult to define. Your service is invisible to the human eye; if you are truly doing your job, someone else may actually take credit for what you do. This helps to explain why building relationships is imperative.

During your start-up:

- *Make lists of people and places where you can begin to build relationships.* We've addressed building relationships with your clients, but you also need to build relationships with other consultants, experts, influencers, community leaders, or others. In every case, you might be able to help them now and call upon them as clients at a later time.
- *Begin to build trust everywhere.* Don't do this as a gimmick to use in the future. Do it because it is the right thing to do. It builds collaboration and inclusiveness. Think about what you do every day to demonstrate honesty, reliability, consistency, integrity, and discretion. Pass it on.

Your Competency Level

You may wish to assess yourself on each competency. Go back to each preceding competency and rate yourself on a 10-point scale. Think of a 1 as representing a *beginner* level and a 10 as representing a *master* level. You will find the eight competencies and the improvement suggestions in Exhibit 10.1. Decide what you could do during your start-up to improve your chances of success. Even better, print the document and use it during your start-up as a reminder of what you need to improve.

Set time aside each year to assess how you are doing as a professional consultant. Your future success is dependent on how well you are doing today. Exhibit 10.2

Exhibit 10.1. Competency Improvement Ideas

Begin with these suggestions to determine how you can improve in each of the competencies as you start your business.

1. **Professional Standards**
   - ❑ *Create your company's guiding principles.* What do you want your company to be known for?
   - ❑ *Think of a company that you respect and interact with.* What does it do that keeps you coming back? How can you build those standards into your business?

2. **Professional Awareness**
   - ❑ *Meet with two consultants you admire and respect.* Ask them how they stay up to speed with the changes within the profession and what they see on the horizon. Ask them what they are reading and who they follow on TED Talks or LinkedIn.
   - ❑ *Identify several blogs written by other consultants you can follow.* Select a couple that seem to keep you abreast of topics that resonate with you and changes in the industry that are important to you and follow them. To start, I'd recommend Andrew Sobel.

3. **Consulting Skills**
   - ❑ *Volunteer to help another consultant—without pay, if you need to.* This will give you an opportunity to view an expert in action. It also gives you a chance to build a relationship with someone to share ideas in the future.
   - ❑ *Learn the right questions to ask.* Andrew Sobel and Jerold Panas's *Power Questions: Build Relationships, Win New Business, and Influence Others* is high on my list of resources.

4. **Communication Skills**
   - ❑ *Tap into your knowledge of communication styles.* If you have never completed an assessment to determine yours, do it today. The DiSC®

Exhibit 10.1. Competency Improvement Ideas, Cont'd

is a good place to start. But don't just learn about your style; learn how to approach and sell to other styles as well. It is unlikely that you will sell to clients with a style similar to yours. You need to internalize the content existing in communication styles.

❑ *Review your last 360-degree assessment.* Look for clues that will help you be a better communicator in your new role as a consultant.

5. **Mindset Success**

❑ *Check your mindset.* What kind of self-talk are you practicing? A proper mindset allows you to address unplanned setbacks as learning opportunities. Although sometimes I do wonder how many more "learning opportunities" I can handle. You need to believe in your business and that you will be successful. Certainly, working on your business is important, too. Chapter Three opens with the quote, "The harder I work, the luckier I get." The combination of a positive mindset and doing what you need to do will lead to success.

❑ *Find your positive corps.* No, that's not a typo for core. I do mean corps—the group of people you will hang around with who will help you maintain your positivity. Meet with them when you are unsure. Celebrate with them when you are successful. And between times, enjoy their presence.

6. **Business Development**

❑ *Take advantage of your time.* You will never have the luxury of so much time for developing business as you do when you start your business. Use that time wisely. Identify the client problems you will solve, ask friends and colleagues for referrals, send personalized letters and emails to potential clients, add testimonials to your website, determine the best way to get your name out there, and finally, revisit (or create) your annual marketing plan and calendar from Chapter Five. Now is the best time to warm up your cold calls following the process in Chapter Five. Use your time wisely.

❑ *Meet with someone who is a friend—but could be a potential client.* Review your business development plans with this person and ask for honest, candid feedback. Take good notes. Do not make excuses. And say "thank you very much" at the end.

7. **Business Management**

❑ *Focus on your less-than-stellar skills.* Yes, you are brilliant at what you do—but can you run a business? Return to the entrepreneur assessment in Chapter Two to determine what you can improve.

❑ *Get your numbers in order.* Review the accounting/bookkeeping process you have chosen. Even if you don't have a dime to post, be ready when your first $10k contract arrives. If you are just starting up, you'll want to focus on how to bring money in and how to prevent it from going out. How can you conserve cash?

8. **Building Relationships**

❑ *Make lists of people and places where you can begin to build relationships.* We've addressed building relationships with your clients, but you also need to build relationships with other consultants, experts, influencers, community leaders, or others. In every case you might be able to help them now and call upon them as clients at a later time.

❑ *Begin to build trust everywhere.* Don't do this as a gimmick to use in the future. Do it because it is the right thing to do. It builds collaboration and inclusiveness. Think about what you do every day to demonstrate honesty, reliability, consistency, integrity, and discretion. Pass it on.

is a professional checkup to determine how you are doing; head to www.wiley.com/go/newconsultingbiech to check it out and download or print a copy.

It is likely that you will be high in some areas and lower in others. It is also likely that you may have been higher in some areas in the past than you are today. After you have completed your self-assessment, you will want to create a professional-developmental plan. The next section will help you with that planning.

CONTINUING TO LEARN

You have an obligation to your clients to improve your knowledge and skills continually. The rapid changes in the world today can turn today's expert into tomorrow's dolt if the person fails to keep up. The professional identifies a developmental plan for continued growth. Let's consider several strategies.

Attend Learning Events

At a minimum, attend your professional organization's annual conference. It may be expensive, but you owe it to your clients to invest in yourself. I can think of no more enjoyable way to learn than to go to a great location, meet new people, renew past acquaintances, and attend sessions in which presenters discuss new ideas and approaches. To top it off, you may very likely go home with a fistful of business cards belonging to potential clients.

You have an obligation to your clients to improve your knowledge and skills continually.

To get the most out of your attendance, be sure to network. Don't sit on the sidelines or retreat to your room during breaks. You will not gain all the value that you can. Instead, go where the action is. Be the first to say hello. Introduce yourself to others and be interested in who they are. Identify common interests and experiences. Trade business cards. If the person has asked you for something or if you want to follow up after the conference, jot a note on the back of the business card as a reminder. I learned early on that if I did not make a note to myself I would get to my office the next week without a clue about who each card matched and what we had in common.

Attend virtual learning events. My email box is filled with offers to attend webinars, teleconferences, and webcasts. Many are free; the rest have a small price tag. All will stimulate learning, produce knowledge, and encourage thinking.

Go back to school. You may not need an MBA, but courses at the graduate level are critical. Take courses in finance, marketing, human performance technology, or organizational change. Take a class to bring yourself up to speed in the area of technology.

Ask Others

Ask for feedback from others on a regular basis. Ask for it from friends, colleagues, and clients. I usually conduct an exit interview to ask clients what they liked about my work on the project and what they wish I had done differently. Ask clients about their most pressing concerns. Although this is not related to your growth, learning something from them may be fascinating, and this will enhance your relationship and your value.

Join an Association or Group

Affiliation with a national or international professional association or group is critical to maintain your professional awareness. Through the group, you will be kept informed of learning events.

Sometimes a professional organization will provide a networking list, designed to provide you with contacts in your geographic location. If not, form your own network. Networking is one of the best ways to continue to learn or, at the very least, to learn what you ought to learn!

Study on Your Own

Reading is one of my favorite methods of learning. The suggested reading list at the back of this book is a place to begin if you are interested in learning more about the business of consulting. If you have not yet read the two books I have referred to several times, you must put them on your immediate to-do list: *Flawless Consulting* by Peter Block and *The Consultant's Calling* by Geoffrey M. Bellman.

Subscribe to and read your professional journals. Read general business magazines such as *Fortune, BusinessWeek,* or the *Harvard Business Review.* Read the same publications your clients read to keep yourself informed about the industry. Read cutting-edge journals such as *Fast Company* and *Wired.* Consulting professionals are voracious readers.

Read your junk mail from your mailbox and your inbox. You will learn what your competition is doing, how to write more effective marketing letters, and how to design brochures. Realize that you will observe and learn from both good and bad examples! Listen to podcasts or audiobooks while driving longer distances.

Identify Resources

Visit your local technology training organization. Check out the classes they offer and other available resources they can lend you. Visit your local bookstore. Browse the shelves looking for trends in the industries you serve and business in general. Thumb through all new books about consulting to determine whether they should be on your bookshelf.

Co-Consult or Train with Others

Consulting with a colleague is a unique way to learn from someone else in the profession. It allows you to observe someone else, elicit feedback, and learn from the experience of working together. Invite colleagues to observe you during a consulting or training situation. Ask them to observe specific things. Sit down afterward and listen to everything your colleagues say. Ask for improvement suggestions.

Create Mentoring Opportunities

Meet with other professionals to discuss trends in the consulting profession. Some consultants form small groups that meet on a regular basis to share ideas, discuss trends, and help one another. Identify someone in the consulting field whom you would like as a mentor. Then ask the person if that would be possible. My mentor and I meet for breakfast four to six times each year. I pay for our meals. This has become the best $20 investment I've ever made. I'm investing in myself.

Develop coaches in your key client industries. This requires effort on your part, because you may not cross paths with these folks on a regular basis. For example, several years ago I found myself working with several utility regulatory bodies. I remembered that my cousin had a friend who held a management position in the same industry. I called my cousin and set up a meeting with her friend so that I could learn more. He became a good friend as well as a resource, and now he calls me for coaching!

Identify where the experts hang out. Then go there. Sometimes this is a related association or an informal group. More seasoned people and those with different experiences can offer you priceless advice.

Aspire to the Best of Your Knowledge

Your clients expect you to be on the leading edge, regardless of your field. You have an obligation to them and to yourself to learn and grow. Learning is an ongoing process, even if you are at the top of your profession. Often it is what you learn *after* you know it all that counts!

Often it is what you learn after you know it all that counts!

BALANCING YOUR LIFE AND YOUR BUSINESS

Many people I meet think of consulting as an exciting, high-powered career: flying from coast to coast, meeting with publishers in San Francisco and executives in New York City, staying at the Madison in Washington or the Ritz Carlton in Dallas, eating at a bistro in Manhattan or a coffee shop in Seattle. I am paid well, dress well, land large contracts, hobnob with the influential and famous. But that's only the first layer.

My friends know what my life is really like: up at 4 a.m. to catch a flight for a noon meeting, spending six hours in an airport because of delayed flights, calling to cancel dinner plans, and finally arriving home after midnight. It is also about eating poorly prepared restaurant food, writing proposals until the wee hours of the morning, and losing a contract due to a technicality. Most of all it is about long hours.

Although you have the freedom to set your own schedule, the truth is that the hours are long. Projects demand your immediate and sustained attention. When you are putting food on the table, you may find it easier to stay glued to the project than to break away. In today's fast-paced world, no one finds balance an easy task. It becomes even more difficult when you are dependent on the success of the project your family now expects you to hold at bay while you attend the annual family picnic in Pauquette Park.

Although you have the freedom to set your own schedule, the truth is that the hours are long.

One of the most challenging issues facing consultants today is achieving a balance between the competing priorities of balancing their lives and their businesses; balancing their families and their work. There's a line that says, "In consulting, you will always have perfect work-life balance. Your work will be your life and your life will be your work. Perfectly balanced." Although it is supposed to be a joke, consultants do need to make an effort to take care of themselves. In most cases, the hours will be long, but you can establish your own guidelines to make a difference.

How can you achieve balance? What can you do?

Identify the Imbalance

Geoff Bellman leads an exercise in which he asks you to identify the three things you value most in life. Write them down. Now scan your checkbook and calendar. Do your choices match the three things you value the most?

Next ask your spouse, a colleague, or friend what he or she believes you value the most. Did that person choose the three things you chose?

Now begin to make real choices. What do you need to do to demonstrate the value you place on the three things you chose?

Make Your Own Rules

You started your consulting business so that you could be your own boss. You can begin by telling yourself what your hours will be. A business takes creativity and energy, so draining yourself becomes counterproductive. Of course, sometimes you stay late or work a weekend simply to meet a deadline, but do not make that your standard way of working. Make up a rule that helps to put your business in perspective. Tell yourself, for example, "If it's not done by 6 p.m., it will wait until tomorrow."

Enjoy the Doing

Don't hurry through each project just to get to the next one. If you love what you do, you may be missing some of the fun! Much of the pleasure may be in the doing. I know this may not curb the hours, but it will make them more enjoyable!

Take Time Off

It is very important to take a break from your business. Go on vacation, even if you just spend a week at home. Invigorate your mind, rejuvenate your body, sleep late, relax, and read something that has nothing to do with work. And it doesn't have to be planned ahead: I love to walk on the beach, so when I finish with a client early or my plane lands in the middle of the day, I might just head to the beach at 2:00 in the afternoon to enjoy the reason I'm doing what I do.

Identify Other Interests

Join a book club. Learn golf. Try embroidery. Fly a kite. Collect something. Visit an antique store. Try hiking. Shop Etsy. Solve a Sudoku. Learn to paint. Take a cooking class. Write poetry. Work crossword puzzles. Refurbish a classic car. Study your heritage. Go for walks. Take an online course. Develop your family tree. Write a letter. Plan a trip. Do it with your spouse, your children, or a friend.

Take Advantage of Being at Home

If you work from your home, find ways and times to get away from it all. Go for a walk at noon. Visit the gym a couple of times each week. Read the morning paper in your kitchen or eat lunch on the deck.

Issues of balance become more acute during transitions. Therefore, if you are planning to transition to consulting, plan the entire transition. Focus on all the important areas of your life: social, family, spiritual, business, education. Identify how the balance might shift initially, and determine how you want it to change and how soon.

To some extent, the issue of balance in life is really one of time management. Don't mistake busy-ness for business. You must prioritize deliberately, based on what you want out of life. Add a few of the following consultant time-management tips to those you already use.

Don't mistake busy-ness for business.

MANAGING YOUR TIME

Time is the one thing we all have access to equally. We all have exactly 24 hours in every day and 525,600 minutes in every year. The truth is that we cannot save time. Time continues to march on no matter what you insist. You cannot save time, but you can *shave* time—shave time from some of the less enjoyable things you must do. As a consultant, you can shave time in two primary areas—running your business and planning your travel. Try some of the following to shave time from each of these areas.

Business Time Savers

Here are some of the ways I've found for saving some time for myself and for managing my business.

The Big Jobs. Work on several large projects rather than dozens of small projects. You invest a great deal of time moving from one client to another, getting up to speed, flying from one coast to the other, reminding yourself of all the personalities, and remembering names. This is why repeat business with the same client is good. I sometimes have two or three projects with the same client at the same time. If I travel to the client's location, I can spend some time on each.

Prevent Scope Creep. Scope creep occurs when a project slowly grows larger than the original intent. This is certainly one of the greatest ways consultants misuse time. Unless you are paid by the hour, scope creep will erode your profits and consume your time. Prevent scope creep with clear, measurable objectives and specific, identifiable timelines and deliverables. Then stick to them.

Tip: Use a survey tool.

If you need to conduct surveys for your clients, subscribe to one of the online survey tools. Several to consider include www.confirmit.com, which offers an industrial strength tool; www.zoomerang.com which costs under $500 for a one-year subscription; or www.sensorpro.net and www.surveymonkey.com might meet your needs. Online surveys will save you time conducting and compiling surveys.

End-of-the-Year Tickler File. I keep an end-of-the-year tickler file for my accountant. It's labeled "Take to Stephanie" and reminds me of all the things that have occurred during the year that I need to remember for tax purposes, legal responsibilities, and personal desires. When something happens, I write a quick note or copy the necessary document and slip it into the file. It's a guaranteed method to ensure that I have everything I need when tax time comes and that I am not at the last minute rummaging through stacks of paper trying to locate an Internal Revenue Service notice or a question from my attorney. You can certainly do that with your mobile phone as well. In my case I have office staff that also add to the file. So a paper file works best. We spend no time trying to organize it until about December 1.

Invoice Ease. Keep an invoice template on your computer for clients who will incur repeat billings. When it's time to bill them, just pull it up, fill in a new date and numbers, and print it. Your accounting system should format it this way, too. When I can accurately predict the billing date and amount, I complete the invoices when I initially schedule on-site dates. Early on in my career, I could return to my office, add a stamp to the envelope, and mail the invoice. Now I email my staff upon completion and they mail (or email) the invoice immediately.

Card Contact. I keep a bundle of greeting cards in my briefcase. When I am on a plane, stuck in a waiting room, or have a canceled appointment, I pull them out to stay in touch with friends, colleagues, and clients. You can certainly text and email from your mobile phone, but there is some added fun receiving an actual paper card with a friend's or colleague's written note.

File Tips. Develop a system that works for you. You must keep up on the filing so you can move through your office, but you also want to find what you filed! We use different colored files to distinguish what's inside: blue for project files, yellow for office files, red for client resources, orange for originals, green for volunteer activities, and so on. We have separate cabinets to separate resources from client work.

Make smart choices for filing your work electronically as well. Establish a system as soon as you can. Think about the best way to file your documents so that you can find them. This works for us. We have five large categories: client work, proposals, accounting, books, and miscellaneous. Client work is all filed by topic area first, then client name, and finally date. We file this way because, when I have a new "cultural change" project, all the files for that topic are together. We keep proposals separate from the client work. When I am ready to compose a new proposal, I do not want to sort through content to find them. This may not work for you. You need to be logical about it and determine what will save you the most time.

Protect Your Time. Calls can interrupt your concentration. If you want to stay focused, accept or return phone calls at a specific time. If you have a number of calls to make, make them in sequence. If the person is not there, leave a time when you can be reached, "I'll be available from 10:00 to 12:00 today."

Follow the same general thinking with email. Select certain times during the day when you will check and respond to emails to avoid being interrupted every few minutes. I like to clear the deck early in the morning and then check email again mid-afternoon. You will save lots of time by addressing all your messages in a focused timeframe.

Travel Time Savers

Travel can be hectic, but I have developed some ways to reduce the hassle and gain time for other activities.

Cash Stash. I have become almost entirely dependent on my credit card. However, there are still some times when I need cash. I keep $42 in the side pocket of my briefcase. If I'm traveling and do not have enough cash in my wallet, this amount will allow me to take a cab, buy a snack from a street vendor, or buy almost anything else that I cannot purchase with a credit card. Two dollars in quarters is handy for plugging a parking meter or a vending machine.

One Travel Agent. Yes, almost everyone goes online to purchase airline tickets. But have you clocked your time? My last purchase took almost an hour. When we travel, we use one travel agent. We get fabulous service from Ginger and her gang. They know our preferences for services and carriers. We email information about our trips to them, identifying times, destinations, and anything special. They email an itinerary back for our approval. They have all of our frequent traveler numbers and enter that information as well. For special itineraries or international travel, they deliver documents to our door. You cannot beat service like that!

Double Up Trips. Use a trip to work with one client and visit another potential client. Add a mini vacation to a special location when working with a client. In this case you will, of course, pick up all additional expenses.

Your Travel Bag. If you travel a great deal, keep the basics packed. I have two of everything: curling iron, hair dryer, makeup kit, toothbrush, and so on. When I return from a trip I replenish anything that I used or emptied, such as toothpaste, underwear, deodorant, or whatever. This ensures that I never forget any of the basics and makes packing for the next trip a breeze.

You will never *find* time for anything; if you want time, you must *make* it. The list in the sidebar is a reminder of time-management tips you probably already know, but may not be practicing. Try them. They work.

---

*You will never **find** time for anything;*
*if you want time you must **make** it.*

Classic Time-Management Tips

Be sure you are doing these at the minimum to manage your time:

- Set your priorities first thing in the morning or the last thing at night for the next day.
- Do your top priorities first.
- Tackle large projects in stages.
- Identify your "best" times—that is, your best time for writing, best time to make telephone calls.
- Use your waiting and travel time productively: make lists, listen to podcasts, answer an email, balance your checkbook.
- Use the notes app on your mobile phone. Select one that is easy to set up and use. High marks are often awarded to Bear, Zoho Notebook, and Simplenote. Some have free versions.
- Carry 3 × 5 cards or a small notebook to write down ideas or reminders. Looking at your phone while in a meeting can make it appear that you are not paying attention—even if you are taking notes.
- Use an action item catcher, one place where you keep a list of all your actions—even those you'll probably remember—and at some point add a due date, what must precede it, and what resources you may need.
- Handle each piece of paper once. Handle each email once.
- Have a place for everything.
- Set deadlines.

Exhibit 10.3, which you can find at www.wiley.com/go/newconsultingbiech, is a time-management log. Although keeping the log is not a way to manage your time better, you may want to collect data to find out where you are spending your time. The log is divided into quarter-hour increments. Track your time for two weeks to obtain a good sample. Diligently record what you were doing and for how long. Next, determine your key job categories. You might include marketing, consulting, administration, and professional development. Add a category for personal things. You can use your mobile phone to do the same, but I just find it easier to hash mark the log. In addition, it is a good reminder when it is lying next to me.

After you have the data, determine what percentage of your time you spent in each category over the two-week period. Is that what you expected? Did you spend too much time in some categories? Too little in others? What can you do to change?

Two time-management tools that I cannot live without are my month-at-a-glance calendar and a session planner for each event. The calendar has room for almost everything that I need to keep myself organized. In addition to meetings and appointments, I have room to include telephone numbers, departing and arrival times for my flights, important monthly reminders, and social engagements. I color-code time spent with clients. I need to see the full month to have a feel for how things flow from day to day and week to week.

The session planner in Exhibit 10.4, found at www.wiley.com/go/newconsultingbiech, has all the planning details for a successful event. I start it the day the project is scheduled. It initially serves as a memory jogger to ask all the right questions. Later it helps our staff to know what needs to be prepared and packed. On-site it provides all the information about where to go for the consult-ant. It also tells staff how to get in touch with the consultant. Rework the session planner until it works well for you to help you manage your time.

Manage your time well—it is your most valuable resource. Guard it jealously. Once it is gone, you will never get it back.

Manage your time well—
it is your most valuable resource.

GIVING BACK

You have received assistance, advice, and ideas from others as you advanced in your career. Now, you are probably asking for more of the same as you consider a consult-ing career. You may feel as if you owe many people. How can you pay them back?

Do the same in return. It takes time to invest in others, and you should always be ready to give back—give back to clients, give back to the profession, give back to your community, and give back to individuals.

Try some of these ideas:

- Mentor someone just entering the field.
- Volunteer your services to a social service organization.
- Volunteer services to a civic group.
- Volunteer to help a children's group.
- Serve on local government or civic boards.
- Provide pro bono work for a local nonprofit organization.
- Send a thank-you card.
- Volunteer to assist inner-city programs during their summer sessions.
- Volunteer to serve on a committee for your professional association.
- Volunteer to speak at your local professional chapter meeting.
- Speak at your local high school's career day.
- Start a scholarship fund.

A Personal Checkup

Earlier in this chapter you conducted a professional checkup. You have read addi-tional thoughts that are more personal, including managing time and giving back to the profession. If you are one of the readers who has been in the consulting field for at least a year, you may want to consider the personal checkup in Exhibit 10.5.

Exhibit 10. 5. Personal Checkup: How Am I Doing?

Think about your personal life.

As a well-balanced professional:

1. Have I determined what I value most?
2. Do I know what I stand for and have I ensured that my business is aligned to those standards?
3. Have I tracked my time on a log and identified the imbalances?
4. How can I reestablish balance in my social, family, spiritual, business, education, health, or other areas?
5. How can I align my time with what I value most?
6. Does what I am doing still excite me and am I having fun?
7. What adjustments must I make to the business to increase my satisfaction?
8. What role do my family and friends play in these changes?
9. How will I know if I have improved one year from now?
10. What can I do to continue to learn?
11. What can I do to give back to the profession?
12. How will I take better care of myself in the coming year?

If you're thinking about being a *consultant*, don't stop there. Be a *respected, knowledgeable, well-balanced* consultant! Be a *successful* consultant. Be a *highly professional* consultant. Be all the things that you are capable of being. *Astound* yourself!

For the Consummate Consultant

You are the CEO of your own professional company. How you present yourself, how you stay up to speed, and how you think about your clients all impact your chances to be a stellar consultant who is constantly in demand. Integrating the competencies into your repertoire and continuing to learn will ensure that you will never be without an engagement.

Get a Mentor. Yes, I mentioned this several chapters ago. If you haven't done it yet, do it now! The sooner the better. Tap someone who is a successful business owner you could easily connect with after work over a beer or coffee.

Share Your Brilliance. Know where your brilliance lies and build your work around it. This will help you zero in on your niche, identify your target audience, create a marketing plan, and save energy by not being all things to all people. What do you do better than anyone?

Play Chess with Your Future. Use your mindset to plan for your future success. You can predict your future by using the same technique excellent chess players use, planning three steps ahead. Start with small things, such as thinking through step-by-step the drive from your office to a new location. Practice planning each step that will occur before you meet with a client. Visualize it. Plan your future out a couple of years. What three steps will you need to take to get there?

Do You Still Want to Be a Consultant?

Life is either a daring adventure, or nothing.

Helen Keller

Nnovember 11. Best day of his life. Yessiree! It's the day he jumped off the treadmill and stopped bucking traffic snarls every day.

Lambert had a traditional start in life. He worked summers at his dad's hardware store, went to college, got a job, got married. He always knew he wanted to be an independent consultant, but it became harder to envision a move when his company continued to give him promotions, increased his salary, provided great benefits, and always gave him a shot at developmental opportunities.

Of course, there was also the other side of the story. All these incentives came with long hours, increased stress, daily traffic congestion, lots of travel, and completing work that no longer excited him. He knew that making the move from the corporate world into consulting would ultimately make him happier. He wanted to control his destiny, but it was going to be difficult for him and his family to lose the stability.

Before he made the leap, he was doubt-laden! But today he was proud of the time he'd spent researching what it would take to make the transition as smooth as possible. He started meeting with consulting vendors and friends and asked them lots of questions. At first he didn't share his plans with them, but one evening over bourbon, his golf buddy, Adam, caught on and said, "Hey man, are you planning to jump ship? Become a consultant like me?" So the jig was up and Lambert admitted what he was thinking about. Adam asked, "Have you told Cheryl and the kids what you're thinking?" When Lambert said no, Adam responded, "Look! Ya gotta tell them. This is a big change. Once you clear it at home, I'll share all the trade secrets."

So that started a weekly Thursday night meeting between the two. Cheryl was fine with Lambert's decision—especially since Adam was providing some coaching. She even offered to go back to her job at the bank now that the kids were in their teens. Adam was great. He'd shared a roadmap with Lambert that presented a combination of information and homework to do between meetings.

Adam suggested that Lambert and Cheryl agree on how much of an income they needed to survive by looking at his current salary and the expenses. The result surprised them. They didn't lead an extravagant lifestyle, so the amount didn't seem astronomical until Adam pointed out some of the other things Lambert would be on the hook for: health insurance, life insurance, retirement savings (which his company had been paying), self-employment taxes, and office expenses. Lambert started to panic, but Cheryl suggested that they immediately start saving and earmark the money for the business.

Adam was patient as Lambert determined exactly what he would do and for whom, what he'd name his business, and why he wanted to work out of his home. He was less patient as Lambert pushed back on talking to his manager about a bridge period in which Lambert would finish up some of the projects he might be working on when he made the transition. Adam had to push Lambert to start planning for his first clients before he quit his job. Adam had shouted, "What do you think? The clients are just going to fall into your lap on your last day of work?" Lambert acquiesced to making a list of 100 people he knew and preparing an announcement that would be sent the day after he left his current job.

Adam helped Lambert identify an accountant and an attorney, select a business entity, develop a business plan, and open a business checking account. Lambert looked a bit shocked one Thursday evening when he realized that he really would be in charge—completely in charge. If he wanted a raise, he'd have to charge more. If he wanted to be promoted, he'd hire a couple of employees. If he wanted to go to the annual conference, he could—as long as his credit card wasn't maxed out!

When Adam suggested he join the local Chamber of Commerce, Lambert realized he needed to meet with his manager soon and work out a transition plan with him. He finally made the big move the night that Adam forced him to name the worst thing that could happen. Lambert acknowledged that the worst thing was that he wouldn't be able to find clients; he'd close the business and go back to his old job.

Now, here he was one year into his company with a new marketing plan targeted to larger companies on the outskirts of Chicago. Lambert knew that owning his own business was not for everyone, but it was right for him. He had even received a job offer from one of his clients seven months into his new role. He was flattered, of course, but he turned it down.

His own consulting company. What a deal! It wasn't until the previous month that he realized that growing up in an entrepreneurial family (his father had owned the store and his mother had been a self-employed home RN) had probably had an effect on his strong need to be his own boss. He decided it was in his genes. Life didn't get much better than this!

■ ■ ■

The most important reason to become a consultant is because you want to do it. If you have reached this chapter and the disadvantages don't discourage you and the challenges excite you, you are ready to develop an action plan that will take you into the world of consulting.

*The most important reason to become
a consultant is because you want to do it.*

This chapter provides an example of a week in the life of a consultant. It raises lifestyle issues that do not fit neatly into other chapters. One of the most salient reasons for becoming a consultant is that you can create the lifestyle you choose. Therefore, this chapter provides visioning exercises that will help you to clarify your future.

If you answer the chapter's title question with a "Yes!" there is an action plan you can use to begin the planning and execution of your consulting practice.

It provides a structure to take you from "I *want* to be a consultant" to "*I am a consultant!*"

Finally, if you are not quite ready, this chapter's Fast Fifty exercise will start you thinking about what you can do next to move "closer to ready."

A WEEK IN A CONSULTANT'S LIFE

It is Saturday afternoon and I am completing this book on my laptop at home. I have written several books and recognize how crucial it is to get this book in on time. I am several hours behind my original schedule today because I was on email for four hours this morning. It seems that most of my clients respond to and initiate email around the clock, every day. I've had my consulting business for over 30 years. I grew the business to a large number of employees and subcontractors. I had two offices, one in Wisconsin and one in Virginia, for 20 years. I wasn't happy in a managerial role and gently downsized my business to where it is now: me, a couple of support staff, and subcontractors when I need them for special projects. I sold my office building in Wisconsin and moved to Virginia.

I will leave on Sunday on a late flight to attend a quarterly meeting at the Center for Creative Leadership (CCL), where I am on the board of governors. Following that meeting, I'll head to New Orleans, where I will facilitate two sessions for ATD's CORE4 conference. ATD is the Association for Talent Development and my professional organization. And then on to Washington, D.C., for meetings with clients. I am fortunate that travel this week keeps me on one coast.

Although this book isn't due until the end of the week, I must complete this manuscript today or tomorrow since I will be immersed in my other obligations. If I do require more than today to finish, my husband will most likely attend a birthday party for the wife of his flying partner alone.

I could take the manuscript with me tomorrow, but I have learned that, if I do, I will not work on it. Therefore, if I am not near completion, I will call my walking partner and cancel our walk along the beach Sunday morning. I try not to cancel with friends too often, but when someone else is counting on me to come through—like my editor is for this book—I need to adjust. I hate to cancel the walk because I've had very little exercise the past two weeks. I've been sequestered away writing with too little sleep and too many calories. I've published over 80 books and the one thing I've learned is that writing can be detrimental to your health!

I can look out my window to a beautiful view of the Chesapeake Bay, which is sometimes distracting and sometimes inspiring. If I look around my home office, I see the stacks that represent several major client projects I will complete over the next couple of months, two book projects I have started, a series of webinars I am designing for a client, and a book-writing retreat I will conduct.

In my briefcase I have a 3 × 6-inch leather-bound annual calendar. It is scribbled full of notations, phone numbers, meeting times, color-coded notes for each client, and locations. I have about eight various colored files—each representing a different project.

There are five blue files, each one representing a client project. One is a three-day team-building session that will be held in Arlington, Virginia. Two blue folders represent year-long projects that I am completing with two private companies. The projects are different and address learning, talent development, change, and Lean Six Sigma. I need to contact both clients this week. Since I will be in New Orleans, I will most likely make those calls in the afternoon when I finish my meetings, since both are on the West Coast. The fourth file belongs to a group of cyber gurus for whom I facilitate a monthly full-day meeting. The fifth blue file represents a design project with a client near Chicago. As I scan the work, I am reminded that I need to design questionnaires and conduct interviews for the design project and the team building. I muse that those five blue folders represent more work than I would have been expected to produce internally in a year. Politics, policies, meetings, and other things prevent internal employees from being as productive as I can be as an external consultant.

There are two green folders, each one representing a volunteer project. I am working with ATD's certification institute to revise the credential for the Certified Professional in Learning and Performance. The second volunteer effort is a presentation entitled "Memory, Motivation, and Mindsets: How Do You Make Learning Stick?" that I will make at a conference in Singapore. Although I am getting a stipend, the association that hired me was not able to pay my typical fee. Speaking at this conference has led me to client work in the past, so I considered it an investment and accepted the assignment.

A gray folder represents a special project. I am the consulting editor for a publisher. Since agility and innovation have become the norm in companies, we want to explore how to tap into the topics and produce something that is practical and useful in today's workplace. I have a list of potential contributors and I'd like to try to reach the editor for a discussion sometime this week.

Pink folders represent marketing. One pink folder contains creative ideas for our Christmas mailing—one of our key marketing activities. The second folder contains the list of 94 experts who contributed to two books I recently wrote: *ATD's Foundations of Talent Development* and *ATD's Action Guide to Talent Development*. We are designing a gift for this stellar group.

An orange folder holds three proposals for which we are awaiting responses. I am carrying them with me in case one of the companies calls and wants something clarified. I am nearly positive that we will not be awarded one of them—I am certain that the company had already preselected the vendor they want to use. However, because they needed a minimum number of submissions, we were caught up in the action. I have never been sure if procurement departments realize that it takes anywhere from four to 20 hours to write a good proposal. I know they can't tell us that someone has already been preselected. But what a waste of time—and in a small organization like ours, no one has extra time.

The yellow folder contains my expense sheet, last week's financial report, the year's income projections, and the monthly expense/budget sheet. These four pages, combined with my calendar, contain enough data for me to make a number of decisions. I keep the spreadsheets on a memory stick as well, in case I need more information while I am on the road. Also in the yellow folder are several real estate descriptions, since I am interested in investing in another piece of real estate.

I have also packed the latest issues of *Harvard Business Review, TD, Fortune, Fast Company,* and the book *Human + Machine: Reimagining Work in the Age of AI* by Paul Daugherty and James Wilson. I can't wait to dive into this book, since this is the direction our companies are going. I hope I find some insight. This is my airplane reading.

Stuck among the folders is a small brochure advertising an e-learning conference. It's Elliott Masie's Learning 2018. It's only a couple of weeks away. My thought process is something like this: "I should go. The fee is high. But the lineup is great. Laura Bush and Dan Pink will be speaking. I'm too busy. But I deserve a break. It's too late to plan anything around the trip. Some of my favorite people will be there. But I really should get that marketing campaign designed. The networking would be great for me. But I will lose a couple of billable days. I will gain knowledge that I need to help my clients. I'll think about it on the plane."

Speaking of planes, I spent an hour figuring out my schedule for next month and turning it over to our travel agent to schedule. It seems to take longer and longer to book my own tickets, so I just let the experts do it. The pocket of my briefcase holds a spare stash of business cards, some cash, and my cell phone. I just downloaded my boarding pass on my phone. My small wallet that holds everything I could ever need (I gave up carrying a purse 30 years ago) is also tucked in the front of my briefcase.

I have several lovely leather briefcases, but I continue to use my black nylon Lands' End model. It is light and easy to swing on my shoulder as I drag one or two suitcases on wheels through airports from coast to coast.

As an added thought, I stuff a dozen catalogs (Lands' End, Bloomingdales, Gumps) in my briefcase (you can always stuff one more thing in it). I like travel. And I like flying. Really!

Even with the stricter travel rules, I like the hustle and bustle of busy airports. I like the takeoff; it gives me a surge of energy. I like the freedom to be unavailable so that I can read without interruption or distraction. I read books (fiction and nonfiction), catch up on my reading of professional journals, and shop. Shop? Yes. I love catalog shopping and find that flights are a great time to thumb through catalogs and rip out pages that picture gift ideas. Later I'll make final decisions about which items to purchase for others or for myself.

I need to plan for the week. When I arrive in Greensboro I will go straight to the hotel. I have an early-morning meeting at CCL. I am working on a special project as a part of my board responsibilities. I have dinner planned with one of the staff and we'll be talking books and writing. The board meeting lasts two days, after which I will hop on a plane and fly to New Orleans. When I arrive in New Orleans I'll need to scout out the presentation rooms since I have activities that are dependent on the way the room is set up. I am pleased that my first session is right after the opening keynote. I have substantial set-up for that session and the placement allows me to put everything out on tables and get organized. I will be up by 5:00 and in the training room by 7:00. My session starts at 9:00.

Thursday night I have promised to meet a colleague for a late dinner. She lives in the New Orleans area and hinted at some potential project. I am not sure if she wants to hire me or pick my brain for ideas. Either way, it's okay. I give a significant number of ideas away. Some consultants chide me about it. But I like challenges, and helping others is good for the soul.

That night I will fly to Washington, D.C., on the redeye. I try not to do this too often, though it was my preference in my early years as a consultant. I need to be with a client on Friday morning for a meeting that starts at 10:30. So I will drop my luggage off at the hotel, freshen up, and head to the meeting. That evening I will probably have dinner with someone from the company. It may be a late night—dinners with clients usually are.

A quick one-hour flight will take me home Friday evening. I'll stop at the office for an hour to check the stacks of messages that have accumulated. Usually there are a few checks to sign. I'll arrive at my door about 11:00 p.m.

This was a particularly heavy travel week. On a typical day I enjoy the newspaper on the deck with a cup of chai and arrive at the office before 8 a.m. Also, I usually hold Friday as a catch-up day. I return phone calls, proof proposals, finish old projects, start new projects, write letters, write a half-dozen notes to clients and colleagues, add my opinions about office issues that concern others, and just catch up on everything else. I typically leave the office around 6 p.m.

Sometimes I stay home on Fridays to work on projects that require more concentration and perhaps go into the office for an hour or two mid-afternoon. A heavy travel schedule makes it difficult to schedule appointments at the dentist and doctor or even to have my hair cut. I count on my staff to make the calls to obtain the appointments. Traveling also makes it difficult to schedule social time with friends. I count on my husband to plan our evenings on the town or to know where the best jazz band is playing. If planning were left up to me, it would be too late to schedule anything, and our friends would all have plans with other people who do not travel.

After reading these paragraphs you may have some questions. Let's tackle some potential questions, as each represents an aspect of the consultant's lifestyle that you may wish to consider before becoming a consultant.

- *Why is she writing a book and why is she so intent on finishing it?* Consultants write books as a marketing tool, to demonstrate their knowledge and expertise, and to share something with the rest of the world.

I write for the joy of writing. Unless you have a best-seller, you will not make money from the book itself. Self-published authors claim that they do make money, but then you need to deal with distribution and other hassles I don't want. I am intent on finishing it on time because I said I would. As a consultant, you will want to build trust with everyone you meet. Everyone is a potential client, and everyone is a potential reference for a consultant. Why do a book at all? Being published is equated with expertise for some, and this allows you to charge a higher fee. I had a once in a lifetime experience this past August when one of my books, *The Art and Science of Training*, made it to the number-one spot on the *Washington Post's* best-selling nonfiction list. It was only at that spot for a week, but that was enough for me. I write for the joy of writing; as a consultant, you may write for other reasons.

- *Why doesn't she take her laptop and finish the book next week?* Consultants owe their clients their undivided attention when they are working for them.

When I work with a client I am completely absorbed by the work at hand. I rarely think about the other projects in my briefcase. I am focused completely on the client for whom I am working. It's difficult to go back to a hotel room after focusing for up to 12 hours on one client and switch gears to write a proposal or even a letter, let alone a book! The long hours require some downtime. If you go out to dinner with a client, you can expect a late night.

- *Why did she spend four hours on email on a Saturday and why is she traveling for business on Sunday?* Weekends may not always be free for consultants. They often see Saturday morning as a catch-up time.

I try to make myself available to all clients at any time. Everyone I work with is busy! I try to keep up with email myself when I can and sometimes schedule telephone calls on the weekend. It is frequently impossible to find a time when two of us can meet in person or by phone. Some of my clients want to talk on weekends and evenings, though I try to discourage it. Other consultants prefer to talk on weekends more often. The Sunday travel is my choice. If I travel on Monday I have lost another billable day. If I schedule a Monday–Tuesday assignment, I could still easily be available for a Thursday–Friday assignment if necessary. In this case the board meeting was planned to start at noon on Monday, but I wanted to meet with my colleague before, not after. As a consultant, you will need to determine how working or traveling will affect your weekends and your lifestyle. You will also want to consider how you will choose to balance being available to clients and still respecting your personal lifestyle.

Are You Motivated Enough to Conquer Niagara Falls?

Annie Edson had led a difficult life. Although she was a teacher, she'd fallen on hard times. She traveled from Michigan to Mexico City searching for work, to no avail. Motivated and determined not to die in the poorhouse, Annie cooked up a scheme to build her wealth.

On October 24, 1901, her 63rd birthday, she hopped in a barrel with her lucky heart-shaped pillow to become the first person to survive a trip over Niagara Falls in a barrel. Her motivation paid off and she became the first person to conquer the falls. Annie lived 20 more years. What does it take to get you motivated?

Perhaps you've started your dream of becoming an independent consultant, but things may not be going as you originally planned. There is too much work, not enough hours in a day, and too little income. You may feel insecure and frustrated. Perhaps you are ready to give up. Don't! Frustration, uncertainty, and self-doubt are all parts of the journey. Before you give it all up, try the advice here to keep you going.

- Fuel your vision with action. Identify three things you will do each day to get you closer to being a consultant.
- Take a break. Perhaps you just need to get away to see it from a different perspective.
- Get advice. Make a date with another consultant, your mentor, or a coach who can help you see what you are missing.
- Change your perspective. Referring to Carol Dweck's work, see your challenges as an opportunity to grow. Tell yourself, "I haven't mastered it quite *yet*." There is power in the word *yet*.
- Revisit your "why." Review the purpose for making the switch. Are you looking forward to living a more purposeful life? Getting out of the rat race you called a job?
- Right-size your expectations. Think about what is reasonable to accomplish at this point. Sometimes it just takes time.

You don't have to go over Niagara in a barrel. There are safer ways to rally your motivation.

- *How often does she cancel social plans for work?* Consultants do not work a typical workday or workweek and may need to switch social and work times around.

I rarely cancel social plans after I make them. However, I must admit that it takes a concerted effort to schedule social activities. I have to think about them a week in advance and put them on my calendar. When I arrive back in town on Friday evening, it is usually too late to plan weekend activities. On the positive side, I have the option to build social time into my workweek. I do not need to ask anyone for permission to take an afternoon off for a haircut. I can add a day to my New York trip for shopping. I can browse in a bookstore on a Wednesday morning as long as I choose. As a consultant, you will have total freedom to set your own schedule. You'll still work hard—but it's *your* schedule.

- *How does the setting affect her work?* Consultants choose where they will work.

My surroundings affect my work greatly. I need the sun and water and a view when I am creating, developing, or designing something new. As a consultant, you will be able to select where you want to live. As long as you are a short drive to an airport, you can live anywhere. One of the best things about my move to Virginia is a shorter drive to the airport. It takes 15 minutes, as opposed to an hour when I lived in Wisconsin. If you decide you do not want overnight travel, you will need to live near your clients.

- *How often does she work at home? What are the benefits? What are the drawbacks?* Consultants can choose to have an office and work only there, choose to work out of their homes, or any combination of the two.

I complete any work that requires creative input in my home office, where I have a separate room furnished with a desk, equipment, and supplies. My office, however, is better equipped, and most of my resources (think books and research papers) are there. In addition, I have staff at the office to support me when I experience a computer glitch or need assistance. These factors sometimes make it easier to work at the office. I have a fax machine, printer, and copier in each location. I travel about 70 percent of the time. Of the remainder, I probably work half at my office and half from home. You will need to determine how having an office in your home will affect your lifestyle. The benefit is that I have total privacy. The drawback is that I can easily be distracted by a half-dozen personal projects.

- *Why does she refer to the color of the folders?* Consultants are always on the go. They need to find ways to have an office-in-a-bag.

The colored folders display what I have to do at a glance: blue for projects, green for volunteer work, and so on. The color coding also simplifies filing and retrieval. Other things that round out my office-in-a-bag include a miniature stapler, Post-it Notes, paper, pens, highlighters, small scissors (small enough to be acceptable to be carried on a flight by TSA), an address and phone listing of key contacts, cash, comb, breath mints, lipstick, a Tide To Go stain remover pen, an extra pair of pantyhose, spare frequent-flyer coupons, and a throwaway rain poncho. I think you can imagine why I need each item. As a consultant, you will determine how much time you will live on the road, out of your car, or at home. In any case, know that you will be busier than you originally expected. Decide how that will affect your lifestyle and what you can do to prepare for it.

- *Why does she use a paper calendar rather than an electronic schedule?* Consultants are usually bouncing from project to project; they need to find ways to be organized.

I personally like to be able to pull my calendar out in a restaurant, the back of a taxi, or anyplace else without depending on my mobile phone. One calendar tracks both professional and social engagements. My friends are all over the United States, and I like to schedule visits with them in conjunction with my travel schedule. I like to see everything I'm doing over several months at the same time. That said, technology allows you more flexibility than you could ever imagine. You will want to determine how technology will affect your lifestyle and what you must do to keep yourself organized. Do what works best for you.

- *Why does she refer to her volunteer work?* Consultants can be role models for giving back to the profession and their communities.

I volunteer because it is good for my soul. I like to volunteer. I did not get where I am without hundreds of generous people giving me something—a lead, a reference, an idea, time, encouragement, or a chance. Volunteering and helping others enter the field is my way of giving back to a profession that has given so much to me. And, on rare occasions, the work leads to potential clients. Although that is possible, that is not the reason you should volunteer. I dedicate a specified number of days each year for volunteer work. Think about how some volunteer or pro bono work can fit into the lifestyle you are creating.

- *Why does she carry the financial information with her?* The financial data tells a consultant if the mortgage will be paid next month.

I carry it with me so that it is readily available if I need to make decisions. Besides, it really amounts to only four pieces of paper that are updated weekly or monthly. They are printed directly from the computer, and I toss old ones away as I receive updates. If I need additional data, it is available on my laptop if I have it and the memory stick in my briefcase. You will need to determine how you will be able to fit data analysis into a schedule that dictates that you will not always be at your desk.

- *What's significant about the reading materials?* Consultants typically read a lot to stay on top of the profession.

What is significant about my reading list is what is missing, more than what is there. Although I have a good selection of professional reading, I typically pack a good fiction book for balance. Not taking a fiction book signals that this is a busy month. As a consultant, you must determine how you will keep up with all your reading.

- *Why can't she decide about attending the conference?* Consultants owe it to their clients to stay on top of issues and solutions.

I know that I need to gain knowledge. I know that I need to attend a conference like the one described. As you read, there are always issues and events that will tug at you. Every argument is viable. You must determine how you will make decisions like this one. The lifestyle you choose will be a factor to help determine which is more important: feeding your brain or feeding your bank account; taking a break from work or catching up on work; capitalizing on an opportunity to hear leaders in the field or capitalizing on an opportunity to market to clients on your list.

- *Why the discussion about a briefcase, purse, and luggage?* Consultants have many things to juggle.

I try to simplify, simplify, simplify! That means ensuring that I have whatever I need wherever I go, but not one thing too many. Simplifying does not mean eliminating everything. If it rains and I don't have a poncho with me, I will need to scurry around solving a different problem. That's not simplifying. I keep a suitcase packed with all the basics; I avoid checking luggage to save time and to avoid the hassle of lost luggage. New rules make it harder and harder to live with only carry-on luggage, but it is possible. See a later question for more details.

If I do need to check luggage, I always have what I need for the first 24 hours with me in my carry-on bag. I need wheels on my luggage so that I can cruise through airports to ground transportation without being dependent on a porter.

You will want to look at the lifestyle you now lead to determine how consulting will add complexity or how it could simplify it. Ask yourself if you have the physical stamina for the rigorous travel that may be required.

- *How much equipment will she pack in her briefcase?* Most consultants carry laptops to use for development and research, plus a cell phone. Some have additional equipment.

I have learned to travel with just my cell phone, although it is turned off while I am with a client. The greatest drawback of instant social contact is that some people believe that you will receive it, read it, and respond immediately! This is not possible when I am with clients, since I do not wish to take time away from them. Therefore, I usually have my associates monitor my email when I am with a client all day. Again, there are pros and cons to all the technological equipment available and you will need to determine what you will require to be efficient.

The greatest drawback of instant social contact is that some people believe that you will receive it, read it, and respond to it immediately!

Tip: Monitor and manage your calls.

Have someone you trust at your office monitor your calls and email while you are with a client. You owe it to your client to be fully present when working with them. Yet others will expect an instantaneous answer. All your clients appreciate your focused attention when they are paying for your time.

I do not want to take my computer on every plane I board. I travel with my laptop if I need it for design, writing, or for a presentation; otherwise it stays at home. Travel has become so inconvenient that I have limited the technology I schlep around with me. And when I do take a laptop, I am more interested in saving my back than how large the screen is. I have found a couple of laptops that weigh only a couple of pounds and do not need their own separate case. They are wonderfully light and serve my purpose beautifully.

- *What's all the fuss about airplanes?* A consultant's travel can take up time, reduce productivity, and affect his or her personal life.

It is not uncommon for me to visit both coasts in one week. I am on an airplane every week and because I do not live near an airport hub, I change planes for most trips. One trip often means four airplanes. Yes, I rack up frequent-flyer miles—over 5,000,000 and still counting. But the drawback that will affect your lifestyle is the difficulty in maintaining balance. Consider two simple things: food and exercise. You really must work hard to eat a healthy diet and exercise while on the road. How will you approach travel as it affects your lifestyle?

Rules about what we can pack in our carry-on luggage have stymied my travel a bit. I still take only a carry-on whenever possible. Here's what I have changed. I purchase the smallest size toothpaste for travel and ask the hotel front desk for additional toothpaste upon check-in. I switched to a solid deodorant and perfume stick. I also pack the fragrance samples found between magazine pages (men, they are available for you, too). When I must, I drop in to the local drugstore to pick up hairspray and other items that do not have a dry or solid substitute.

- *Why are the details of her schedule significant?* A consultant's schedule is usually hectic.

The week that I described is pretty typical. I don't try to get my week down to 40 hours. I don't think I will ever try. I love what I do, and I have created ways to build things other than work into my work schedule. Who do you know who can shop in New York City one week and in San Francisco the next? How many employees can take time off for a haircut or to browse a furniture store during the week? Who do you know who can work at home by choice? Who do you know who could take a stack of journals and sit next to the ocean to catch up on his or her professional reading? Although I may have worked over 50 hours in addition to travel time in one week, I will have many opportunities to balance those hours. Your lifestyle could change dramatically based on schedule alone. Will you have your family's support for a dramatic change?

Your lifestyle is yours and yours alone. Decide what you want your lifestyle to be as a consultant. Let's try some visualization activities to help you clarify what you want your consulting lifestyle to be and to help you plant that lifestyle firmly in your mind so that you are more likely to create it.

Tip: Take it with you when you travel.

Download your favorite book or podcast to your phone for your travel. Interested in leadership? Check out Halelly Azulay and her podcast series. You can download and subscribe to The TalentGrow Show: Grow Your Leadership and Communication Skills by Halelly Azulay on iTunes.

VISUALIZING SUCCESS

A friend of mine was a high school state champion tennis player. Her coach required her to spend hours visualizing success. She visualized herself completing specific strokes perfectly. She visualized herself winning a match. She visualized herself as a champion. Coaches of many other sports use visualization as well. They ask athletes to close their eyes and visualize what the pass feels like leaving their hands, what the wind feels like against their faces, what the ball looks like going through the hoop, what the crack of the club against the ball sounds like.

You can do the same thing. You can be your own coach. Of course, before you do that you must have a clear picture of the kind of future you want. Turn to Exhibit 11.1. This exercise will help you determine how you want to live and work—how you want to spend your time. Find a quiet place—one where you are sure you will not be interrupted by a phone call, a visit, or a nagging chore. Take at least an hour to complete the exercise. Take more time if you can. Put it aside. Sleep on it. Feed your subconscious by thinking about it before you sleep. Then dream about it. Pull it out again and fill in more details. Now discuss it with your significant other. Make additions or deletions.

Place your visualization exercise in a safe place, perhaps in your end-of-the-year tickler file—or perhaps you want to give your dream one year. Make an appointment with yourself one year from now to review your desires. Schedule your appointment just as you would schedule an appointment with a client. *Really*! If you don't schedule it, you'll forget it. Realize that you may not have achieved all that you identified. Realize also that some things may have changed. In any event, you will most likely learn much about yourself and what is important to you.

Create a "successful future" file to keep your ideal future in front of you. You may wish to place your Visualize Success exercise in the folder. However, because pictures speak louder than words, shout your future by collecting pictures such as the following and keeping them in a file:

- Magazine pictures of people engaged in a hobby you want to begin.
- Snapshots of you and your family or friends having fun together.
- Pictures of the results of something you want to find time to do, such as a gourmet meal you want to try cooking or a handcrafted oak desk if you want to try woodworking.
- An advertisement for the condo you want to purchase.
- Cartoons that depict your special situation.

- A travel flyer advertising a vacation spot you want to visit.
- A picture of the scene you want to view outside your office window. (For years, my picture was of the Chesapeake Bay!)
- A dollar bill with a larger figure written on it representing the amount you want in your savings account!

Periodically sit down with your file to remind yourself of what success looks like to you. It will keep you focused on your future. I guarantee it!

TAKING ACTION

I subscribe to the belief that everyone should love what they do and do what they love. Money will follow in one way or another. Life is about passion.

Is Fear of Failure Holding You Hostage?

Consulting can be unpredictable. But if fear is stopping you from moving forward, preventing you from following your passion, you may be giving up the biggest reward of your life. Sure, there is fear in change: fear of the unknown, fear of failing, fear of being judged.

Let's be reasonable. How often have you failed in your lifetime? If you are considering becoming a consultant, you've likely had very few failures. Oh sure, there was the time you and your frat brothers decided to have the fireball express zoom out the second story window of your frat house—on fire, of course—on Halloween. Yeah, that was a failure. And if you can remember others, it is only because there were so few of them and we always remember our vivid failures better than our successes.

This book provides you with step-by-step guidance for what you need to do, and you are developing a sound business plan. Your mentor (you do have a mentor, don't you?) will stop you from doing something stupid. Get moving. Dale Carnegie said, "Inaction breeds doubt and fear. Action breeds confidence and courage. If you want to conquer fear, do not sit home and think about it. Go out and get busy."

Try reframing your fear. Tell yourself that you are doing what's right for you, that it is exciting and forward-leaning. You will be more successful by moving than stagnating, so find something you can do every day to move closer to your dream.

> ### Is Fear of Failure Holding You Hostage?, cont'd.
>
> I nearly drowned when I was a kid, so it's natural that I'd have a fear of water (well, that's what I tell myself). I also love swimming. To get over my initial fear, I dive into the deep end of the pool first. Getting that nasty feeling of fear out of the picture allows me to enjoy swimming. I'm not saying you should dive in without a plan, but I do think you can take actions that move you forward.
>
> Do you remember Adam's tactic with Lambert at the beginning of this chapter? He asked Lambert to name the worst thing that could happen. You can do the same. If fear is holding you back from taking the plunge into the deep end, think about your actions and name the worst thing that could happen to you. Perhaps the worst thing is not trying. . . .

I once heard a speaker say that only 2 percent of all Americans have the discipline to achieve their dreams. Of those who do not achieve their dreams, 23 percent do not know what they want and another 67 percent know what they want but do not know how to make it happen. The remaining 10 percent know what they want and how to get it but lack discipline to follow through. In which category will you be?

If one of your dreams is to become an independent consultant, turn to Exhibit 11.2. It provides you with an outline to begin to put your plans on paper. Why not start today?

GET READY, GET SET . . .

Perhaps you have read this far in this book. You're interested, but you are not quite ready. Perhaps you think you need a little more experience. Perhaps your financial situation is not stable enough to take the risk. Perhaps you are satisfied with the job you now have. But someday. . . .

What can you do? Don't lose the spark. Turn to Exhibit 11.3 and list 50 things you can do to move closer to becoming a consultant. List everything that comes to mind as fast as you can, such as read another book, join a professional organization, interview a consultant, take a course, attend a conference, invent a name for your consulting practice, identify a client with whom you would choose to work. All suggestions are good. Don't pause to judge or prioritize them now. Just write. Ready, set, go!

Exhibit 11.1. Visualize Success

Take a few minutes to imagine a successful future for yourself. Think in terms of three to five years. Describe your successful future.

Part I. Professional

1. Describe your professional goals. (What is your title? What do clients say about your work? What do your colleagues say about you?)

2. Describe your interactions with your clients. (What are you doing? Where are you doing it? How does it feel? To whom are you talking?)

3. Describe your work more thoroughly. (How many people are around you? What is their relationship to you? What work excites you?)

4. Describe the logistics more thoroughly. (How much do you travel? Where? For how long? Why? What does your office look like? Where is it? What is the view outside your office window?)

5. Describe the results of your work. (What honors or awards have you received? What is your annual salary? What profit does your business make? How much is in your retirement account? Your savings account?)

6. What other professional dreams do you have? (What other professions? What other work?)

Exhibit 11.1. Visualize Success (Cont'd.)

Part II. Personal

1. Describe your personal goals. (What are you doing? What percentage of your time is spent pursuing personal goals? Where are you? With whom?)

2. Describe your interactions with family and friends. (What clubs have you joined? What vacations have you taken? What are you doing? Where? With whom? How does it feel?)

3. What do you do when you are alone? (What are you reading? What are your daydreams? Where are you?)

4. What are you learning? (Are you taking classes? Did you earn an advanced degree? Where? How? Why?)

5. What personal skills have you acquired? (What hobbies are you trying? What sports are you participating in? With whom? How often?)

6. Describe the logistics of your personal life. (Where do you live? What is your living space like? What kind of car do you drive? How are mundane chores completed?)

Exhibit 11.2. A Consultant's Action Plan

Instructions: As you complete each step, check the box. The numbers in parentheses refer to exhibits in this book.

1. Do you know enough about the consulting profession?
   - ❑ Interview consultants you know. (1.1)
   - ❑ Read about consulting. Scan the reading list at the end of the book.
   - ❑ Compare your values to the requirements of consulting.

2. Are you a match for the profession?
   - ❑ Compare your skills and characteristics to those required of a consultant. (2.1)
   - ❑ Measure your propensity as an entrepreneur. (2.2)

3. Do you know enough about consultant billing practices?
   - ❑ Calculate your financial requirements. (3.1)
   - ❑ Read about consulting billing structures.

4. Are you ready to start?
   - ❑ Describe your business, its services, and its products.
   - ❑ Identify your market.
   - ❑ Analyze your competition.
   - ❑ Assess your skills.
   - ❑ Name your business.
   - ❑ Determine your pricing structure. (3.2, 3.3)
   - ❑ Identify start-up costs. (4.2)
   - ❑ Select an accountant.
   - ❑ Determine your business structure.
   - ❑ Check on zoning laws, licenses, and taxes.
   - ❑ Select a location.
   - ❑ Develop a business plan that includes:
     - ❑ Business description
     - ❑ Marketing plan (5.1)
     - ❑ Management plan
     - ❑ Financial plan (4.3, 4.4, 4.5)

Exhibit 11.2. Action Plan, Cont'd.

- ❑ Select a banker, attorney, and insurance broker.
- ❑ Arrange for financing or set aside capital for a worst-case scenario. (4.6)
- ❑ File documentation to register your business legally.

5. Are you consistently marketing your services?
   - ❑ Complete and follow your marketing calendar. (5.3)
   - ❑ Identify potential client organizations and research them. (5.4)
   - ❑ Introduce your services with letters and telephone calls. (5.5)
   - ❑ Call on organizations in person. (5.6)
   - ❑ Maintain a client contact log. (5.7)

6. Do you have a handle on your expenses?
   - ❑ Maintain a monthly expense record. (6.1)
   - ❑ Track petty cash and expenditures. (6.3, 6.4)
   - ❑ Monitor invoices. (6.5)
   - ❑ Project revenue. (6.7)
   - ❑ Invoice clients in a timely manner. (6.6)
   - ❑ Track the time and cost of specific projects. (6.8)
   - ❑ Compare project profits. (6.9)

7. Are you building professional client relationships?
   - ❑ Clarify expectations during the contracting phase with each client. (7.1)
   - ❑ Build a partnership with each client. (7.2)

8. Are you ready to grow?
   - ❑ Explore various ways to build your business. (8.1, 8.2)
   - ❑ Ensure that expectations are clear when using subcontractors. (8.3, 8.4)

9. Do you consistently practice the highest ethical standards?

10. Are you professional in every respect?
   - ❑ Improve your skills.
   - ❑ Balance your life and your business. (10.2, 10.5)
   - ❑ Manage your time wisely. (10.3)
   - ❑ Mentor others.

11. Do you enjoy the profession as much as you thought you would?

Exhibit 11.3. Fast Fifty

Instructions: List 50 things you can do to move closer to becoming a consultant.

1.	26.
2.	27.
3.	28.
4.	29.
5.	30.
6.	31.
7.	32.
8.	33.
9.	34.
10.	35.
11.	36.
12.	37.
13.	38.
14.	39.
15.	40.
16.	41.
17.	42.
18.	43.
19.	44.
20.	45.
21.	46.
22.	47.
23.	48.
24.	49.
25.	50.

What can you do with your 50 ideas? It would seem natural for you to begin to put a plan together for how to go from here to there. *The New Quick Start Guide,* another book in this series, can help you simplify the planning process by providing you with a series of questions, a list of ideas, and plenty of room for planning.

Remember, it takes as much energy to wish as it does to plan. So go ahead. Wish on paper and it becomes your plan.

Wish on paper, and it becomes your plan.

For the Consummate Consultant

This book has been filled with ideas and suggestions to answer your concerns and questions. It has even presented the difficulties of consulting. If you still want to be a consultant, don't let anything hold you back. Find your focus, collect your confidence, and start acting on your action plan! Practice persistence, perseverance, and patience to achieve your passion. You will be successful. I look forward to seeing you on the consultant trail.

It's All About Focus. You start with a vision for your consulting business and then funnel all the ideas down to what you will do, with whom, where, and why. Your focus will lead you to a good strategy. Your focus will be even better if you know when to say no. The tighter your focus, the faster you'll grow.

Stop-Doing List. Make a stop-doing list—all those things you've been doing for years—in order to find time to do all the new things you want to do.

Have Plan B. Always have a Plan B. That's just common sense. However, be sure to give Plan A a complete chance. Give it time. Give it tactics. Give it positive energy. Don't panic too soon before you switch to Plan B.

A Bonus for the Consummate Consultant

Fly High and Remember the Reality. You've chosen to follow a different path. Good for you. The reality of it is that you are going against the wind. And, you do realize that an airplane must fly against the wind in order to take off—right? So turn into the wind. Meet the challenges and resistance head on. File your flight plan. And take off! You are sure to land successfully at your destination.

HELPFUL RESOURCES AND LINKS

- Business Owners Idea Café; www.businessownersideacafe.com
  An online site that provides articles, resources, and ideas to start and run a business.
- Entrepreneur.com; www.entrepreneur.com
  An online resource providing ideas and articles for start-ups and new companies.
- Equiteq; www.equiteq.com
  The leading M&A advisor for consulting firms that helps consulting firm owners prepare for sale by growing profits, revenue, and equity value.
- Ewing Marion Kauffman Foundation; www.kauffman.org
  A foundation that provides entrepreneurs with education, tools, and resources to break down barriers that stand in the way of starting and growing their businesses.
- ISA—The Association for Learning Providers; www.isaconnection.org
  An association dedicated exclusively to the needs of owners and executives of the leading training, learning, and talent development firms.
- Nation1099; www.nation1099.com
  A web publication for freelancers and consultants, where you'll find articles, tools, and interviews of interest to small business.
- National Association of Women Business Owners; www.nawbo.org

An association that provides resources and networking opportunities for women-owned businesses.

- Professional Independent Consultants of America; www.picanetwork.org
  A national membership organization that provides consultants with education, tools, advice, partner services, and community.
- PwC Talent Exchange; www.talentexchange.pwc.com
  A marketplace where consultants can connect to projects and opportunities within PricewaterhouseCoopers.
- SCORE; www.score.org
  A volunteer-supported organization that offers live and recorded webinars as well as in-person events at more than 300 chapters; it also pairs new small business owners with mentors.
- StoryBrand; www.StoryBrand.com
  A company that helps businesses clarify their messages and create clear and focused websites.
- Top Consultant; www.Top-Consultant.com
  An online talent marketplace dedicated to consultants.
- Vistage; www.vistage.com
  A peer mentoring group. Dun & Bradstreet 2017 data shows that member companies grew 2.2 times faster than average small U.S. businesses.
- Your Consulting Course; www.yourtrainingconsultingbiz.com
  An online course for new consultants with an ongoing offering to learn what's needed to start your business.
- YPO; www.ypo.org
  A global platform for chief executives to engage, learn, and grow, with 26,000 members in 130 countries.

READING LIST

Bellman, G. M. (2002). *The consultant's calling* (2nd ed.). San Francisco, CA: Wiley.

Biech, E. (2000). *The consultant's legal guide.* San Francisco, CA: Wiley.

_____. (2003). *Marketing your consulting services.* San Diego, CA: Pfeiffer.

_____. (2015). *101 ways to make learning active beyond the classroom.* Hoboken, NJ: Wiley.

_____. (2015). *Training and development for dummies.* Hoboken, NJ: Wiley.

_____. (2016). *Change management training.* Alexandria, VA: ATD Press.

_____. (2017). *The art and science of training.* Alexandria, VA: ATD Press.

_____. (2018a). *ATD's foundations of talent development.* Alexandria, VA: ATD Press.

_____. (2018b). *Starting a talent development program.* Alexandria, VA: ATD Press.

_____. (2019). *The new consultant's quick start guide: An action plan for your first year in business.* Hoboken, NJ: Wiley.

Biech, E. (Ed.). (2001). *The Pfeiffer book of successful team-building tools.* San Francisco, CA: Wiley.

Block, P. (2011). *Flawless consulting* (2nd ed.). San Francisco, CA: Wiley.

Clark, D. (2017). *Entrepreneurial you.* Boston, MA: Harvard Business Review Press.

Cohen, S. (2017). *The complete guide to building and growing a talent development firm.* Alexandria, VA: ATD Press.

Consulting.Com. (2018). *How much do consultants make?* Retrieved at https://www.consulting.com/consultant-salaries.

Cope, K. (2018). *Seeing the big picture: Business acumen to build your credibility, career, and company*. Orem, UT: Acumen Learning.

Daugherty, P., & Wilson, J. (2018). *Human+ Machine: Reimagining Work in the Age of AI*. Boston, MA: Harvard Business Review Press.

Dweck, C. (2016). *Mindset: The new psychology of success*. New York, NY: Penguin Random House.

Entrepreneur Media Staff. (2015). *Start your own business* (6th ed.). Irvine, CA: Entrepreneur Press.

Halls, J. (2017). *Rapid media development for trainers: Creating videos, podcasts, and presentations on a budget*. Alexandria, VA: ATD Press.

Heisler, K., Southhall, M., & Cardec, L. (2016, December 12). *Randstad US study projects massive shift to agile employment and staffing model in the next decade*. Randstad North America. Retrieved at https://www.randstadusa.com/about/news/randstad-us-study-projects-massive-shift-to-agile-employment-and-staffing-model-in-the-next-decade/.

Henry, P. (2017, February 18). Why some startups succeed (and why most fail). *Entrepreneur*. Retrieved at https://www.entrepreneur.com/article/288769.

Hofferberth, R., & Urich, J. (2015). *2015 professional services global pricing report*. Liberty Township, OH: Service Performance Insight. Retrieved at https://www.kimbleapps.com/site/wp-content/uploads/2015PSPricing_Kimble.pdf.

Hyatt, M. (2018a). How to write better blog posts with a simple template. Retrieved at https://platformuniversity.com/blog-post-template/.

_____. (2018b). *Your best year ever: A 5-step plan for achieving your most important goals*. Grand Rapids, MI: Baker Publishing Group.

Lewin, M. D. (1997). *The consultant's survival guide*. New York, NY: Wiley.

Lewis, L. (2000). *What to charge: Pricing strategies for freelancers and consultants*. Putnam Valley, NY: Aletheia Publications..

Linamagi, T. (2015). The most common reasons startups fail. *Fast Company*. Retrieved at https://www.fastcompany.com/3044519/7-of-the-most-common-reasons-startups-fail.

Manyika, J., Lund, S., Bughin, J., Robinson, K., Mischke, J., & Mahajan, D. (2016). *Independent work: Choice, necessity, and the gig economy*. San Francisco, CA: McKinsey Global Institute.

McGovern, M. (2017). *Thriving in the gig economy*. Wayne, NJ: Career Press.

Miller, D. (2017). *Building a story brand: Clarify your message so customers will listen*. New York, NY: Harper Collins.

Moss, W. (2005). *Starting from scratch: Secrets from 21 ordinary people who made the entrepreneurial leap.* Chicago, IL: Dearborn Trade Publishing.

Peters, T. (1997, August–September). The brand called you. *Fast Company*, pp. 83–94.

Pink, D. (2002). *Free agent nation: The future of working for yourself.* New York, NY: Hachette Book Group.

Pofeldt, E. (2018). *The million-dollar one-person business.* New York, NY: Penguin Random House.

Schein, E. (2016). *Humble consulting: How to provide real help faster.* Oakland, CA: Berrett-Koehler.

Shefsky, L. E. (1994). *Entrepreneurs are made, not born.* New York, NY: McGraw-Hill.

Silberman, M., & Biech, E. (2015). *Active training: A handbook of techniques, designs, case examples, and tips.* Hoboken, NJ: Wiley.

Sobel, A., & Panas, J. (2012). *Power questions: Build relationships, win new business, and influence others.* Hoboken, NJ: Wiley.

Sobel, A., & Panas, J. (2014). *Power relationships: 26 irrefutable laws for building extraordinary relationships.* Hoboken, NJ: Wiley.

Stein, C. (1994, November 15). Millions for their thoughts: Management consulting finds big, profitable place in cutthroat economy. *Boston Globe*.

U.S. Small Business Administration. (2016). Small business profile. Retrieved at https://www.sba.gov/sites/default/files/advocacy/United_States.pdf.

ABOUT THE AUTHOR

Elaine Biech is a consultant, trainer, and the author of the *Washington Post*'s number-one best-seller *The Art and Science of Training*. With more than three decades of experience and 80-plus published books, she has been called "the Stephen King of the training industry."

Elaine is president of ebb associates inc, a strategic implementation and leadership development consulting firm, where she helps large organizations work through large-scale change. She has presented at hundreds of national and international conferences and has been featured in publications such as the *Wall Street Journal, Harvard Management Update, Investor's Business Daily,* and *Fortune.* Her books have been published in a dozen languages, and several have received national awards.

Among her extensive body of published work are *The New Consultant's Quick Start Guide* and *Training and Development for Dummies.* She has authored ATD's flagship publications, *The ASTD Handbook: The Definitive Reference for Training and Development* and *ATD's Foundations of Talent Development.*

Elaine is a dedicated lifelong learner who believes that excellence isn't optional. She delights in helping leaders maximize their effectiveness and guiding organizations through the current business churn. Customizing all of her work for individual clients, she conducts strategic planning sessions and implements corporate-wide systems, such as quality improvement, change management, reengineering of business processes, and mentoring programs. She is particularly adept at turning dysfunctional teams into productive ones.

As a consultant, she has provided services globally to the U.S. Navy, China Sinopec, China Telecom, PricewaterhouseCoopers, Banco de Credito Peru, Minera Yanacocha, Lockheed Martin, Newmont Mining, Outback Steakhouse, the Department of Homeland Security, the FAA, Land O' Lakes, McDonald's, Lands' End, Chrysler, Johnson Wax, the Federal Reserve Bank, American Family Insurance, Marathon Oil, Hershey Chocolate, NASA, Newport News Shipbuilding, the Kohler Company, ATD, the American Red Cross, the Association of Independent CPAs, the University of Wisconsin, The College of William and Mary, and hundreds of other public and private sector organizations to prepare them for current challenges.

The recipient of numerous professional awards, Elaine is a consummate training professional who has been instrumental in guiding the talent development profession for most of her career. A long-time volunteer for ATD, she has served on the association's national board of directors, was the recipient of the 1992 ASTD Torch Award, the 2004 ASTD Volunteer Staff Partnership Award, and the 2006 Gordon Bliss Memorial Award. In 2012, she was the inaugural CPLP Fellow Program Honoree from the ASTD Certification Institute. Elaine wrote the first ASTD Training Certification Study Guides.

Elaine was the 1995 Wisconsin Women Entrepreneurs' Mentor Award recipient and has served on the Independent Consultants Association's Advisory Committee. She is currently on the ISA—The Association for Learning Providers board of directors. Elaine is a member of the Center for Creative Leadership's (CCL) board of governors and is the chair of CCL's Research, Evaluation, and Societal Advancement Committee. She is also a member of CCL's executive committee and the editorial board.

INDEX

Big Four accounting firms, 12
Bill paying, 162
Block, Peter, 29, 147, 183–184, 195, 279
Blogs, 130, 245
Bonuses, 11–12
Bplans.com, 95
Brand. *See* Image
Budgeting, actual vs. projected, 162–164, 163*e*, 181, 182
Buffett, Warren, 255
Building a Story Brand (Miller), 129
Building Your Training Business, 82
Business acumen, 237
Business cards, 118
Business development assessment, 280–281, 284–285*e*
Business directories, 84
Business expenses. *See* Expenses; Record keeping
Business growth, 219–253; decision-making about, 219–221, 226*e*, 231–233, 249–252; expectations for, 21; geographical expansion for, 247–249; myths about, 21; partners for, 227–230, 228–229*e*; practices vs. firms, 231; record keeping for, 183–184; staff for, 221–225, 231–233; stages of, 222–223; staying small vs., 252; subcontractors for, 234–238, 236*e*; without adding people, 238–247
Business interruption insurance, 169
Business management assessment, 281–282, 285*e*
Business name, 82–86
The Business of Consulting (Biech), 184, 231
Business plan: business management assessment, 281–282, 285*e*; development of, 89–96, 90*e*; following, 249; marketing plan, 91, 93, 118–128, 121*e*, 123*e*, 127*e*; need for, 89; now vs. forever plans, 104; research before starting business, 10–16, 23–28, 24*e*, 25*e*; Small Business Administration for help with, 90; structure of, 90–91, 90*e*
Business structure: business plan on organization and management for, 93; choosing legal entity for, 14, 85, 87–89; expectations for, 22; and part-time consulting, 14; self-employed independent consultants, 15–16; subcontractors, 14

C

Calculation method, for fees, 52–55, 54*e*
Calendars, 312
Capital investments, 161, 184
CareerJournal (*Wall Street Journal*), 10
Careers in Business, 41
Carnegie, Dale, 317
Cash flow: management of, 156–164, 163*e*; and petty cash, 172–175, 173*e*, 174*e*. *See also* Invoices; Record keeping
C corporations, 87, 89
Certificate of Trade Name, 85
Certification and credentials, 11, 33, 278
Characteristics of consultants, 31–50; assessing personal situation for consulting, 43–45; and avoiding mediocrity, 42; entrepreneurial characteristics, 45–49, 47–48*e*; ideal consultant skills, 41; and motivation, 31–33; personality and consulting profession, 25–28, 25*e*, 39; precautions about consulting, 49; roles of consultants, 40–42; skills for success, 33–39, 34*e*. *See also* Motivation
Charging (what to charge), 51–77; 1% Rule, 63; 3 x Rule, 52–55, 231–233; assessing personal situation for, 55–56; business expenses and, 70–71; and characteristics of consultants, 36; defining billing time, 68–69; discussing money issues with clients, 75–76; estimating income needs for, 52–55, 54*e*; ethical issues of, 73–75, 255–256, 263–265; expectations for, 51–52; increasing charges, 71–73; myths about, 17–18; prepayment discount, 159; pricing structure choices for, 64–68; rate calculators, 59, 61, 63; and satisfaction guarantees, 76; setting, 56–64, 57*e*, 60*e*, 62*e*; and understanding competition, 77; *What to Charge* (Lewis), 162
Client-consultant relationship, 187–218; adding value in, 204–211; building relationship with individuals, 214–215; consulting competency assessment, 282–286, 285*e*; expectations for, 21–22; improving, 211–214; initial contact, 187–189, 191–192; and listening importance, 193; phases of building, 193–204, 196*e*, 201–204*e*; post-project maintenance of,

fees for, 71; image conveyed by, 105–108; and image of business, 105–108; and invoicing, 157; mailing, 117–118, 157, 170; mailing lists for, 117–118; marketing, 134; sending lumpy envelopes, 134, 139, 151; time savers for, 294

Credit: credit cards and cash flow, 160–161; lines of credit, 160; payment via credit cards, 158

CUSTOMER (Commit, Understand, Strengths, Team, Observe, Measure, Expect to succeed, Recognize importance), 216–217

D

Daily rates, 56–61, 57*e*, 60*e*, 64–65, 69

Data-collection step, 197–198

DBA (Doing Business As) certificate, 85

Deception, recognizing, 270

Deloitte, 11, 12

Deming, W. Edwards, 115, 151

Design: business cards, 118; logos, 106; websites, 129

Directories, 84

Disability insurance, 168

Discounted fees, 74–75

Diversity, 266–267

Domain names, 84

Donations, 166

Double dipping, avoiding, 264

Dues, 162, 166

Dweck, Carol, 279–280

E

ebb associates inc, 82, 83, 107, 132

Edison, Thomas, 273

Edson, Annie, 310

Einstein, Albert, 1

Electronic billing systems, 157, 293

Employment. *See* Permanent employment

Entertainment expenses, 166

Entrepreneurial characteristics, assessing, 45–49, 47–48*e*. *See also* Characteristics of consultants

Entrepreneur (magazine), 46, 96

Entrepreneurs Are Made, Not Born (Shefsky), 26

Envelope system, for expenses, 164–165

Equiteq, 220, 325

Ernst & Young, 12

Errors and omissions (E&O) insurance, 168, 261

Estimated taxes, 171

Ethical issues, 255–272; in client-to-consultant transactions, 268–270; codes of ethics, 270–271; in consultant-to-client transactions, 258–265; in consultant-to-consultant transactions, 265–269; for fees, 73–75, 255–256, 263–265; friendship with clients, 214; and image of consultants, 256–257, 260; in international situations, 271–272; refusal of assignments because of, 150–151, 190; of using subcontractors, 237

Ethics Today Online (forum), 271

ExecuNet.com, 16

Expenses: advertising, 125, 165; for entertainment, 166; envelope system for, 164–165; and ethical issues, 262, 264; expectations for, 17–18; for insurance, 168; and interest, 169; for meals, 169; for office equipment and maintenance, 168, 170–171; for overhead, 52–56, 59, 70–71; for presentation materials and equipment, 179; for professional development, 170; for reference materials, 166; of subcontractors, 236*e*; and taxes, 164–165, 171; tracking, 164–172, 167*e*; for travel, 69, 166, 167*e*, 169; for websites, 165. *See also* Charging (what to charge); Record keeping

Expertise: and characteristics of consultants, 38–39; consultants as subject-matter experts, 3–4; and consulting fees, 69; expectations for, 19, 20; gaining experience as consultant, 108–111; myths about, 19; and setting fees, 57; in specialty fields, 133–134, 313; understanding trends, 133–134. *See also* Charging (what to charge)

F

Failure, fear of, 317–318

Family and friends: family support for consulting business, 44; loans from, 101; support system for positivity, 280

FastCompany (magazine), 81

Fast Fifty, 318–324, 323*e*

Federal employer-identification numbers (FEIN), 88

128–130; survey tools, 292; websites, 84, 128–130, 165

Interns, 128, 238

Interviewing: for employment with consulting firms, 13; for researching consulting profession, 23–24, 24*e*

Invoices: and business image, 107; collections, 179; customizing, 176; for international business, 249; late payment for, 161–162; monitoring payment of, 157–158; "paid-when-paid" terms, 235, 266; promptness of, 156–160; record keeping for, 175–179, 177*e*, 178*e*; for small businesses, 161; templates for, 292–293

J

Jefferson, Thomas, 257

Job listings, 16

Joint ventures, 240–241

Junk mail, 133–134, 288

K

Kay, Alan, 120–122

Keller, Helen, 301

KPMG, 12

L

Labin, Jenn, 65

TheLadders.com, 16

Land O'Lakes, 216

Late payment, 161–162

Learning 2018 (Masie), 306

Leasing vs. purchasing, 161

Legal entity of businesses: corporations, 87, 89; limited liability companies (LLC), 87–89; partnerships, 14, 85, 87–88; sole proprietorship, 85, 87–88. *See also* Business structure

Legal issues: contracts, 55–56, 148–149, 195–196, 196*e*, 227, 235, 237, 265; intellectual property, 247, 262–263; legal fees, 165; letters of agreement, 149; liability, 88, 168; licenses, 169. *See also* Business growth; Insurance

Lewis, Laurie, 162

Lifestyle. *See* Balance of life and business; Characteristics of consultants; Family and friends

Limited liability companies (LLC), 85, 87–89. *See also* Legal entity of businesses

Limited partnerships. *See* Partnership

Line of credit, 160

LinkedIn, 107, 129

Listening, importance of, 193

Loans: record keeping and expense of, 169; for start-up business, 101

Logos, 106

Lumpy envelopes, 134, 139, 151

M

Mailing: of lumpy envelopes, 134, 139, 151; mailing lists, 117–118; Priority Mail, 157; record keeping and expense of, 170

Maintenance expenses, 170–171

Management consultants, defined, 15

Marketing, 115–151; and advertising, 125, 133–134, 165, 245, 288; attracting high-value clients, 209–210; business development assessment, 280–281, 284–285*e*; and characteristics of consultants, 35; clients' word-of-mouth, 135–136; cold calling, 141–145, 142*e*, 144–146*e*; and competition, 133; evaluating client base and setting fees, 71–73; expectations for, 20–22; financial issues of, 136–140; finding new clients with, 135–136, 141–147, 142*e*, 144*e*, 145*e*, 146*e*; mailing list for, 117–118; marketing consultants' fees, 68; marketing plan, 91, 93, 118–128, 121*e*, 123*e*, 127*e*; market research, 95, 133–134, 143, 288; materials needed for, 105–108, 118, 165; mistakes made with, 119; need for, 115–117, 131–132, 140; networking for starting business, 109–111; organization for, 118; personalization of, 135; proposals, 66, 69, 148–149, 158–159, 293; record keeping and expense of, 165; sales required by employed consultants, 11, 12; scheduling, 131; skills needed for, 27, 35; social media for, 128–130; strategy for, 132–133; testimonials for, 118; thank you messages/gifts, 118, 134, 137, 139, 141, 151, 269; trends, 133–134; value proposition, 13, 36, 104, 210, 250; websites for, 84, 128–130, 165. *See also* Business plan; Refusal of work

Marketing Your Consulting Services (Biech), 140

Masie, Elliott, 306

Mastermind groups, 250

Materials. *See* Marketing; Presentation materials and equipment; Reference materials

MBO Partners, 15, 16, 251

McGovern, Marion, 63

McKinsey, 11

Meal expenses, 169

Mediocrity, avoiding, 42

Meetings: and characteristics of consultants, 37; initial contact with clients, 187–189, 191–192. *See also* Charging (what to charge)

Mentors, 223, 288

MicroWorkers.com, 240

Miller, Donald, 35, 129

The Million-Dollar One-Person Business (Pofeldt), 15–16

Mindset success, 279–280, 284e

Motivation, 301–324; Action Plan for, 321–322e; and appeal of consulting, 1–3, 8–10, 31–33, 51–52, 79–80, 301–304; Fast Fifty for, 318–324, 323e; overcoming fear of failure, 317–318; rallying, 310; Visualize Success for, 316–318, 319–320e; week in life of a consultant (example), 304–315

Myths about consulting: avoiding politics and paperwork, 18–19; business growth, 21; consultants' charges, 17–18; expertise, 19; getting started in consulting, 20–21; image of consulting, 20; time management, 19–20; truths vs., 21–22

N

Name of business, 82–86

Nation1099, 59

National Speakers Association (NSA), 245

Networking: for business growth, 250–251; for business planning, 96; and client-consultant relationship, 216; expectations for, 21; for marketing, 136–137; and professionalism, 286, 287

New clients, finding, 135–136, 141–147, 142e, 144e, 145e, 146e. *See also* Marketing

Niche market: avoiding excuses about, 105; business plan on, 91, 93; defining consulting specialty, 104; identifying, 102–105; identifying ideal clients, 103–104; target market vs., 102–103; value proposition for, 104

Noncompete agreements, 237, 265

O

Objections, responding to, 207

Office equipment: for copying, 106–107; purchasing vs. leasing, 161; record keeping and expense of, 168, 170

O'Mara, Julie, 266–267

Onboarding process, 198

1% Rule, 63

Online courses, 135, 243–244

Operating losses: carrying, 156; understanding, 181–184, 185e

Organization: calendars, 312; and characteristics of consultants, 36; filing systems, 293, 305–306, 311–312; for marketing, 118; for travel, 313–314

Overcommitment, avoiding, 36, 259–260

Overhead expenses, 52–56, 59, 70–71, 170

P

"Paid-when-paid" terms, 235, 266

Panas, J., 278

Partnership: advantages of, 14; for business growth, 227–230, 228–229e; collaboration with consultants, 241–243; as legal entity for business, 88; limited partnership, 85; virtual partners and joint venture, 240–241. *See also* Legal entity of businesses

Payroll services, 182–183

Payscale.com, 61

Peale, Norman Vincent, 79

Pension plans, 170

Performance percent fee, 68

Permanent employment: for consultants, 11–13; consulting contracts with former employer, 55–56; frustration with, 1–3; hiring staff (*See* Business growth); IRS on independent contractors vs. employees, 235–236; and part-time consulting, 50, 108

Per person pricing structure, 67

Personal financial statements, 100

Personalization: for client-consultant relationship, 214–216; of marketing, 135, 139

Peters, Tom, 66

Petty cash, 172–175, 173*e*, 174*e*

Photos, 212–213

Pink, Dan, 5

Podcasts, 246

Pofeldt, Elaine, 15–16

Positioning strategy, 122–124, 123*e*

Positive thinking/messages, 46, 47, 50, 141, 155–156, 267, 279–280

Power Questions (Sobel, Panas), 278

Prepayment discount, 159

Presentation materials and equipment: as client cost, 70; copying and printing, 166; record keeping and expense of, 179

Price fixing, avoiding, 61

PricewaterhouseCoopers (PwC), 12, 16, 250–251

Priority Mail, 157

Problem solving: and characteristics of consultants, 35, 37, 40–42; customized solutions, 208; helping clients recognize value, 205–208

Pro bono work, 70, 110

Productivity of consultants, 198–200

Product market, for expansion, 245

Professional development: for professionalism, 286–289; record keeping and expense of, 170; for start-up business planning, 95, 109–111

Professionalism, 273–299; balancing life and business for, 289–291; defined, 274–275; personal checkup for, 297–298, 298*e*; professional development for, 286–289; self-assessing consulting competencies, 273–286, 283–285*e*; time management for, 291–297; and volunteering, 278, 297. *See also* Ethical issues

Professional liability insurance, 168

Profit, understanding, 181–184, 185*e*. *See also* Record keeping

Project-based fees, 66

Project initiation fees, 158–159

Proposals: as cost of doing business, 69; developing, 148–149; including project initiation fees in, 158–159; Requests for Proposal (RFP), 66; special delivery for, 149; time savers for, 293

Prosperity, portraying, 155–156

Q

QuickBooks Pro, 164, 166

R

Randstad US, 5

Rapid Media Development for Trainers (Halls), 246

Record keeping, 153–186; business time savers, 291–294; cash flow management with, 156–164, 163*e*; and characteristics of consultants, 36; invoicing and charging client for expenses, 159, 175–179, 177*e*, 178*e*; need for, 153–154; and petty cash, 172–175, 173*e*, 174*e*; planning for worst while portraying prosperity, 155–156; for revenue projection, 179, 180*e*; for tracking expenses, 164–172, 167*e*; types of, 155; for understanding the numbers, 181–184, 185*e*

Reference materials: finding time for, 313; loaning, 184; record keeping and expense of, 166; resources for, 287; subscriptions, 162, 166

Referrals: by clients, 135–136; referring work to colleagues, 139–140, 261

Refusal of work: to avoid overcommitment, 36, 259–260; due to ethical issues, 150–151, 258–259

Registering a business name, 85

Relation, Requirement, Relatable, Rationale questions (4Rs), 205–208

Relationship management. *See* Client-consultant relationship

Rent, 170

Repair expenses, 170–171

Repeat business, 189–191

Research: analysis of present situation during start-up, 120–122, 121*e*; asking questions of clients/potential clients, 145*e*, 191–197, 205–208; data-collection step, 197–198; disclosing need for, 259; interviewing consultants about profession, 23–24, 24*e*; market research, 95, 133–134, 143, 288; networking for conducting mini-research, 216; questions to ask before starting business, 80–81, 278. *See also* Start-up businesses

Retainers, 67

Retirement, 170
Revenue projection, 179, 180e
Review. *See* Assessment
RFP (Requests for Proposal), 66
Risk, tolerance for, 26
Rockefeller, John D., 16

S

Sales and selling: business plan for, 93; and characteristics of consultants, 35; helping clients recognize value, 205–208; hiring staff for, 225, 231–233; mistakes of, 210–211; required by employed consultants, 11, 12. *See also* Marketing
Satisfaction guarantees, 76
Savings accounts, 172
ScalablePath.com, 240
Schedule: availability to clients, 309; avoiding overcommitment, 150–151, 190, 259–260; balance of life and business, 289–291, 297–298, 298e, 311, 315; for bill paying, 162; calendars, 312; effective date for proposals, 148–149; for estimated taxes, 171; for marketing, 125–126, 127e, 131, 136; repeat business, 189–191. *See also* Time management
Schedule C, 88
Scope of work: clarifying, 195; for market pricing strategy, 73–75; scope creep, 66, 292; and setting fees, 57–58. *See also* Refusal of work
S corporations, 87, 89
Search Engine Optimization, 129
Secretary of State offices, 89
Self-discipline, 27–28, 318
SEP IRA, 170
Shefsky, Lloyd E., 26
Sherman Anti-Trust Act, 61
60-second sound bite, 147
Sleep, need for, 26
Small Business Administration, 90
Sobel, A., 278
Social media, 107, 128–130
Social responsibility, 260
Society for Business Ethics, 271
Sole proprietorship, 85, 87–88. *See also* Legal entity of businesses

Solutions. *See* Problem solving
"So You Want to Be a Consultant" (Biech), 8
Spam, 133–134, 288
Staff, hiring, 182, 184, 221–225, 231–233. *See also* Hiring
Standards, for professionalism, 276, 283e
Start-up businesses, 79–113; accountants for, 86–87; business plan development for, 89–96, 90e; failure of, in first five years, 45; financial considerations for, 96–100e, 96–102; gaining experience for, 108–111; image projection for, 105–108; legal entity for, 14, 85, 87–89; myths about, 20–21; naming the business, 82–86; niche market identification, 102–105; questions to consider for, 80–81, 278; Start-Up Checklist, 111–112; success vs. failure of, 81. *See also* Charging (what to charge); Consulting competencies; Marketing; New clients, finding
Status reports, 175
Stein, Charles, 5
StoryBrand, 35
Students, working with, 128, 238
Subcontracting: for business growth, 234–238, 236e; ethical issues of, 265–269; "paid-when-paid" terms of, 235, 266; for start-up business, 110
Subscriptions, 162, 166
Survey tools, online, 292

T

Tag lines, 82
Talent development, 37
Talent Exchange (PwC), 16, 251
The TalentGrow Show, 315
Talents/tolerance of consultants. *See* Characteristics of consultants
Target market vs. niche market, 102–103
Taxes: and accountants, 86–87; carrying operating losses, 156; for different legal entities of businesses, 87; estimated, 171; federal employer-identification numbers (FEIN), 88; home offices, 102; independent contractors vs. employees, 235–236; record keeping and expense of, 171; Schedule C, 88; 1099 vs. W-2

designation, 15, 236; tracking expenses for, 164–165; and using subcontractors, 234

Teaching, 243–245

Temporary services, 239–240

1099s, 15, 236. *See also* Subcontracting

TESS (Trademark Electronic Search System, U.S. Patent and Trademark Office), 84

Testimonials, 118

Thank you messages/gifts, 118, 135, 137, 139, 141, 151, 269

3 x Rule, 52–55, 231–233

Thriving in the Gig Economy (McGovern), 63

Tickler files, 292

Time management, 291–297; business time savers, 291–294; expectations for, 17–20; myths about, 19–20; session planner, 296–297; sleep and, 26; time-management log, 296; tips for, 295–296; travel time savers, 294–295; vacation time, 290

Tips: business growth, 227, 236, 240, 244, 245, 246, 247, 248, 249; characteristics of consultants, 35, 41, 44, 46; client-consultant relationships, 198, 200, 212–213, 216; consulting profession information, 10, 11, 16, 27; ethical issues, 262, 271; fees, 59, 61, 64; financial issues, 157, 182; marketing, 126, 141, 149; motivation, 314, 315; professionalism, 278, 291–293, 295, 296; record keeping, 160, 164, 175, 176; start-up business, 84, 87, 90, 95, 96, 102, 106

Toptal.com, 240

Trademark Electronic Search System (U.S. Patent and Trademark Office), 84

Trademarks, 84, 85

Traditional employment. *See* Permanent employment

Travel: advantages and disadvantages of, 11, 12; automobile expenses, 166, 167e, 169; ethical issues of charging for, 262, 264; example, 307–308; fees for business expenses, 69; organization for, 313–315; record keeping for, 158–159, 172, 179; time savers, 294–295

Trust, building, 282

Twain, Mark, 259

Twitter, 129

2 x Rule, 52–55

U

UpWork.com, 240

U.S. Patent and Trademark Office, 84

Utilities, 172

V

Vacation time, 290

Value: adding value in client-consultant relationships, 204–211; attracting high-value clients, 209–210; value proposition for niche market, 104

Value-based fees, 68

Visualize Success, 316–318, 319–320e. *See also* Positive thinking/messages

Volunteering: to give back to profession, 278, 297, 312; pro bono work, 110; for start-up business, 109

W

W-2, defined, 15

Walkaway rates, 63, 75

Wall Street Journal, 10, 95

Watershed Associates, 262

Websites: domain names for, 84; for marketing, 128–130; record keeping and expense of, 165

What to Charge (Lewis), 162

Women-owned businesses, 227

Wood, Tom, 262

Word-of-mouth marketing, 135–136

Workers' compensation, 169

Work-life balance. *See* Balance of life and business

Workplace 2025 (Randstad US), 5

Writing: of books, 245–246, 308–309; for business growth, 245–247; skills needed for, 26–27. *See also* Proposals; *individual titles of books*